CAMBRIDGE LIBRARY COLLECTION

Books of enduring scholarly value

Religion

For centuries, scripture and theology were the focus of prodigious amounts of scholarship and publishing, dominated in the English-speaking world by the work of Protestant Christians. Enlightenment philosophy and science, anthropology, ethnology and the colonial experience all brought new perspectives, lively debates and heated controversies to the study of religion and its role in the world, many of which continue to this day. This series explores the editing and interpretation of religious texts, the history of religious ideas and institutions, and not least the encounter between religion and science.

A Memoir of the Rev. Henry Watson Fox, B.A. of Wadham College, Oxford

George Fox (1810–1886) compiled this memoir of his younger brother to inspire Rugby schoolboys to emulate this devout alumnus and become missionaries themselves. It was first published in 1850; the 1880 edition reissued here was the sixth printing and included a new preface and appendix recounting the successful establishment of the Rugby Fox Mastership at Masulipatam, India, where Fox had preached among the Telugu people of the British Madras Presidency. Containing an impressive quantity of personal letters and excerpts from his journal, the book provides insights into Fox's spiritual development and religious trials in the first half of the nineteenth-century. It includes unsympathetic accounts of the Telugu and India in general, but also recounts Fox's missionary strategies and goals, often reporting specific conversations or incidents. This content provides useful source material for scholars studying the British mission to India, the British empire, or nineteenth-century personal devotion.

T0381751

Cambridge University Press has long been a pioneer in the reissuing of out-of-print titles from its own backlist, producing digital reprints of books that are still sought after by scholars and students but could not be reprinted economically using traditional technology. The Cambridge Library Collection extends this activity to a wider range of books which are still of importance to researchers and professionals, either for the source material they contain, or as landmarks in the history of their academic discipline.

Drawing from the world-renowned collections in the Cambridge University Library, and guided by the advice of experts in each subject area, Cambridge University Press is using state-of-the-art scanning machines in its own Printing House to capture the content of each book selected for inclusion. The files are processed to give a consistently clear, crisp image, and the books finished to the high quality standard for which the Press is recognised around the world. The latest print-on-demand technology ensures that the books will remain available indefinitely, and that orders for single or multiple copies can quickly be supplied.

The Cambridge Library Collection will bring back to life books of enduring scholarly value (including out-of-copyright works originally issued by other publishers) across a wide range of disciplines in the humanities and social sciences and in science and technology.

A Memoir of the Rev. Henry Watson Fox, B.A. of Wadham College, Oxford

Missionary to the Telugu People, South India

GEORGE TOWNSHEND FOX

CAMBRIDGE UNIVERSITY PRESS

Cambridge, New York, Melbourne, Madrid, Cape Town, Singapore,
São Paolo, Delhi, Dubai, Tokyo

Published in the United States of America by Cambridge University Press, New York

www.cambridge.org
Information on this title: www.cambridge.org/9781108008372

© in this compilation Cambridge University Press 2009

This edition first published 1880
This digitally printed version 2009

ISBN 978-1-108-00837-2 Paperback

Grendamour

A MEMOIR

OF THE REV.

HENRY WATSON FOX, B.A.

OF WADHAM COLLEGE, OXFORD;

MISSIONARY TO THE TELUGU PEOPLE, SOUTH INDIA.

BY THE

REV. GEORGE TOWNSHEND FOX, M.A.

New Edition.

LONDON:

THE RELIGIOUS TRACT SOCIETY,

56, PATERNOSTER ROW; 65, ST. PAUL'S CHURCHYARD,
AND 164, PICCADILLY.

PREFACE.

UPWARDS of thirty years have elapsed since the decease of my brother Henry, during which period four editions in England, and one edition in America, of his Memoir have been published, and have long since been exhausted. It might have been supposed that after the lapse of so long a period the interest originally excited by his missionary enterprise and premature death would have died out, but the facts introduced in the Appendix will serve to refute this impression.

Some months ago my friend, the Rev. John Sharp, formerly missionary at Masulipatam, wrote to me, complaining that my brother's Memoir had been so long out of print that even at Rugby a copy was not to be had; and hence that neither the boys themselves, nor sometimes the preachers of the annual sermon, could obtain information of him whose name had become associated with what is now an established organisation in connection with Rugby School.

He strongly urged upon me to bring out a new edition, which I consented to do, and offered it to the Religious Tract Society, who considerately undertook the responsibility.

The present edition, in a slightly abridged form, will, I trust, meet the requirements of the case, not merely in Rugby, but likewise amongst those who take an interest in the missionary cause throughout the kingdom.

I should have hesitated to take this step if it had not been for Rugby ; but remembering the interest which the Memoir excited in bygone years in the minds and hearts of many Rugby schoolboys, and that we are indebted to its perusal for having given the first impulse to several persons, and amongst others to one who is now a bishop, in the missionary field, I commit the new edition to the blessing of God, with the prayerful hope that it may be accompanied with similar results.

G. T. FOX.

Durham : *September*, 1880.

CONTENTS.

———◇———

CHAPTER I.

CHAPTER VI.

CHAPTER VII.

CHAPTER VIII.

CHAPTER IX.

CHAPTER X.

LIST OF ENGRAVINGS.

RUGBY SCHOOL.

A MEMOIR

REV. HENRY WATSON FOX, B.A.

CHAPTER I.

BIRTH—EARLY EDUCATION—REMOVAL TO RUGBY—CORRESPONDENCE
WHILST THERE.

HENRY WATSON FOX, son of the late George
Townshend Fox, Esq., of the city of Durham,
was born at Westoe, in the county of Durham, on
the 1st of October, 1817.

The history of his childhood furnishes no circumstances worthy of being mentioned : his disposition was
naturally amiable and tractable ; his early education
was conducted under his parents' roof, and at the age
of eleven, he went to the Durham Grammar School,
where he continued till his removal to Rugby, in
February, 1831, at which time he was thirteen years
old.

The remainder of his education he received at Rugby
School, where he continued for six years, until his

B

removal to Oxford, and thus enjoyed the benefit of
Dr. Arnold's instruction and example, during the most
vigorous period of his valuable life; that instruction
was not thrown away, nor that example without its
influence, as will appear in the course of the following
correspondence. During his residence at Rugby School,
and especially towards the latter part of it, when he
had the privilege of coming into closer contact with
Dr. Arnold, he contracted the greatest affection and
reverence for his character; whilst the simple Christian
instruction, which he so faithfully delivered in the
School Chapel, produced a strong and abiding impression upon his heart; so that it may truly be said, that
the classical knowledge and intellectual development
which he acquired at school, were the least of the
blessings he there received : for though other influences
were co-operating during that period, yet the control-
ling power of Dr. Arnold's mind in forming his
Christian character was of the highest value, and to
the end of his days was ever remembered by him with
affection and gratitude.

I may here mention that my brother enjoyed the
advantages of a careful education at home, as well as
those which have been referred to as arising from his
connection with Rugby School. Much seed had been
sown in days of childhood, and thus a good foundation
of religious knowledge had been laid—such knowledge
as can be received before the Holy Spirit has taken of
the things of Christ and shown them to the soul. And
no influence was so happy, or proved of such lasting
benefit, as that which his eldest sister exercised over

him during his holidays; when he was in the habit of
reading with her regularly, and of receiving instruction,
which, though for a season it lay dormant, and seemed
to produce no impression upon the heart, yet in due
season sprang up and brought forth fruit.

The first communication of a religious character
which I can remember having held with him, took
place in the year 1833, and is still vividly impressed
upon my memory. I well remember the discourage-
ment which I felt at finding, as I imagined, no
response, after having read to him, one Sunday, and
conversed with him about the value of his soul and
the duty of serving God. He appeared uninterested,
and made no reply ; but, as the following letter
afterwards informed me, his countenance had not
been a fair index of his heart :

Rugby: Nov. 10, 1833.

MY DEAR GEORGE,

As you wish me to write to you before I go home, and
as I have both opportunity and will to do so now, I shall
set about it. I did not indeed know or expect that you
were so near me, and I could have wished that you had
come to see us ; but it is, as you say, best perhaps that
you did not, as you would certainly derive more pleasure
from Mr. Gisborne's society, than from coming to see
us. * * Perhaps you recollect a conversation you had
with me one Sunday at Durham ; that conversation did
me most inestimable good, for which I have to thank
you ; for before that, I had become almost, I may say,
callous, or at least lukewarm in religious matters. But
that first roused me, and it being followed by reading
with Isabella at Cullercoats, I have become alive to my

situation : I see how great is sin, and to what extent I have sinned, and hope that God will now forgive me ; but still I feel myself constantly led away by temptation, in one shape or another, and still have a great repugnance to looking back on the actions of the day. I now follow a practice which —— advised me to, and from which I feel great benefit ; that is, before I leave my room in order to go to the bed-room, to pray heartily to God, instead of, as I used before to do, merely saying my prayers before I got into bed ; and if in these I was disturbed by other boys talking, I used to go to bed and to sleep, without offering up any prayer from my heart, and without having even asked forgiveness for the sins of the past day. I have been this evening reading one of Dr. Whately's Essays, on comparing the life of a Christian with that of children, wherein he shows how little we know of God, and in how confined a sphere ; what low and earthly ideas, our very best must be, concerning the Divine Being. We have lectures from Mr. Price on a Sunday evening, and partly from what he said, and partly from my own thoughts, the following idea arose, which, though new to me, has undoubtedly occurred to most persons, namely—that an additional reason for turning to God early in life is, that as the faculties of the body are more developed by exercise, even to the last period of one's life, so a person, the longer he lives in the fear and love of God, the more righteous and more fit for heaven he becomes. I must leave off now for want of time : which though generally an idle excuse, is not so in this case, as it is now nearly bedtime, and I shall have no time to finish this letter next week, so now—Good night !

Your affectionate Brother,

H. W. Fox.

Some religious impressions had been made upon his mind, however, at an early period, as the following letter to a school-fellow will show. It seems that being confined to a sick-room, this boy had spoken to him seriously; but at that time, as too often happens under similar circumstances, the counsel, instead of being gratefully received, was unthankfully rejected, and caused rather a breach of friendship. His friend having removed to Harrow, it led to a correspondence, of which the following letter forms a part:

To M. BUCKINGHAM, ESQ., DR. LONGLEY'S, HARROW.

Rugby: Oct. 30, 1834.

MY DEAR BUCKINGHAM,

You will, no doubt, be much astonished at receiving a letter from me, so long after our correspondence had closed; and especially as I was the party who put an end to it. I now write to ask your pardon for so doing, and to express my sincere sorrow for it. Do not think these expressions are feigned or exaggerated; for though our acquaintance was but very short, yet it was blessed by the hand of God, and you were made by Him the first instrument to call me to Him: at first, as you may remember, I obeyed the call, but after you left I fell away again, and on your writing to me—as religion was *then* a disagreeable subject to me— I did not answer your letters, and so the correspondence broke off. I now beg of you, that, if you can forgive me, you will be so good as to renew it. I recollect you told me that you were brought to the knowledge of God by an elder sister, and this has been my case: about a year ago my eldest sister and brother took great care of my religion, and have, by God's blessing, bestowed on me the best gift they could have given me; or rather not they, but God. I have often thought of you since you left, but more especially lately, and have intended for some time to write to you, but have had no opportunity before this; and now, though

later, I hope you will not reject this letter. Since you
went away from here, nearly three years ago, great changes
have taken place in myself, my friends, and the school.
From the "shell" I am now advanced to a high place in
the "sixth," and my mind and faculties have had a great
change;—but this is too egotistical and boasting. Again
and again, as I go on writing, I constantly think how you
will receive this, and am afraid that you will not take
it well; but pardon what is amiss, and believe me

Your affectionate Friend,

HENRY W. FOX.

I may here observe how greatly they err, who
mistake naturally amiable dispositions for Christian
principle. My brother, as a boy, was of a very kindly
and endearing temper; but for all this his heart was as
thoroughly alienated from God as other persons'. This
sad disease of human nature exists in every heart, till
it has been changed by the Holy Spirit; and though
the symptoms may be modified, and its deformity
sometimes concealed by a fair outside, or by amiable
dispositions, yet the malady remains, and man's heart,
in its relations towards God, is all wrong and all
corrupt, till Divine grace shall work the change.

The following letters will furnish abundant illustrations of this, showing that whenever an attempt is
made by any one to bring his own heart into obedience
to God, there a struggle and a spiritual warfare will
spring up,—there inward toil and difficulty must be
encountered,—there the heart will show its enmity to
God, its alienation from Him, its unwillingness to love
and serve Him.

It may seem to require an apology for publishing

the letters of so young a person, at a time when his mind was imperfectly developed, and his Christian experience of the most juvenile character; but I have ventured to do so under the impression that more instruction may be derived to those who are of like age, and under similar circumstances, by tracing the early workings of God's Spirit upon a school-boy's heart, than by having the character of a mature and experienced Christian presented to them.

The feelings, the sympathies, the affections of a school-boy are more likely to be enlisted by a record of the trials, temptations, and spiritual progress of another school-boy, than by the example of an older person, with whom he can have no fellow-feeling, and few sentiments in common.

I would fain hope that there is a better spirit abroad in our public schools at the present day,—that there are more of what Dr. Tait so well terms "thoughtful boys," whose minds are opening out under right influences, early to realise the great ends of their being; and I shall greatly rejoice if I am permitted to furnish any instruction for that very important and interesting part of the community—the boys of our public schools; by presenting to them the spiritual progress and career of grace, of one who, like themselves, was a boy at a public school. It is for their sakes chiefly, that I have yielded to the importunity of friends, and have sacrificed my own feelings, by venturing to spread out before the public eye, much that was of a private and domestic character—thus invading, as it were, the sacred precincts of the social hearth.

Rugby : Wednesday, Feb. 19, 1834.

MY DEAR ISABELLA,

I received your kind letter by Robert, for which I am much obliged to you. Now that I am come here, I have fallen into such a vortex of temptation, that I scarcely know what to do, and they chiefly come on so insinuatingly, that I can scarcely perceive them at first. The two greatest are, I think, pride of heart, in thinking myself better than others, in comparing myself with others ; and though in my understanding I see how wicked I am, yet my heart is so sinful that it is with difficulty I find means of repressing such thoughts. The other temptation is, wasting time, which comes on by little and little, but which I hope soon to be able, with God's assistance, to overcome. I find myself so sinful, that were it not for Christ's blessed promises, I could scarcely fancy He would hear me ; but He has felt the infirmities and temptations of man, and from thence I derive my comfort. And on account of the very temptations I meet with here, I ought to rejoice and be thankful to God, that He has given me such opportunities of becoming more perfect and patient than I could otherwise hope to be ; but I, as well as you, am anxious and fear greatly lest I should fall. During the day I feel myself clinging to this world too much, and if it were not for my devotions—evening and morning—I feel I should quite forget my Maker : I intend therefore to read the Bible several times during the day, for there is such a blessing in the Holy Scriptures, that they always inspire one with good thoughts, and set me forward afresh to follow the precepts laid down in them. Oh, if they were taken away, how could man exist ? I often follow the plan of Wilberforce Richmond, of reading the Psalms and praying over them ; I find them so full of beauty and comfort, so full of holiness, that they quite refresh my soul. I constantly wish I was with you, but God's will be done :

if He will it, we shall meet again, when I shall be able to talk to you and learn from you many good things.   I pray for you continually.

There is a very interesting case here.   There is a little boy about fourteen years old, in other respects a nice little boy, and one whom I was rather fond of : but, the other day, in talking with him, I discovered he never read his Bible ; in short, he knew nothing of the Christian religion.   I have been endeavouring to impress on him the awfulness of his state, but he seems scarcely to care whether he is lost or saved.   He understands neither heaven nor hell, nor that he is born for any other state than this,—that is to say, he does not *feel* it to be the case : he has apparently been completely neglected at home with respect to religious matters.   Now I want to know how to proceed with him—how to open his mind—for I think when he once perceives in his heart, how wicked he together with all others are, that he will be more able and willing to understand the truths of the Gospel. When I have got him to do anything right rather than what is wrong, I generally discover it is done merely because I asked him ; and this doing what he thinks I wish, together with other points, shows that he has naturally a good heart, but that it wants cultivation.   Oh, how thankful I ought to be to God that He has given me such good and kind parents, and brothers and sisters : for, as Sumner says, we should be thankful that we were not born in an heathen country, and that we are placed in a land where the Gospel is preached, for it is by no merit of our own that we are not condemned to darkness and ignorance.   Dr. Arnold, in his sermon on Sunday, used a simile I thought particularly beautiful.   In talking of those who seek God in this world,—they are, he said, like those foreign plants which we see here flourishing, but not having flowers or fruit ; we see that this is not their proper place, and that they must have some other place where they come to full ripeness.   Both Robert and I con-

stantly make use of the books you wrote out for us, in which
we find great use. That God may requite to you the good
you have done us, is the constant prayer of

Your affectionate Brother,

HENRY W. FOX.

Rugby : March 1, 1834.

MY DEAR GEORGE,

When I returned to school this half I was wofully disappointed. I had a great friend here ; and though I had
spoken but little on religious points with him, yet I expected
that on that subject our hearts would be knit together, but
alas ! I find that he is little actuated by Christian principle :
not that he is a bad boy, in the eye of the world, but it is
almost only when duty and pleasure run together that he
follows the former. The following verse struck me the other
day on this point ; " Yea, mine own familiar friend, in whom
I trusted, hath lifted up his heel against me." Psalm xli. 9.
Not that I mean that he is no longer an acquaintance, but I
find that I can no longer make him my friend ; our two
grand pursuits being so different. So that, besides my own
family, there is not a human being who is my *intimate*
friend. It is in this situation that I find how kind God is
to me, He is my all to me : while I am here I am separated
(except for Robert) from all (whom I know at least) who
seek the same God as I do, who run along with me ; I am
here a solitary being, but still I am happy, because God is
with me.

Your affectionate Brother,

H. W. FOX.

Rugby : Thursday, March 6, 1834.

MY DEAR ISABELLA,

* * * I am glad to be able to say that I was partly
deceived in my old friend who is here, for I thought he was

far too fond of the world; but on talking with him lately, I have discovered he is more willing to turn to God than I had expected,—in fact I have great hopes of him. I am, however, disappointed in another point; namely, a boy who was once a great friend of mine, but who, for various reasons, has not been such a one for the last half year, and whom I was endeavouring to assist, has put an almost insurmountable bar to my progress with him. I have in this instance particularly felt what you mentioned in your letter : "That God alone giveth the increase, and without that, how useless are the efforts of man !" Whenever lately I have spoken with this boy on religious subjects, he has refused to answer questions; will not say a word on the subject, and does not attend to what I am saying. He fancies that he can serve God and mammon; he used to answer my exhortations to him, "*that I was going too far*," and that he did not think it necessary to avoid *small faults*, but because they were small (though he could not deny they were faults), he quite neglected attending to them. I have, therefore, since he refuses to listen to a conversation, determined to write out different things for him, to the best of my power, which I hope with God's holy assistance may be to his advantage. I have already written out one paper for him, pointing out the chief points of the Christian religion, yet without immediately applying them to him. I intend next to remark on several of the faults I have observed in him lately, which he does not feel to be faults. I was the more disappointed in him, as I had before found him willing in the general, but when I came to particulars, and he saw he must give up certain pleasures if he would give himself entirely to God, then he thought he had gone far enough, and I had gone too far; for God tells us to go as far as we can. But this last-mentioned boy is not the one I told you of before; he is improving; he *feels* what it is to be endeavouring to do one's best, but yet he is scarce strong enough to resist temptations

which I point out to him as wrong, yet which he has all his
life-time believed to be perfectly innocent. I find it is very
difficult to persuade him, and some others, that any common
amusement is wrong ; all the world, they say, do such and
such a thing, and certainly all the world will not go to hell.
But with God's grace all will, I hope, go well with him.

While I am thus talking to and thinking of these three,
I am afraid lest I should, by seeing their faults, fancy
mine own smaller; humility is, I find, a very difficult thing
to attain, and doing good from the motive of pleasing God,
still harder. I have to struggle very hard for this last, for
when I do anything right, I do it too often for my own sake;
that is, falsely thinking at the moment that it will advance
my salvation : but of late God has had mercy on me, and I
have been able to discover the system of faith. I was much
obliged to you for your kind letter. Give my love to all.

Your affectionate Brother,

H. W. Fox.

Rugby : March 17, 1834.

My dear Isabella,

I received your letter dated the 10th, yesterday morning.
I am very much obliged to you for it, it will do me a great
deal of good, and it has warned me from doing a great
injury : for, on Saturday evening, I induced the "silent
boy" to talk, and he informed me he had been silent because
I had so constantly been speaking to him on religion.
During the conversation, he told me he intended to serve
God wholly (which I thought a great point gained) : and
next he confessed he was not so doing at the time. He
asked me then, whether I thought it wrong to read light
books and do lessons on a Sunday. I was struck quite
with astonishment at the question, and I answered that I
certainly did. He said he thought the contrary, and his
only argument was, that if he was not so doing, he would

be thinking of something wrong, and therefore it was *right* to do lessons on a Sunday : he perfectly *understood* what keeping Sunday holy was, viz. : endeavouring to think on God only ; but he could not get it out of his head, that because he would (or rather thought he would) be doing worse, that therefore the end justified the means. He acknowledged he had *never* tried to keep, for one whole Sunday, his heart on God, yet because he had tried for one hour, he thought it was impossible that man could help thinking of things wicked in themselves on a Sunday. But I cannot help thinking that those reasons were put forward as an excuse, and that in his heart he felt it to be wrong. I urged him to try the very next day. But I have not yet learnt whether he did so or not. With respect to " Amusements," I believe I used the word in too general a sense when I wrote to you ; but your observations on that subject are very true and just. I may, perhaps, and I believe I have often, spoken of religion to these boys as leading to other pleasures besides what they now enjoy, and have perhaps made them view it in a gloomy light, as they did not understand nor feel how great the new pleasures would be. But what I meant in my letter by amusements, were amusements more or less sinful ; such as, for instance, wasting one's money over trifles and sweetmeats ; or wasting one's time in reading a book when we ought to be doing our lessons, and such as those,—not drinking—for, as I said in my last letter, that is almost extinct. For my little pupil I have constantly changing hopes and fears : at one moment I see outwardly no hope of him, and again shortly I am quite rejoiced. I trust, however, that Christ will not let him fall back again after he has now been once called. Last evening in particular, God had great mercy towards him and assisted him. I at last persuaded him to overcome a great temptation, namely, copying his exercise, and to do it himself. I consider this a very great point gained,

for it is showing his faith by works. I have been particularly happy lately; I read over again the account of
Wilberforce Richmond's latter end and death. I was
struck still more than I was the first time, with the beauty
and simplicity of it; with his sincere faith and trust in
God; since then I have been able to keep God continually
in my heart, which I was not able to do before: I have
therefore derived such comfort and happiness, that I hope
never to lose that gift. But still sin clogs me greatly : I
get proud, and fancy I do *any thing good* of my own self :
at least I feel it to be so, though I know full well that I
am exceedingly sinful, and that the very thought I had just
been indulging in (viz, of pride) was very wicked in itself.
I derive very great comfort from reading the Bible every
day. I understand it better and better, and see the meaning of the various passages in it in a more forcible light.
I always find the Sunday too short for what I want to do
on it. I therefore intend to make some other day during
the week like a second Sunday, and, except my lessons,
read and think of nothing, save God only. Many others
here think, as I used to do formerly, that Sunday is too long,
and therefore spend two or three hours in bed longer than
usual, and spend the rest of the day in listlessness, or
perhaps worse; never thinking what a blessing they are
throwing away. I feel now, as you told me you did, that the
Sabbath is quite a rest from the worldly thoughts of the
other parts of the week. Last Sunday was a most beautiful
day, and I took a walk by myself into the country, and
never felt so happy before. I continued for more than an
hour praising and praying to God, and thanking Him. I
shall never neglect it again : I felt it as a preparation for
heaven.

Your affectionate Brother,
HENRY W. FOX.

Rugby: April 7, 1834.

MY DEAR ISABELLA,

You will be thinking, I suppose, that as I have not written to you lately, I am too busy to do so. I am ashamed to say it was not from that cause, for we have just had three whole holidays, during which I had no lessons to do, but I neglected through laziness to write to you. I have in truth spent a very bad Easter, very lazy I was all the time, and I have just returned to working again. I had intended to have read several books during the holidays, but I neglected them, and have not kept half my resolutions. All this shows how very weak I am, and how unable I am to resist extraordinary temptations. I can manage to resist, and often to overcome, my every-day trials, because I have experience of them and am aware of their approach; but when those come which I am not so much accustomed to, or if my old ones come on me in a new shape, then I fall a victim to them. When I know and have determined in myself that anything is wrong, then I generally overcome it, but my greatest difficulty lies in making out whether the thing is wrong or not. I have of late been able to see all my sins so clearly (that is, all I consider sins), that I scarcely could dare to look up to God, or pray to Him, were it not for His gracious promises. I have given over all hopes of persuading the formerly "silent boy" by speaking to him, for he over and over again says, he is convinced of what he holds to be true, and that he will not change his opinion : or if he does enter into conversation about keeping the Sabbath holy, he merely repeats his foolish arguments over again, and will not attend patiently to what I say in answer to them. In this case he seems unable to connect what I say to him, though in general he is clear-headed enough. He is evidently not affected by my arguments, for every Sunday he continues to do his lessons, &c. Instead, therefore, of talking to him on the subject, I am writing out for him the best arguments I can think of, which I shall have finished in about a week. * * * I was thinking to-day what an inducement there is to convert any one who wanders from the truth, to convert him from the error of his ways; for we are told that God and the angels in heaven rejoice when one sinner turns to heaven; and how great must be the honour and glory for him who is the instrument of joy in the heart of our heavenly Father: the same reasoning applies, indeed, in every case where we do good from a right motive; but this case struck me to be so much stronger than most others.

Tuesday, April 8.—I was, as I mentioned in the beginning of my letter, very wicked all last week. I lived without God in my heart. I was ruled by my own wishes, not by what was right; all that time I was very unhappy. This is a strong instance to me, of not only the vanity of the pleasures of this world, but also of their nauseousness, whilst we are without God. I have no one to turn to but God; no one, save Him, can relieve me in my necessities and troubles, and no one like Him is so merciful and sparing. I often thank Him that He has spared me so long, and not cut me off in the midst of my unrepented sins. I might have been at this moment in hell, bemoaning my folly and wickedness. But, blessed be God, He has, by your instrumentality, called me unto Him.

Your affectionate Brother,
H. W. Fox.

Rugby: May 13, 1834.

MY DEAR GEORGE,

 * * * * I am sorry we shall be unable to see each other for a long time; but though far distant, we may yet constantly communicate with one another, and it will be a great consolation to think that our thoughts are constantly on one and the same great object. What I have always till

now found my greatest difficulty has been prayer. I could offer up words, but as I could have no idea of God, I felt I could not offer up my heart to Him : but lately, on thinking, and at last feeling, that God is always present in my inmost soul, I can heartily ask for what I need, and often, and continually throughout the day, keep my thoughts on Him, which I used to find almost impossible. I derive the very greatest advantage from this, for whilst I am continually keeping my heart with God, it is contrary to my very nature to commit sin against Him ; that is, at least, known sin. I feel and know that all this has not been through my own means, but through the grace of God alone. I also have had my eyes opened, to view my wickedness and depravity, and God's purity and holiness. I was before, as it were, covered with darkness ; I could not see anything though I tried. But now these things stand before me in glaring colours, and I almost wonder God has not yet cut me off, or even now allows me to live on in the many sins I daily commit ; for notwithstanding the greatest care, I am constantly falling into, and often yielding to temptation : the greatest is lying in bed in a morning ; it is of all the most difficult to overcome. It thus appears how vain and futile are all men's endeavours unless they be assisted by God's grace. I often find that those temptations which outwardly appear very small, and which one would almost pass by unperceived, are the very strongest which attack me. There is the continual whispering in my ear—This is but a small sin, it maketh no matter to commit it ; and thus I sometimes yield. But I find my only true test of right or wrong is to ask myself whether I do it from a motive of pleasing God. I find, as you mention in your letter, the great advantage of reading the Bible, with an earnest desire and prayer to understand it : often the mean-ing of a before-hidden passage breaks in upon me in a way which quite astonishes me. I have got, therefore, a very

C

small pocket edition of the New Testament, to carry about
with me always, that I may use it whenever I have an
opportunity.

Your affectionate Brother,
HENRY W. FOX.

Rugby: June 5, 1834.

MY DEAR ISABELLA,

    * * * * I lately discoursed again on the Sabbath-question
with the boy I before mentioned, and he seemed, though he
did not acknowledge it, to be somewhat convinced. He
candidly confessed that it was not for God's glory that he
did his lessons, &c., on a Sunday. He seemed not to understand that we must " do all things for the glory of God."
This is a matter I have found very difficult in myself to feel
thoroughly, for I am unable to see individually, how each
little action I may do, is to the glory of God ; for many
seem to be perfectly indifferent to do, or to be left undone.
However here, as elsewhere, faith must come in and lead me
at last to understand what I am as yet too blind to see.   I
am sorry to say that B—— has been fighting with another
boy ; this fighting is one of the worst evils of this school,
and I am utterly unable to understand Dr. A.'s conduct in
not forbidding fighting.   That he must know it to be wrong,
I am convinced, and unless it be that he thinks forbidding it
will be of no use in stopping it, I cannot conceive why he
does allow it to continue.   I was talking on this subject the
other day with Mr. C——, who perfectly agrees with me.
Fighting, I am glad to say, does not often take place ; but
twice within the last month or two, there have been bad
cases.   In the first, one of the boys was within a few
moments of dying, but has at last recovered ; and the second
is this one of B——, who fainted and was unwell for a day
or two after. * * * * I feel so happy now ; I have at last
been able to overcome my greatest temptation, viz., of lying

in bed too late : and on examining myself in an evening, I generally find that God has enabled me to overcome every known temptation during the day. I used before to get up sometimes, and lie in bed sometimes, but now at last I have more firm trust on God, and I have been enabled to rise the moment I am awakened. I used to trust too much to my own efforts, and to think over-night, how easy it would be to rise the next morning : but, alas ! if I trusted not in God, I used to go to sleep, without getting up. I still feel great difficulty in the evening, in examining my motives for various actions during the day ; I often cannot recall them ; often, perhaps, because I had done them from no particular motive. I am glad to say, that the friend I before mentioned in this letter, has been persuaded to leave off several wrong things, and I have more hopes of him than of any others here. His conscience seems to be touched, and he feels it, though he does not confess it. But H—— is no better than before, if not worse. He has no steadiness, nor strength, nor does what I say to him have any weight : he does not think, or I am convinced he would not say or do what he does.

Your affectionate Brother,
H. W. Fox.

Rugby : September 2, 1834.

My dear Isabella,

I received your letter on Sunday, as you expected, and return you many thanks for it. Though I have found less difficulty than I usually have found in returning to my school duties, yet I feel the change still irksome and difficult to be borne up against. I have got settled to my work, but not quite to my habits, and not having got again accustomed to a regular rule for spending the day, I frequently waste some part; not, however, in absolutely doing nothing, but time slips away in getting ready and beginning. On looking back to the holidays, I find much of my time has been lost in the same way, for though I was *busy* at my lessons almost all the day, yet on the whole I have done but little ; I have, however, acquired a habit of doing something at least, for hitherto during former holidays, I have never done anything worth mentioning. I have already begun what you advise in your letter, namely, selecting some prayers ; but I have done it from Bishop Ken, rather than from Wilson ; as I thought those in the former better suited and more applicable, than those in the latter. I have now a matter to talk about, which it would have been better to have mentioned to you during the holidays, but I have such a great dislike to converse personally on such subjects ; it is, I now think, a foolish and perhaps wrong dislike, but I could not then overcome it, and I therefore now mention it in writing. It is, how to be sure that I am in the way to heaven, not inquiring of the truth of the Bible, but how to find it out in my own heart. For I believe the Articles of the Christian faith, and that not what I do of myself, but the death of Christ, brings me to heaven : at the same time I have some love of God (but very little, I fear), and *some* of my actions are done for His sake, and I try to do all so by His assistance ; now, is this the beginning of what is requisite ? Is not faith a junction of belief and works springing from love to God ? I am, as you may well suppose, very anxious on the question ; and on examining myself on the point, I fear I do not do enough for God's sake, and thereby have not sufficient faith. I find it is so difficult to separate in my head faith and works ; for as the former is more than belief, and in part consists of the latter, they seem to approach each other's nature. I wish you would be so good as to set me right on this subject in your next letter.

Your affectionate Brother,

HENRY W. FOX.

Rugby : September 7, 1834.

MY DEAR ISABELLA,

I received your most excellent letter this morning, and was exceedingly comforted and strengthened by it ; for being, I thank God, able to answer most of the questions in the affirmative, I received assurance that I have at least *some* faith. Since the time of reading it, my happiness has been growing greater and greater, and I have passed one of the happiest days I have as yet spent ; though I have not been blessed with that exquisite joy, and as it were foretaste of heaven, which I have sometimes met with, yet my happiness has been deep, though quiet, and continued ; and I know no better way of employing a few minutes this evening, than in returning thanks to you, and through you to God. For, my dear sister, I always consider you as one of my greatest bless-ings, for you have been God's instrument in recalling me from the deadness and corruption of sin to newness of life, and to a firm hope in Christ. I have been this day examin-ing myself in the most doubtful points of my faith ; for, strange it is, the most doubtful parts have been the most vital parts ; for I have never till to-day had a clear concep-tion and firm belief that my salvation is from Christ alone and entirely ; and that my own good deeds are worth nothing in God's sight. My chief difficulty is now, in praying to God, for His Son's sake, for I do not feel at the moment of praying, the necessity of so doing : deceiving myself by thinking God will hear me because He is merciful, and not *merely* for Christ's sake. This one day has been of more benefit to me than many days, for I have considered and learnt many things which I understood not before. We had a most excellent sermon from Dr. Arnold this evening, explaining the duty of obedience to masters ; that it was only then truly shown, when in some matter indifferent in itself, we obey them because they command us, and not because of any servile hope or fear from them. He took his text from the first lesson of the evening, and referred to that in the morning; also saying, that the two afforded examples of the greatest obedience and disobedience. I feel great advantage from his sermons, for he addresses us practically, as well as generally on doctrinal points.

Friday, 12th.—I had not time to finish this letter on Sunday, so that it has been lying in my drawer for nearly a week, but unwilling to allow a week to pass without your hearing from me, I again take up my pen, and shall endeavour to send the letter by this morning's post. I feel now, even stronger than at first, the good effects of your letter, for having now received a sure hope of salvation, and a better understanding of the way, I have more peace, and am able to love God better; for before I was (and I am afraid I am in some degree now) in the habit of believing that good works work salvation, or rather, not believing, but having a hankering feeling that such was the case. I now, however, feel myself liable to the danger of believing, that what I henceforth may do is of no consequence, and the struggle is sometimes very hard, but by God's help I am able to overcome it. * * *

Your affectionate Brother,
HENRY W. FOX.

Rugby : March 24, 1835.

MY DEAR BUCKINGHAM,

My writing for the Prize Essay has prevented me from answering your letter sooner ; but I am at last freed from all work of that kind, and am glad to be able to write to you again, which, as it is the nearest approach to speaking to you is very pleasant to me. * * * I have this morning been reading the "Dairyman's Daughter," in Richmond's "Annals of the Poor" : a book you have probably read before, but which I have been reading for the first time. I shall always think of it as an especial means of grace to me, for it has been so blessed to me, as to open my eyes to many of my secret and besetting sins—as self-confidence and deadness of faith—which are hard to discover and to root out : yet God has now in His mercy assisted me, or rather, I should say, done the work wholly Himself, of restoring me to a better knowledge of Him : for I do not think, on looking back, that I have ever had true faith : I have always had some trust or hope in my own works. I have often, or rather generally, endeavoured to do good, in order that *I might be saved thereby*, instead of acting on the true motive of love and thankfulness, and trusting implicitly to God that He would take me to His heavenly kingdom for His *Son's sake.* And even now, I find it difficult completely to eradicate this evil motive and self-confidence from my heart. * * * Dr. Arnold has just instituted a new practice, which I think was much needed, and it is to be hoped that it will extend farther than at present. In addition to the prayers in the big school, we now have a prayer before beginning our first lesson, in order that we should begin the day by asking God's blessing on our endeavours. I only trust that it may be a means of making many of us pray more than we do : for I cannot help thinking that especially in the higher part of the school, a very great deal of irreligion, if not infidelity, exists. * * * I find it a very difficult point to manage in my duty as præpostor, namely, to draw the line between " official " and " personal " offences—to discover where I feel revenge, and where I do anything to enforce the power which properly belongs to me. I think I may learn from this not to desire earthly power, as it only increases our difficulties and temptations : God alone can teach me aright. To Him, therefore, I pray, and do you also pray for me, that I may have wisdom and strength to execute judgment rightly.

Your affectionate Friend,

HENRY W. FOX.

Rugby : April 13, 1835.

MY DEAR ISABELLA,

 * * * I feel every day an increasing desire of becoming a clergyman. I desire to be always employed in more immediately serving God, and in bringing many souls unto salvation. I am aware that we can do our duty and a great deal of good in every station of life; but I think a clergyman is more particularly appointed to do good, being a light set upon a hill. I have hitherto, and I know you have at home also, looked forward to my going to the Bar, but it is not so now,—it can scarcely ever be too late to change my prospects. If it is particularly the wish of my father and mother and you all that I should fulfil the original proposition, I willingly acquiesce; but if it is indifferent, or of no great importance to you, I should prefer very much to enter the service of the Church. However, whichever profession I may hereafter follow, my present and future (for some years at least) studies will suit both; I wished, however, to mention this desire of mine to you. Dr. Arnold has made a great improvement in the public prayers; for besides the prayers which are read when we first assemble in the morning (to which I fear few attend), we have now, immediately before our first lesson, a prayer to ask God's blessing on us for the day. * * *

Your affectionate Brother,

H. W. FOX.

Rugby : August 30, 1835.

MY DEAREST ISABELLA,

I cannot refrain from writing to you now to express my happiness, my great and exceeding joy, which I have received from the Lord. During the holidays, indeed, I was constantly led astray by the pleasures and amusements of the world, and though frequently called again by God to return to Him, as often as I turned I fell, for I did not

enough trust in Him ; nor was I able to turn more stead-
fastly to the way of salvation, till the very last day I was
at home ; which day was to me the beginning again of
serving the Lord ; and during my journey, especially during
the first night, I had leisure and opportunity, and God gave
me grace to pray fervently to Him for grace and strength to
resist my temptations ; and I have most mercifully been
heard, so that this week has been to me one of very great
joy and growth in grace ; but this afternoon, during the
service, I experienced more happiness, and a greater foretaste
of heaven than ever before, especially during the singing of
the hymn, " From Egypt's bondage come," and particularly
of the words, "We are on our way to God." Oh, then I felt
the great mercy of our Saviour in leading us to Himself, and
the greatness and majesty of Him to whom we are led. I
have been reading the life of Henry Martyn (for which I
have to thank George, as being a means both of great profit
and pleasure) and I have derived the most instructing lessons
from it. I found how much the enjoyment of things of this
world have hold on me, and when I consider his state of
giving himself up to be a missionary, and asked myself,
Could I give up home and the pleasures and happiness I
enjoy from worldly objects, to do this laborious work for the
Lord's sake ?—I found the weakness of my love to God, and
my need of constant prayer that I may set my affections on
things above and not on things below ; that I may confide
my present as well as my future happiness to my heavenly
Father, and make God my all in all, my desire, my happiness,
and my hope.

Wednesday, Sept. 3.—I am only able, on account of
business, at present, to write to you by fits and starts, as I
can catch a few minutes now and then. Though at the
beginning of the half I am in the middle of an exceedingly
busy week, for my lessons of course occupy a large portion
of my time, indeed larger than before, for we have had

some additional ones imposed, and· I have received a sudden call for articles for the Rugby Magazine. I am appointed also one of the Committee for the examination of the articles; and these things together have kept me so busy, that since Saturday morning (Sunday excepted) to the present moment, I have been as hard at work as possible all day, with the exception of an hour's walk each day, and I shall have similar occupations for the remainder of the week. But in the midst of all my business, I trust I do not forget the end and aim of it all, namely, that I may the more glorify God; still I find it a very great difficulty and temptation, to be able to give up so little time daily to the immediate service of Christ. I have begun searching the Scriptures for a settlement of the various articles of faith, and I find it an excellent plan for acquiring an accurate knowledge of the Bible and the situation of various passages, and I each time discover more and more how our religion must be sought for through many indirect passages, and from the whole tenor of the book; for instance, I have found no passage *exactly* defining faith, but collating several, I have gained my end. I also now, chiefly from M—— F——'s advice, keep an occasional journal of my spiritual state, and I trust I shall find it useful. I have, as you know, long kept a daily and particular journal, but this is a more general and of a very different character.   *   *   *

Your affectionate Brother,

H. W. Fox.

Rugby : Sept. 10, 1835.

MY DEAR GEORGE,

  *   *   * Baxter has done well in laying out so very plainly how that we must not seek our rest here, and I feel it every day more and more, for as I pass through this vale of tears (well may it be called so) my natural man lays hold on every thing it meets with, and clings to them eagerly; and often

have I to thank God for showing me that this is not our abiding-place, by showing me the folly, the weakness, and sad deformity of all worldly things ; how even the most innocent pleasures must be used—not abused—must be made means to lead us on our way to God, and not to merely delight ourselves in them : home, for instance, and the holidays, though they ought to be a time of great spiritual advancement, become to me a snare and a temptation, and the half-year at school a *comparatively* lighter time. Yet here I have a large stock of temptations and difficulties which need constant struggling with ; and they too show that a state of warfare, such as a Christian life must always be, cannot be " our rest." I often long to leave this sinful world (I mean one in which *my* sins are so many) and be at rest ; but I am reconciled to do God's will and remain here as long as He shall ordain, as Baxter says :

> " If life be long, I will be glad,
>   That I may long obey ;
> If short, yet why should I be sad,
>   That shall have the same pay ? "

One of my most difficult *outward* causes of temptation is my great quantity of business, which is at present so large, that merely doing the work for the school leaves me scarcely any time for devotional exercises ; yet as this is not of my own ordering, I believe it will work for my good, by making me more constantly to rest on God for grace and assistance, and teaching me to make use of even the shortest periods, for the purpose of prayer and meditation. * * * I have to thank you very much, my dear George, for the " Life of Henry Martyn," which you gave me ; for I think from no book did I ever experience so much good, so much urging to be more diligent and zealous in God's service, and knowledge of how much I fall short of even what a good *man* can acquire. I like the book the more as giving Henry Martyn's *own*

thoughts and feelings, and showing us an example of the
inner man, that we may derive good in that part of ourselves,
and such improvement in the heart more especially.

Your affectionate Brother,
HENRY.

EXTRACTS FROM AN EARLY JOURNAL.

RUGBY.—*Wednesday, Sept.* 23, 1835.—I did not rise
when first called—I attended ill to my devotions, public and
private—No verse—I was very unkind to M——.   I do not
recollect yielding to temptation—I have wasted much time—
I have done but very few things for God's sake—I have been
proud and very cold-hearted — Conversation poor — My
thoughts have been seldom on God—I have trusted in myself
and been very worldly to-day ; God be merciful to me a
sinner.

Sunday, Oct. 11.—On rising and during dressing I
did not give my [thoughts to God—I read the Bible with
attention and prayer— My morning devotions were from a
cold and worldly heart, and to morning service I was
miserably inattentive, but to the afternoon service I attended
better—I have kept my thoughts much on God to-day, but
in a fearful, faithless state—I did not thank God for my
meals—Much of my conversation has been trifling, and little
for others' good.

Sunday, Nov. 1.—On waking and during dressing I
was cold-hearted—During morning service I was very
inattentive : during evening somewhat better, but at prayers
very inattentive—I have endeavoured to keep the day holy,
and at times have had great joy in contemplating my Saviour,
but at others have been cold and my thoughts wandering—
My conversation has been often worldly and light—I rise
very late, though wakened repeatedly—Last night I went to

sleep with vain thoughts ; I yielded to temptation in not rising earlier—I am very proud—proud of my very humility —I am very unthankful for God's infinite love—I have in some, but not many things, really sought God's service—I have had some love, some faith, but yet weak ; but God has been very merciful to me.

Saturday, May 23, 1836.—R—— sent up T—— for excessive fagging and bullying—On Monday, the 6th, inquired into the right of sending up a præpostor, and it was settled for the future, that if necessary the matter must be laid before the sixth, a majority of whom alone can send a præpostor up.

Saturday, June 13.—This was Dr. Arnold's 42nd birthday. He dined with his children, and afterwards played a game at cricket with them.

Aug. 29.—Elected a member of Committee of Rugby Magazine, also of that for the books of the reading-room.

Oct.—Chosen president of the Debating Society.

SUBJECTS FOR SELF-EXAMINATION.

1. Did I perform my devotions last night, and were my thoughts on God ?

2. When I awoke, were my first thoughts on God, and what was my state of mind while dressing ?

3. How did I perform my devotions, private and public ?

4. Did I rise when first called ?

5. How did I do my lessons ?

6. Have I wasted any time ?

7. Have I obeyed all that are placed over me ?

8. Have I spent my money in the best way I could ?

9. Have I in any case behaved uncharitably ?

10. Have I loved God with my whole heart, not allowing any other object to interfere ?

11. Have I, in all I have done, sought to do His will ?

12. Have I been humble towards God and towards man ?

13. Have I, in conversation, sought to do good ?

14. Have I yielded to temptation ?

15. Has my conduct been influenced by the opinion of the world ?

16. Have my thoughts been constantly heavenward ?

17. Have I at all trusted in myself, either for salvation or strength ?

18. Have I been thankful ?

19. How did I read the Scriptures ?

20. Am I cherishing any idol in my heart ?

Rugby : Oct. 25, 1835.

My dearest Isabella,

I take up my pen to write to you in a very mixed state of mind, partly mourning for the weight of my sins, partly rejoicing for the mercy God has shown me. I am just come to the end of a Sunday, one of the most unhappy, but, I trust, not unprofitable, I have had for long past : for I have just finished a week with more than usual backsliding and coldness towards God—chiefly the immediate effect of a neglect of my daily devotions and self-examination, and have been passing to-day weighed down by the weight of my sins, unable through my wickedness and hardness of heart to look up unto God, and feeling all the bonds of sin upon me. But it is good that I have been thus troubled and brought low, for I am thus taught the hateful and miserable nature of sin, and again and again I am forced to see, spite of myself, my own wickedness of heart, and to feel my own weakness, and thus to throw myself entirely on God. And He this evening has raised me somewhat from my low and dark state to some perception of Him : yet how thick and dim is the glass we still see Him through, and how much need have I to come closer to Him. Yet whither else can I go ? No one but He hath the words of eternal life, and that alone is worth living for. Oh ! how unspeakable are the riches of His mercy, and how eternal is His love : to bring us back again and again when we fall away from Him, and again to teach us how gracious He is. In truth eternity itself cannot be too long to praise Him in : and yet this life must also be spent in that same service of praise and love, though these be mingled oftentimes with troubles, and groanings, and tears ; and be often hid from us by some earth-born idol of our own creation.

Tuesday, Oct. 27.—To-day again I have been blest by great peace of mind and by strength to continue aright ; this I feel more than I have generally felt before, for it has always happened that my days of coldness towards God and unwillingness to serve Him, have been some of the week-days, and my days of greatest peace have been the Sundays ; on which I have often looked forward to the coming week with great fear and almost horror, expecting to be again swallowed up by the world ; but now I am going on with my usual avocations, yet feeling in me that peace of God which passeth understanding, and a firm hope of eternal salvation through Christ, and feeling also that between to-day and to-morrow there is no great and marked difference to break in upon my comfort. I thank you very much for your advice about my anxiety for the exhibition ; and I think I fully feel how much I must humble myself, and how much there is still in me of self, which must be rendered up wholly unto God. This anxiety has been exercising very bad effects on me, by leading me to work for the exhibition, and hiding God from me in all my daily school-work ; but I pray daily that I may be led more and more " to do *all* things for Christ's sake." * * *

My dearest Isabel,

I am your affectionate Brother,

HENRY.

Rugby : April 17, 1836.

My dearest Isabella,

I find I have *two* letters of yours still unanswered, which makes me begin this sheet to you rather than to Anne. * * * * I have just returned from visiting a poor sick woman, who is, and apparently has long been, a sincere Christian ; and though she was unable from weakness to say much, yet I have received much good from witnessing how a Christian is supported in the most trying hour, and in again viewing how transitory and empty is this world and its goods ; and I find that this last especially is a lesson which I have constantly to learn afresh ; for I live in a state to see the best and most desirable parts of this world ; in boyhood, free from most outward cares and troubles, and with many pleasing and exciting things in prospect ; all this naturally draws me down to the level of the things of this world, and I need constantly to see poverty, weakness, and misery, in order to call to mind that all present things are quickly passing away, and that my affections must be more and more set on things above. I feel a very great temptation attacking me now, in the form of a love of this world, which has come upon me from the prospect of the examinations at the end of this half-year ; for these are constantly before my eyes, on account of my preparations for them, and I am led to look forward to them as the end to which all my present labours are to be directed, instead of doing all things directly for God's sake ;—this necessarily brings a great darkness over me, since I am tempted to have another object in view instead of Christ ; but yet with the temptation God gives a way to escape, and I trust and pray, that by His grace I may not only come out of this trial unhurt, but improved by it. I read in Dr. Arnold's sermons to-day, that " if we have truly tasted that the Lord is gracious, our only reason for wishing to remain on earth, must be to further His kingdom," and I thought how very true, and yet how many other motives do we allow to come in the way—how many other ties to earth do we make for ourselves ! Oh, how very weak and inconsistent are we, and how very sinful ! and how thankful should we daily be, that it is not on our own works that our salvation rests ; and yet even, though we ought to be, and perhaps are, thankful that such is the case, how fain would we try to seek our salvation by our works, and put our trust in them, if we were not constantly checked, and called to remember how sinful they are, and how weak we are.

Your affectionate Brother,

HENRY.

Rugby : May 20, 1836.

MY DEAR FATHER,

Though I begin this letter so soon, yet as I intend it to reach you on your birthday, I must begin it by wishing you many happy returns of the day, and I pray God that they may be also both happy and blessed. * * * I wrote a day or two ago to G——, and have heard from him that I must be in Oxford on June 24th ; the examination begins next day, and the result is given out on the 30th. I shall come down the same evening, and begin the exhibition-examination on the 1st of July (Friday), and shall leave Rugby on Tuesday, the 5th. I shall write immediately the result of each examination is made known ; but I beg you not to rest too much on my chances, which even I cannot now determine, nor shall I be able till the matter is settled. For Wadham, the chances are perhaps rather against me, as a school-fellow who is about my equal tries with me, and I cannot tell what other competitors I may have ; for the exhibition, the chances are about equal, there being two boys whom I fear. But, at any rate, I shall endeavour, that if I fail, it shall not be by want of diligence now ; and if in my

D

letters I have mentioned anything about plans for the holidays, do not think that they occupy my time or attention, but are merely fancies flitting across my head now and then. But, however the event of the examinations may turn out, I know that it will be by God's guidance, and I trust I may not only be content, but glad to receive that allotment which He knows to be best.   I have had some severe struggles with myself : but God has given me His strength, and has enabled me to be willing to commit myself and all my concerns to Him.   I should very much like to succeed according to your wish ; but it may be best for us all that I should not, and then we shall all have need to be thankful that matters have not gone according to our short-sighted wishes, but have been under the direction of Him, who looks not only on our worldly benefit, but on what most forwards us in our approach to His holiness.   As my time draws to a close here, I feel a great deal of pain at parting with old scenes, and leaving school seems to be like leaving the world ; for though one rejoices to go away and be at rest, and enjoy the presence of Christ eternally, and would not return for worlds, yet there is a feeling of pain at parting with what has been so dear on earth ; and the leaving my study for ever will be painful, for it has been the place of my joy and sorrow for the last five years, and has also been the scene of my first opening views of religion, and where for two years and a half I have offered up my daily prayers, and have received so many tokens of God's grace, and mercy, and love.   And yet it is better that these ties should be broken, for it teaches me more manifestly that our rest is not here.   To-morrow I shall receive the Sacrament the last time while I am at Rugby, and much need have I to be exceedingly thankful to my God and Redeemer, for His having so often vouchsafed me the means of attending at His table, and of enjoying the blessed promises of His Word ; for if it was not for His grace, I might be now entirely

ignorant of Him, and be one of those who go away from His
table careless of His goodness.

Your very affectionate Son,

HENRY W. FOX.

Rugby: June 13, 1836.

MY DEAR ISABELLA,

Though I have not been able to manage that you should
receive a letter from me to-day, yet I have found time to
begin one, and I have not thought the less of you, but when
you will receive this one I cannot tell, perhaps scarcely
before the end of the half. I am heartily wishing that time
was come, for I am quite tired out with school-work for the
present, and wish to be at home among you again, and have
some rest and quiet; and besides the weariness of merely
finishing one labour to take up another, I often feel tired of
having nothing but boys' company. * * * But my weariness of school is a very partial feeling; and who can be
unhappy that is a Christian? It is enough to know that our
present situation is of God's appointment, to make us content
and happy in it; and as I know that it is only the feeling of
His presence which can in any circumstances confer happiness, it is rather a mark of weakness of faith to be always
looking forward to some future part of this life, as being
happier than the present, and not to enjoy what God gives
us at present. I am sure you will rejoice in my joy, at
having at last found a person sincerely desirous of becoming
a Christian; he is a boy about fifteen years old, and I first
became acquainted with his state by his coming to me about
a month ago, and inquiring whether I thought he could go
to the Sacrament, considering his state: by this he meant
that he was so sinful. I found that God had been working
in him for some time, but he was yet dark with respect to
the knowledge of many necessary things:—since then we

have met every Sunday evening, and I have endeavoured to teach him from the Scriptures, and explain them to him; he appears very sincere, and has gained more knowledge since I first spoke to him, and though the time we shall have been together will be short, yet I pray and believe that it has been made a means of strengthening his faith, and in leaving him I shall have little fear (I mean humanly speaking) of his relapsing, for God has truly called him, and will uphold him. We had a very nice meeting here about a week ago, for the Church Missionary Society; Baptist Noel was present, and gave a very interesting account of the Missions in the East, especially of an entrance into China : he made me remember Henry Martyn. The assembly was addressed by several other clergymen, and it was very delightful to retire for a while from the bustle and worldly-mindedness of my general scenes and companions, to be amongst those whose only aim was to advance their Saviour's kingdom, and who were talking of Him alone; it was very refreshing and useful to me, and may perhaps be the cause of still more good; for what Mr. Noel spoke so earnestly about—the want, not of funds merely, but of missionaries—has much more than ever before led me to think seriously of so employing the talents which God has given me, but of this I wish to speak more fully during the holidays.

Your affectionate Brother,
HENRY.

Rugby: June 23, 1836.

MY DEAR ——

Instead of sitting alone, and in the sick-room, as I am doing at present, writing a letter to you, I ought to be far away, " skiffing to Iffly and back," but so it is, our fixed plans are not at our own disposal, but are changed when we least expect it : for about a year I have been looking forward to having at least a struggle for a scholarship ; but last

Saturday I was taken ill with the chicken-pox ;—lay in bed
Monday and Tuesday, and am now incapable of going up,
and almost of going out ; at least, I have not been out of
doors yet, though I hope to do so to-morrow. I have not yet
written home, so must ask you to send them some notice of
this interruption of the proposed plan, and tell my mother
not to be at all afraid, as I am quite recovered, as far as
health goes, except my weakness, which will be gone in a
few days, and my plum-pudding face, which will not, I hope,
last above a week ; I have had the peculiar felicity to have
enjoyed the disease in a *marked* degree, having not less than
100 or 120 fine blushing roses on my face, and as many
more on the rest of my body ; at present they have turned
to a fine glossy black colour, and I believe will continue the
same till they are pleased to drop off as unceremoniously as
they dropped in. This has happened at an unfortunate time,
as we call things unfortunate ; but as it was not in our own
hands, but in His who has knowledge and power infinitely
beyond ours, we have no more reason to call it unfortunate
than the contrary. It is not our own will or good we seek,—
and He knows the best, both what is best for us, and how
we may be better enabled to work to His glory ; that was to
be the only end of my gaining the scholarship, and if He has
seen fit to use other means, and of course better, and for us
(as He promises) also better, what cause have we, or desire
ought we to have, to repine ? I at first felt a little disappointment, but I have been enabled to look on it in a con-
tented and thankful manner, and now I am only afraid lest
my father should be much disappointed ; though for my
own sake I would rather that it should be as it is, than that
I should have tried for it and failed, as that, I think, would
have disappointed him still more.   *   *   *

Your very affectionate Brother,

HENRY W. FOX.

Durham : August 29, 1836.

MY DEAR GEORGE,

I thank you for your letter of June 7th, which I received a few days ago : the subject you have spoken of in it has been for a long time, I assure you, a matter of consideration with me, but I do not think that, till very lately, I have entered upon it with a single heart.   It is with shame and sorrow that I have to say, that from the time I was first brought to a knowledge of God, I have scarcely ever walked with a single and entire devotedness to His service : there may have been short times, perhaps for a few hours or days, in which God has been the only object of my desire, but for three years I have had a snare in my path, and have been endeavouring to unite a love of God with a love of the world : and of course the latter has been too frequently gaining the ascendency.   When I look back on this period, I have more and more need to render thanks to God that He has not cut me off for my hardness of heart.   But, praised be His name, He has at last, I believe, brought me to love Him alone, and given me strength to cast away the sins that beset me ; so that now, though my spirit is constantly attacked by, and too often yields to, the enticements of the world, yet I am enabled to set my heart on Him only.   And now that I am freed from having a worldly object constantly before me, I have much greater peace and comfort in Christ —much, very much more—than I have enjoyed for many months, or I may say than I have ever had : now I feel that I can do all things through Him that strengtheneth me ; but only *through Him*.   Hitherto my holidays have been to me a constant source of trial, and of sorrow afterwards ; this year (I know not why—I have not deserved it, and it is through His great mercy alone) God has granted that they should be to me a season of great joy and comfort, and I trust I may be enabled to make them a useful time of pre-paration, for the change in my scene of life upon which I am

just about to enter. To return to the subject of your letter,
I believe that now I am seeking sincerely how I may best
glorify God by my choice of a profession, and that is the
sole object I have; but it was some time before I could
entirely cast away earthly advantages from my view. As
far as I can judge at present, my views agree with yours. I
seem to be rather fit for the ministry than the bar; and
physic, though opening very many means of doing good,
has never occupied my attention. My own desires are
certainly for the first of the three, and my attention is
frequently drawn to view its peculiar duties, so that I should
in some respects be more prepared beforehand for it than
for the others. But I have still some years before I need
make a definite determination, and I trust that God will
hear my prayers to the effect that I may be guided aright
in my choice. I thank you deeply for your letter, which
has been of very great use to me; for your assuming in it
that the glory of God was my only object, made me feel
guilty and aware that such was not the case; it has been
the beginning of my throwing myself entirely on Him. It
is, indeed, an exceeding great mercy to be enabled to have
an abiding sense of our acceptance with God through Jesus
Christ's merits, not by our own. There is the point;—we
are so sinful and so weak, that when once our eyes are
opened, we must despair of salvation by our own means.
And how great is the peace and comfort to feel that our
sins, however heinous they may have been, are blotted out
by Christ's sacrifice, and that our imperfect prayers are
heard, and our works of love accepted through Him, and for
His sake; it is, indeed, a joy unspeakable, and a peace
which the world cannot give or take away. The chief
danger I fear now is, lest I should become proud, and fancy
it is my own doing, or my own merits, which have brought
me to so happy a state; for if we avoid one error, it is
difficult to keep in the straight path; but we are tempted

to fall into the opposite one, and humility is only to be learnt after frequent backslidings. But strange it is that such beings as we, who have most cause of all created things to feel shame, since we alone are fallen creatures, should ever be in danger of becoming proud of our good things, which indeed are not ours, nor of our doing.   *   *   *

Your affectionate Brother,

HENRY W. FOX.

WADHAM COLLEGE, OXFORD.

CHAPTER II.

MY brother left Rugby at Midsummer, 1836, and began his residence at Wadham College, Oxford, in October of the same year.

His correspondence during his career at Rugby has shown a steady development of mind, and a healthful progress in divine knowledge and grace. I cannot refrain from observing, how much more happy was his course than that of many enjoying similar privileges, who neglect opportunities, waste time, and, worse than all, quench the impressions which the grace of God is making on their hearts, instead of cultivating and carefully improving them.

But the object of this memoir is instruction, not panegyric, and I shall not hesitate, therefore, freely to expose the errors into which the subject of it fell; for as much instruction may be derived from the warning voice of those who have erred (if duly heeded), as from the example of those who have walked according to the right rule.

The removal from school to college is a very critical period of life; the reins of personal discipline are of necessity somewhat loosened—the boy has been merged in the man, the *toga virilis* assumed, whilst too often no advance in manliness of mind or strength of character has been acquired, so needful for the scenes of temptation that are in store.

It is not to be wondered at, that so many persons assembled together in this dangerous transition-state, with passions strong and judgment weak, should furnish an atmosphere very unhealthy for sound and vigorous life, and should render that period, which is under any circumstances fraught with danger, yet more hazardous; and so it has always proved that many, too many, make utter shipwreck of their hopes for life during their university career, adding nothing to their stock of knowledge, but largely to their storehouse of vice. It would be unjust, however, not to admit that a more healthful element, some better blood, has been infused into our universities in latter years; and that there is so fair a proportion of men disposed for study and for mental culture, and better still, for spiritual improvement, in our universities at the present day, that any young man who is desirous of following out these, the legitimate objects of his residence there, will meet with sufficient countenance, and friends enough to support him in so doing.

My brother went up to Oxford fortified by the grace of God, and better prepared to withstand the temptations of university life than most at his age; yet for all this, it proved a season of peculiar trial, during which, though he lost not his foothold entirely,— though he was graciously preserved from vice,—nay further, maintained to a certain degree his Christian

character and his Christian warfare, yet he received a
check—his course, for a time, was no longer onwards, but
backwards, and he became the victim of that enemy, so
destructive to the Christian life, a spirit of backsliding.
It may be useful to trace this decline to its origin; for
though in his case, it proved, happily, only the prelude
to a more vigorous renewal of God's grace in his heart—
and in his worst estate he bore, to the outward appearance of man, the character of a moral and religious
person—yet such decays of piety are fraught with
danger of the most destructive character, and often
result in a total and final apostasy from the grace of
God; leaving their unhappy subject a prey to all the
hardening influences of formality, and a conscience
seared with a hot iron, where once all was tender,
promising, and gracious.

1. The first error, by no means an uncommon one,
into which my brother fell, was that of not being
sufficiently choice in the selection of his companions;
associating with many who had no sympathy with him
in divine things, and whose influence could only be that
of deteriorating the better impressions by which his
own heart was already pervaded.

2. He contracted a violent passion for boating, in the
pursuit of which amusement, he found it difficult to
stop at that point which yields healthful exercise; but
became so enamoured of the sport as to spend on it
many precious hours, to which study was properly
entitled. The probability is, that very few have had
better success than he had in this respect, and it may
be a subject of careful consideration for those who are
similarly circumstanced, whether it be wise or prudent

to incur the hazard of being thus carried away ; for in
a solitary pursuit there is no other obstacle to contend
against but one's own will : whereas in boating, the
peculiar relationship of the members of the crew, and
their mutual dependence, give them an influence upon
each other's minds, which few are able to withstand ;
and the result of which often is, a waste of time, the
formation of friendships most undesirable, and an
extravagance of which the loss of money is the least
part of the evil.

3. A want of regular habits and of fixed times, both
for study and devotional purposes, were consequences
very likely to result from such associations, and such
was the case ;—but beyond this, my brother's decline,
at its worst point, went not. The grace of God had
been too deeply rooted, and his conscience was too
sensitive, to allow of his falling away entirely, from
Him to whom he had early consecrated his heart.
Besides this, he had other healthful and corrective
influences acting upon him ; amongst which may be
mentioned his connection with the Sunday-school of
St. Ebbe's, and his acquaintance with Mr. Champneys,
at that time the valuable curate of the parish ; he also
had a district for visiting the poor ;—to which must be
added, the happy influence of domestic affections, and
a frequent correspondence with his sister. Thus, therefore, though to the eye of the world there was not
much to complain of,—nay, if he had not previously
been the subject of deeper impressions, and a more
vigorous piety, one would have rejoiced, even at that
measure which still remained, when most palsied by
lukewarmness ; nevertheless, the disadvantages which

he experienced from the causes already detailed, were
serious and permanent. He was not prevented from
reaping, to a certain extent, those advantages of mental
culture and intellectual development, which our universities, beyond any other sources of education, are so
well calculated to confer, when their course of study
is severely pursued to the end : but he did fail, as he
himself often afterwards lamented, of obtaining the full
benefit which he might have derived from his residence
at Oxford ; and it was mainly owing to this cause, that
the expectations of his friends were not realised, and
the standing he had gained at Rugby not maintained ;
so that, though he took a respectable degree, those
higher honours, of which he at one time gave promise,
were not obtained.

Writing to a friend shortly after he had taken his
degree, he expressed himself as follows :—" I trust your
course at Cambridge may be a more steadfast and
Christian one than mine was at Oxford.   If I may
be allowed a word of advice, I should say, consider
the object of the university, viz., the education of the
mind, and formation of habits, and set yourself to
fulfil it ; and consider in and for whom you are to do
it, and be much in communion with Him who is the
highest blessing."

The altered circumstances in which my brother was
placed, no doubt added greatly to his temptations on
entering upon his university career.

Whilst at Rugby he had enjoyed the advantage of
discipline, that " pressure from without," which was
greatly serviceable in helping the conscientious workings of his own mind ; so that habits of study, and a

system of living by rule, were more easily attained. Now the great advantage of this to the spiritual life need hardly be pointed out. Early rising, with a period of healthful prayer and study of God's Word, before entering on the duties of the day, gives vigour and nerve to the soul, enabling it to discharge its duties with energy and perseverance.

Again, at Rugby, during the latter period of his course, he had the advantage of being in the sixth form, which gave him the office of præpostor; and it is curious to observe what a control this sense of "office" seems to have exercised even upon boys who were not governed by higher motives: a feeling of *esprit de corps* prevailed throughout the body; they felt that upon them rested, in a great degree, the discipline, the credit of Rugby; they were strongly impressed with a sense of their importance, in the exercise of their præpostorial duties, and very high notions were entertained of "the dignity of the sixth."

No doubt some self-conceit and self-sufficiency were infused by such feelings, but the standard of conduct was elevated by it decidedly. I speak more especially of those who had not higher motives to govern them, but even those who had would feel assistance from such external influences.

At Oxford these advantages were lost, and, what would be more injurious, perhaps without being perceived. In the place of discipline came perfect freedom —no external helps towards regular habits—so that except the warning voice of conscience, there was nothing to check self-indulgence, lying in bed, waste of time, unprofitable lounging companions.

Such are the temptations common to all, who are
transferred from a public school to university life, and
it is therefore the more important to contemplate them
beforehand. These, too, are the temptations to which
the steadiest are exposed, as well as others—the
peculiar snares of the better class of men. But surely
a university course ought not to be one of a negative
character, content to escape unscathed by vice; rather
should it prove fraught with the highest intellectual
and moral benefits, and be that season of life when
habits are formed, and principles of self-control
acquired, which shall fit the future man to fulfil his
destinies in the highest and noblest manner.

My brother took up his residence in Oxford at the
most critical period in the history of our Church and
university, which has occurred since the Reformation.
That party was just being formed, whose object of
" unprotestantising the Church of England," has since
been by themselves publicly avowed, but was then
secretly and dishonestly concealed, till the proper time
should come. Those men enjoyed at that day a repu-
tation which they have since forfeited : their novelty,
their earnestness of mind, the show of holiness and
devotion, the touching pietism of their early writings,
all tended to procure for them great admiration from
the unwary, and those who were unable to discover the
secret purpose at which they were aiming.

Others there were, it is true, Fathers of our Church,
whose experience in the things of God enabled them to
detect the counterfeit from the first, and to point out
the unsound theology and Romanising tendency of
the party. In vain they raised their warning voice,

pointing out the necessary result of such doctrines—that
they who honestly pursued them to their legitimate
conclusions must end in Rome : a prophecy which has
been so fully realised by later events as to confirm the
soundness of views and clearness of perception which
influenced those who gave it utterance.

But such wisdom was not to be looked for from inex-
perienced youths, and without question much evil was
imbibed at that period, by those who were to be the
future ministers of our Church, the sad effects of which
we are feeling at the present day.

There are those who were at Oxford with my brother
who trace his decay of piety and increased worldliness of mind to this cause, viz., his having embraced
those unsound views of theology, which were fashion-
able in the university at that day, under the influence
of some with whom he was necessarily brought in
contact, whilst pursuing his studies there. But after
a careful investigation of his journals and letters I
cannot agree with them. It is evident that for a
period he was dazzled by the appearance of those
men, and frequently spoke in their favour, and that
he really misunderstood them; but that any of their
doctrinal errors were imbibed by him does not appear ;
in fact, there is the clearest evidence to the contrary.
And I am fully persuaded that it was owing to the
ordinary process of lukewarmness, arising from the
causes I have already detailed, that his course was
backward during his residence at Oxford, and not
forward.

After what I have said, some perhaps may draw
conclusions stronger than are intended, but I would

again repeat it, that the decay of piety in my brother's
mind at this period was strictly spiritual,—that his
moral character throughout was irreproachable,—that
his heart was ever more or less struggling under the
superincumbent weight of lukewarmness, and mourning
over the loss of God's presence and favour.

Wadham College: Nov. 4, 1836.

MY DEAREST ISABELLA,

Though it is now past 10 P.M., yet if I do not at least
begin a letter to you, I do not know when I shall be able
to do so ; and I suppose that if I were not to write soon,
you would think that my long silence was occasioned by
some other reason than want of time. This has to me been,
very often, formerly, a reason for delaying letters, and is
now ; but the want arises from very different causes : for
though I have enough work to do, yet a good deal of my
time has been hitherto taken up with engagements to my
numerous friends to breakfasts and winings : in the former,
from 9 till 10 A.M. is thus spent to no great use ; in the
latter from 6 to half-past 8 or 9 P.M., with little more profit,
except as affording plenty of time for conversation. These
occupations have been the more numerous from my meeting
with (in addition to the many old friends I have) several
new ones at this college. * * * I have entered a
Sunday-school, which contains 160 boys, and is conducted
in a very able manner by Mr. Champneys, the clergyman,
who is a most excellent person. On Sundays, except for
morning and evening chapel, I am free all day, as far as
regards the college, and thus am perfectly able to give two
hours to the school. Emeris has, through some one else,
become a teacher at the same place. I have found this
change of life a very great trial indeed : for independently
of the broken-up state in which my time has till now been

E

(I hope that in a few days more I shall have done with all invitations), I have been frequently tempted, and yielded to the temptation, of foregoing my mid-day devotions : and thus when the morning has been spent in continual application of my mind to classics, and the afternoon and evening been frequently spent in others' company, you will know that when my devotions have been neglected, I have been worldly-minded in the extreme : this has kept me in a very low state of love to God, till the last few days, when I have been enabled by His grace to resist more successfully the inclinations of my heart. I have all along found the morning and evening service in chapel of great benefit; and instead of growing weary from the constant repetition of the same service, I grow more and more to like it. How daily does one's experience of the wickedness of the heart of man increase. I find mine continually drawing me back to the world, and always at variance with God; and every season of backsliding feeds afresh the half-extinguished flame of sin in it, and the fight has to be fought again. But still, notwithstanding all this knowledge, I am ever yielding to some temptation : I often think of that line of the hymn, "Cleanse me from its guilt and power!" And the days are fast passing away, and the time will soon be at hand, in which the weary shall be at rest, and not only so, but rejoicing in the glory of God. I have already, in spite of the unfavourable weather, become a great waterman. On my third day of rowing, I went down to Abingdon in a four-oar, during which I rowed more than eleven miles, and yesterday the same crew of us went above eight miles, of which the first four was in the rain, and for above a quarter of an hour in the heaviest storm of rain and hail I have ever felt ; but we pulled through it, and none of us have taken any harm from it. * * *

Your affectionate Brother,

HENRY W. FOX.

Louth : Jan. 9, 1837.
MY DEAREST ISABELLA,

* * * Perhaps you will be rather astonished to hear
that I am now strongly tempted to be idle, and it has been
one of my besetting sins during the last term ; I have always
had this as a temptation, but at Rugby I was generally
enabled to resist it, and I trust I shall again be able to do
so when I return. * * * * I am not astonished at your
being anxious respecting me at college, for it is indeed a
place full of temptations of every kind, both outward and
inward : I am tempted on the one hand to be idle by a
hundred different temptations ; and then when I work I am
tempted to do so for the sake of worldly honours and
rewards, and the very work itself is always leading me away
to be worldly-minded. But next term I expect to have a
great assistance, by visiting the poor regularly ; for as far as
I have hitherto done so, I have found great benefit from its
spiritualising my mind. I have not yet overcome my old
habit of laziness in rising, and I feel it to be a constant
source of ill to my soul, either causing me to hurry my
devotions, or to neglect some of my daily work.

Your very affectionate Brother,

HENRY.

Wadham College : June 10, 1838.

MY DEAREST ISABELLA,

* * * I never knew so much wickedness in myself, so
much innate sin, growing apace and overrunning all things,
the moment it was unchecked by the grace of Christ. My
dear sister, you can no doubt feel for me, but you can
scarcely know the extremity of my sin, and the blackness
of my heart ; the frequent entire neglect of God in private,
which made its appearance, even before men, in the form of
carelessness, and the laying hold on the world again, and its
pleasures ; the dimness of the spiritual light ; so that these

things which before had been plainly sinful and hateful
were now become doubtful, and many which before had
been disallowed were admitted; nay, even *now*, I scarcely
dare say that I am out of the slough, so often and often do
I fall back, even when I have been somewhat brought back
to God, and then to think that this is the case with one who
has had committed unto him, not five, but ten talents, for
here am I surrounded, as it were, by every means of grace,
if I choose to make use of them ;—daily prayers, outward
assistances of regularity of mind and habits, good sermons,
truly Christian and wise friends, Sunday-schools, visiting,
and every assistance which books can give :—all this, and
yet so neglected, and I, who am here placed in a most
responsible situation, as a light upon a hill, have become
darkness ;—how much evil I have done, not to speak of the
absence of good to those around, I dread to think of ; but
Christ, who loves us better than we know, deigns to call us
brethren.   *   *   *

Your affectionate Brother,
HENRY.

St. Bees : Aug. 23, 1838.

MY DEAR ISABELLA,
      *   *   * I often find myself deceiving myself by fancying
utility in some pleasure which has perhaps nothing but the
pleasure to recommend it in reality ; thus I am not always
careful about my society, apologising to myself, that to mix
in this or that sort, it may be rather lower than my rank, or
less moral than ought to be, is useful, in order, both in
endeavour to raise those who form it, and to learn men's
manners and minds under every form. I have been passing
by no means a happy time at Ambleside, as far as regards
my state of mind, and I have been in a situation in which I
do not recollect to have been before, though I have known
of it from the writings of others. During my moving about,

I was generally in so unsettled a state, my attention so constantly caught by some novelty or amusement, that I fell into a very careless and godless state.   I cannot tell how low my heart sank in forgetfulness of God, even though I continued my forms of devotion.   On my arrival at the Lakes, my quiet situation, and sudden change of habits from idleness and irregularity to steady reading, gave me every opportunity of returning to God; but here He has used punishment for my sins, and after having a thousand times used mercy, shown in immediate reception after falling away, He has now hid His face from me : I feel as if I could not come near Him, and my prayers are full of darkness and want of faith.   I know that even my present coldness is an additional cause of this state, but it is more than usual.   I desire to bow myself under this trial too, and oh, I desire to struggle after Christ.   I know that He has not altogether given me over to my own wickedness, or else He would not have left this desire after Him in my heart, and I can trust that He will receive me again—nay, does now receive me through His own blood, but that He is using correction to warn me against my sins, and to show me more plainly what are the fruits of following the world.   I have gone many steps backward ; I find myself ever looking forward to some earthly place of rest, and I seem not to realise Christ's kingdom.   Oh, what a miserable sinner I am, to be but now entering into God's service, so long after He has called me, and after so many great and manifest mercies to me !   I sometimes look forward, that probably in two years, or a little more, I shall be a clergyman ; and if I am no more advanced during that time, than I have been during the last two years, how shall I teach, who shall need teaching in the very elements myself ?   *   *   *

Your affectionate Brother,
HENRY.

Oxford : Friday, Oct. 20, 1837.—On Saturday S. H——
and I travelled through pretty hedge-woodlands to Newark,
where we stopped to see the Castle.   Proceeded *solus* in a
fly to Rugby, and as I approached that dear place, all glad
thoughts stirred within me, and my heart leaped to recognise
in the moonlight each scene of my boyhood.   How kindly
too was I received by Mr. and Mrs. Price, and was there not
cause for giving of thanks in all this happiness?   Next
morning I went to chapel, and entering that place of
worship where I first and so often enjoyed in fulness the
presence of God's Spirit, and hearing that same beloved
voice, and seeing those well-remembered faces, filled me with
such an unearthly ecstasy, that I trembled, and could scarcely
stand—for a year had I been looking forward to that
moment, and the reality surpassed the expectation.   And
here I desire to record my intense and heartfelt respect,
admiration, and love for Dr. Arnold, and I wish always to
praise God for His great kindness in having placed me under
him, as from him, as a means, is derived all that I have of
use or of pleasure.   Again did I receive from his hands the
Lord's Supper,—again did I see him ascend the pulpit, and
hear his words of wisdom and of truth.   *   *   *   I wish to
repeat what delight it was to return to old scenes, and places,
and friends.   Rugby is my polar star, and I think of it
daily.   Oh, dear beloved place !

Durham : Sunday, Jan. 14, 1838.—Lord ! do Thou occupy
that place in my heart, which has been emptied of its former
possessors, and which is indeed Thy seat by right.   I desire
to love my Saviour, but I do so very little.   I am about to
enter on some severe trials at Oxford, by leading a different
life, and endeavouring to make all things subservient to the
will and glory of God ; (alas ! how I have hitherto conformed

to the world, and led an inconsistent life,) but to do this my hope is in Christ, who is my Redeemer. Oh, may He be also my exceeding joy !

Oxford : Feb. 2, 1838.—I live much more by myself, and am able to mingle much more in religious conversation. I begin again, after a lapse of a year and a half, to take a great delight in reading, and begin to read more steadily.

Sept., 1838.—During my stay at Frome my life was inconsistent with my profession, and I laid a great stumbling-block in the way of ——, who was quite irreligious herself, and observing how ill my conduct agreed with my language, took, as she told me, a greater objection than ever to religious people. I desire to bewail my sins and backslidings. As a general fault, my want of love to God is chief ; I can love men enough, but feel little of a similar love to God. As to the means of grace, I am careless and sluggish. I know that prayer, thanksgiving, and Scripture-reading are the very life of the Christian ; and he lives or dies according as he uses those. And I oftentimes propose to continue more instant in prayer, but I am ever neglecting : in the morning I am frequently hurried by late rising, at mid-day my heart is cold, and I generally put off, and thus neglect prayer. At evening, I too often lie down in unrepented sin, braving God's wrath, or at most spending a few cold moments in prayer, and I accept the most paltry excuses for neglecting to read God's Word. My Sundays are cold and worldly : I sometimes enjoy the public services very much, but I misspend in idle conversation, sleep, or foolish thought, much of the afternoon and evening ; so that I go to bed cold-hearted and godless, and have no strength for the coming week. In particular offences I am very guilty. I am inactive and indolent, and give way to temptations, even when known as such. Nor am I watchful to avoid and resist them ; nor do I fly to Christ for assistance when under them. And so in outward words and acts, I am inconsistent with my professions,

and I fear I was a great snare to many during my visit in the
summer, and at Kirk Michael : in fact, in outward things,
what difference is there between me and any moral person ?
How do I let my light be seen ? How do I fight against
Satan in the hearts of others ? O Lord, forgive me my
great falling-short in this point ; for I am set on a hill, yet
show no light. How many will there be who, from the
depths of hell, will accuse me of not having warned them,
or of having encouraged them by my example in their evil
courses.

So passed the first two years of his university life :
a better day seems to have dawned upon him with the
third ; and though there are few records remaining of
that period, it is evident that the struggles of which he
complained, had produced a more vigorous renewal of
the warfare ; and that instead of sitting still and complaining, he had been led into the heat of the battle,
and there gained a victory over his own heart, which
resulted in establishing the supremacy of God's authority, and of bringing into subjection those principles
of resistance against God, which still remain in the
believer's heart, and so often cause him trouble and
sorrow.

With this revival of God's work in his heart returned those early thoughts of devoting himself to a
missionary life, which had engaged his mind as far
back as his school-boy days. There is an intimate
connection between love to God and to man : where
the former decays, the latter will not long remain—at
least, the heart will refuse to respond to all calls which
involve self-denial, and require the exercise of a
spiritual mind. To look out upon a world dead in

trespasses and sins, ignorant of a Saviour's love;—to feel their misery, to be willing to hasten to their rescue ;—this, no man ever yet has done, in whose heart the love of God has not established itself, with great vigour and much power.

CHAPTER III.

MY brother took his degree on the 4th of December, 1839, but resided for some months after at Wadham. During this period his mind was deeply exercised in coming to a decision on the important step, which now pressed itself upon him—that of becoming a missionary to the heathen.

He was ordained deacon by the Bishop of London, on the 21st of December, 1840, and married at Bagborough, Somersetshire, on the 30th of December, to Miss Elizabeth James, daughter of the late G. H. James, Esq., of Wolverhampton.

Previous to these events, he had come to the decision of devoting his life to the missionary cause : he offered himself to the Church Missionary Society, and the field of labour to which his attention had been directed was that of the Telugu people, or Northern Circars, who inhabit a district of South India, north of Madras, numbering ten millions of people, to whom, though subject to British rule for eighty years, no clergyman of the Church of England had ever been sent.

By a singular coincidence, the Rev. Robert T. Noble, of Sidney Sussex College, Cambridge, had had his attention drawn in the same direction, and they both offered their services for the same people, unknown to each other, at the same time.

One of the most painful trials of the missionary career, or at least that which is first encountered, is the separation from friends and home, which it involves. But surely this ought not to be a sufficient reason to justify parents in refusing their children, or children in refusing to go, when called of God on so high and holy an errand. We find parents ready to give up their children for secular pursuits, gladly sending them to the same country, and submitting to the same separation, for worldly considerations; whilst those who profess and call themselves Christians are not willing to do that for Christ, which every one rejoices to do for the world. Herein the children of this world are wiser in their generation than the children of light; but it is a sad reflection, that the paucity of Christian missionaries is owing, to a certain extent, to the unchristian conduct of parents calling themselves the followers of our Lord. Many a young man, with a heart beating high for God's glory, has been hindered of his proper destiny, and prevented from carrying out his purposes of love to the heathen, by the selfish love of parents, who are only willing to part with their children, when worldly honour and wealth are the price paid.

Such obstacles, by the blessing of God, stood not in the way of my brother's course; both his parents assented to his plans, and so entered into the spirit of them, as to rejoice in the privilege of having a son willing to consecrate himself to so noble a work : and such was the grace and blessing of God upon that surrender, that when my brother was obliged to return home by the afflictive providence that befel him ; so far from meeting with opposition to his return to India, he was further encouraged in the prosecution of his sacred work, by all who had the warmest affection for him, and the deepest interest in him.

But though Christian principle will lead to the surrender of that which is dearest to the heart, when the glory of God and the honour of Christ are at stake, yet the sacrifice cannot be otherwise than painful : and that pain is increased, by the fact that the influence of Divine grace upon the heart, tends to soften, purify, and refine the affections, and to unite more closely those hearts which have in Christ a common bond of union and affection. The separation about to be made was at that time looked upon as final, and my brother's character was so endearing, that it seemed to all as if we had given up the choicest member,—him whom our hearts could least afford to spare : yet surely, when making an offering to God, it should not be the maimed or the lame, but the choicest of the flock.

At the time of his departure, nearly the whole family happened to be assembled in London, and it was there that the painful separation took place, on Saturday, the 6th of March, 1841 ; whence he and his wife proceeded to Gravesend, but were detained, contrary to expectation, until the 8th, when they embarked in the ship "Robarts" for Madras.

A very vivid recollection of that season is impressed
on my own mind, but I have no desire to dwell upon
the painful feelings of such a parting, for it ill becomes
a Christian to attach undue importance to a sacrifice,
which is daily made for worldly ends, and nothing
thought of.

The contrast, however, between the plans which have
the glory of God for their end, and those which have
not, is most striking in their results.   There is a
security against disappointment in the one, which is
no where else to be found in this world of change and
chance.   For, however the Christian's plans may fail,
however his hopes be disappointed, there is to himself
no loss, his life has not been thrown away, his time
has not been squandered, and his soul is in peace ;—
whereas, when secular objects are the end of pursuit,
and God's glory is not considered, if the object of desire
fail, whether it be honour, emolument, or what not,
there is nothing left, nothing for the soul to fall back
on, and the results of life are an utter blank.   Nay, if
those objects be attained, is the result any better, or
the prospect more cheering, when the hand of death
separates the possessor and his possessions ?

To JOHN EMERIS, ESQ.

2, *Oriental Place, Brighton: Jan.* 9, 1840.

MY DEAREST JOHN,

*   *   *   *   My next subject is regarding poor me.   I
have been casting about an old question, which I have long
put off as out of season, but which now presses upon me in
full force, because now is the time for decision.   I mean the
question, " Must I be a minister in England, or among the

heathen ? " I am not aware that I have any new reasons on the subject, nor that I see them more strongly than before ; but in times past I had to say to myself, " This is not a question to be at present decided while I am yet in education for the ministry generally." Now, however, when each day tends to fix my situation in life, and a decision either way would alter my plans, even for the morrow, I am obliged to give a definite answer to the ever-intruding question : and I see not what other answer I can give than this, " I must be a missionary." My reasons are, as I dare say you know, simply these—that there is an overwhelming call for missionaries to the heathen, and we, the Church of England, have been bringing down punishment on our heads by our neglect in not hearing the call : that thus some one *must* go, and if no one else will go, he who hears the call (peculiarly adapted for the service or no) *must* go. I hear the call, for indeed God has brought it before me on every side, and go I must. My external qualifications of health, strength, and spirits are rather in favour of my aptness, and my internal qualifications are my only drawback : for so great, so honourable, so important a charge is it to be entered upon, that I shrink to think that a being so worthless, so wicked, so very wicked and faithless, should presume to offer himself for it. But better be it filled by the weakest of the weak, than by none at all ; and God can give me strength. As often as I turn the question in my mind, I can only arrive at the same conclusion, and weak and earthly as are many of my present motives for going (for I am full of romantic fancies), yet I see reasons far beyond these motives, and pray that my heart may be filled by more worthy motives, and a pure and single love of men in Christ ; and I know that when I enter on my labours, such fancies will be driven away like chaff :—nay, I accept them rather than nothing, to be a sort of temporary balance to the contrary feeling of pain, in the thoughts of separation

from home and friends. My brother Charles has all along
urged me to take this course, and within these last few days
I laid my case before Mr. Elliott (you know whom I mean),
whose advice I felt confident I could receive ; for he knows
my situation in the family, in life, etc., and is a man of
excellent judgment, and considerable experience ;—he strongly
confirms me in the view I take of it, and he has shown me
an extract of a letter from the Rev. Mr. Tucker, in Madras,
on the subject of a new Mission in India, where all is ready,
people, scholars, house, chapel, school-funds, etc.:—all except
a man to fill the place of missionary ; he speaks in the same
terms as I have often heard and thought, of the imperative
duty of the Church to send out educated missionaries, and
not merely men raised from the poor, to whom to be a
missionary is an exaltation even in a worldly view.   I have
not yet fixed, but I believe I shall do so before many weeks
are passed.

Now, my dear John, I write all this to you, to ask you
for your prayers on my behalf, that I may be guided by
Christ's Spirit in my decision, and supported by Him under
all trials.   Oh, I do so dread my inconsistent life : an
intended missionary, and yet a careless liver.   Do pray for
me that I may walk more firmly in my conversation with
others.   Also I wish for your straight-forward advice ; what
do you think to be my duty?   I do not feel any tie, to
country, family, or friends, which might not equally apply
to every missionary who ever left this land.   *   *   *

Your ever affectionate Friend,
HENRY W. FOX.

EXTRACTS FROM JOURNAL.

Brighton: Jan. 6, 1840.—The question so often put off
is again brought before me, for now is the time to decide.
I am strongly called on to go, because there is no one
else will answer the loudly-echoing challenge of "Come

over and help us!" which rings out from heathen lands;
and there is nothing peculiar to detain or unfit me. So I
have stated my case to Mr. Elliott, asking his advice: his
and Dr. Arnold's are the only two I shall ask.

Jan. 9.—This morning I had a note from Mr. Elliott,
enclosing part of Mr. Tucker's letter from India, which
contained the following information: "They are contemplating a mission in the Telugu country, which for eighty
years has been under British government: the population,
about ten millions, living in towns and large villages on the
coast to the north of Madras. Amongst them there are
only six Protestant missionaries—*not one* of the Church of
England. For eighty years we have neglected it utterly.
This is the last attempt that will be made: everything is
ready except the missionary."

Brighton : Jan. 13.—I still feel bound to be a missionary,
chiefly because I hear and am ready, while none others, so to
say, will attend to the call made: and I feel the call abroad
to be stronger than at home : 1st, because the want numeri-
cally is a thousand-fold greater.—2nd, because here the seed
is sown—we have ten thousand clergy, and many are daily
pressing into orders, but abroad the seed is yet unsown, and
of course no fruit can be expected if we wait till doomsday.—
3rd, our colonies and our trade can be given us for no
purpose but to spread the Gospel : and where are the
ministers ?—4th, though some of the apostles stayed in
Judea, yet Paul, Mark, Silas, and many others travelled
abroad. My great desire now is that my heart may be made
single, so that my motives for going or staying may be simply
the saving of souls to Jesus' glory; but at present they are
mingled with a thousand feelings of romance and heroism.
And oh, my God, my God, men are perishing, and I take
no care ! I am able now to live more to God in prayer and
faith. I am in a particularly happy state of mind, full of
thought. I know that *my* Redeemer liveth.

Brighton : Jan. 21, 1840.—I have been very happy ; all the early part of the vacation my mind was in a state of very great activity, so that almost every sentence I heard made a train of thought arise, often even to a painful extent. I soon felt the happy effects of living nearer to God, peace and content. I then too read somewhat, and wrote a good deal.

Oxford : Feb. 16, 1840.—On January the 23rd, I proceeded to London and stayed till the following Monday ; one of my chief objects was to gain a sense, as far as I could, of the evil and wicked state of that great Babylon, which in some degree I did. The poor fallen women whom I met by night, and the weak men too, the busy, godless, unloving faces, whom I met in multitudes by day, all oppressed my spirit. I spent the Sunday at Whitechapel with S——, and there again entered, in another way, into a perception of the wants of spiritual instruction in the metropolis. I did all this with the object of giving as much weight as possible to the home demands, in order to make my decision more candid ; but all these sensible sights did not outweigh my former sense of the needs abroad. This is to me a quiet time, and I am thankful to God that He has enabled me to continue my devotions, and not fall back into worldliness. But I am at present in a very unhappy state. I am sorely tried by want of faith ; no scepticism, but an inability to realise and feel, either my own sinfulness or Christ's redeeming power; and I am often unable to reach to Him in prayer, so that I go mourning all the day long : I doubt not that it is the effect of my past sinful life, and intended as a scourge to humble me and bring me near to God. I have no sort of ease except in prayer, and I am constantly, as it were, driven to pray ; but even then, my prayers are cold and heartless, and so faithless. I pray continually for more faith, and I can just cling to Christ, and that is all.

Oxford : March 16, 1840.—How small the finite ! how

F

incapable of containing or satisfying the infinite! I have been raised above and beyond the world, and felt how all around is but a vesture, and God, the Infinite, the Eternal, has been very present and visible to my soul; and thanks and glory be to Him, that He has revealed Himself to me, in His Son, by His Spirit, and I am able to cast myself, my sinful helpless soul, on Jesus Christ: yea, thanks to Him, He has received and upheld me; I can look on God as my Redeemer. After many vicissitudes, many risings and fallings, He has brought me still closer to Himself; praise be to Him!

Friday, March 27, 1840.—This is a day much to be remembered in my household; for to-day I have come to my final decision to be a missionary. I am well satisfied and convinced as to this being my true course of duty, and I thank God for so making it plain to me. Emeris sat with me during the evening, and we prayed together for guidance, and help, and comfort in our absence. It has been a formal decision, because I have for some time felt it could not be otherwise. I am willing and thankful to be permitted to give myself up to do God's service, by preaching to the heathen and leaving father and mother, brothers and sisters, home and friends: yea, and if it please Him, life itself. It is an honour too great for me. Oh, may grace be given to me to serve Him in it! I have of late been able to feel more sure of my salvation in Christ—to lay hold on His cross with more confidence: would that I took up my own cross more diligently! I can love Jesus more, for I know Him more as my Saviour; and I am well content to be cut off from social ties and joys, and to give myself up entirely to promote His kingdom, for it is He who has called me to it, who has given me grace to devote myself, who is indeed my all in all. I sometimes feel great consolation in the thought, "This God is our God for ever and ever." A second letter from Dr. Arnold concurs with my plan as

a missionary. Thus has God opened my way on every side :
praise be to His name !

Keswick : Sunday, Aug. 2, 1840.

MY DEAR MOTHER,

I write to you because my heart and my head are full of
many things ; and it is to you that I wish to utter them. I
have to thank both you and my father for giving consent to
my plan of being a missionary ; and a hundred times have
I had cause to thank you in my heart for it, and to feel the
comfort of it ; but I wish, and it is for your own sake that I
wish it, that you gave your consent, and now concurred, more
willingly and heartily ; not merely *allowing* me to go, but
with zeal *sending* me forth ; and I wish this, not because you
should destroy the feelings which cause pain at the prospect
of my departure, nor because I think it a light thing that you
should have given even a half-willing consent, but because
our gifts to God should be given with the whole heart.
" God loveth a *cheerful* giver ; " and if such be the spirit in
which we should give our gold and silver, how much more
should it be that in which we should give our own flesh and
blood ! Nor is it only yielding to a fancy of mine, or to my
judgment that the missionary sphere is the one most needing
assistance, that I ask of you to give both liberally and cheerfully, but I ask of you heartily to acquiesce in the guidance
of God's providence. I believe, from the bottom of my
heart, with that strong sense of certainty and assurance, which
is only given to us on important points, that the missionary
course of life on which I am about to enter, is my peculiar
mission and work, for which I was brought into this world ;
and that, unless I was to follow the course so providentially
and clearly pointed out to me in my heart, I might, so far
as my peculiar work of life is concerned, as well be in my
grave : and were I now to resist the light I have, or had I
neglected to follow where the light (once not so clear) led

me, it would have been in no wise inconsistent with God's
providence and mode of dealing with us, to have taken me
away from all work, either by lingering disease, by death, or
other means. For every soul born into this world has its
own peculiar mission; and to the soul that strives to know,
the knowledge of its mission is given, which, if it refuse to
follow, woe be to it. I do not ask you to rejoice because
I am about to leave you; I know that you will have sorrow
on that account—and for myself as great a sorrow is waiting,
and is already besetting me—but I ask you to feel joy that
I am about to enter on my great work, and that this work
is one so honourable, and which, even among those men
who know what real honour is, receives so much estimation.
For myself, I look on myself as entering (unworthy as I am)
on an office which entails more glory on its holder than any
bishopric, or any civil situation could bestow on man.
Were I seeking honour, and were I most ambitious, I could
not, with the views I have now of temporal and spiritual
things, desire a post more glorious than that of being a
pioneer in a land, in which I hope and believe the Christian
Church will hereafter be triumphant. I entreat you, my
dear mother, to let the true view of my prospects, the joy
which must thence arise, contend with and put down the
pain arising from the temporal view of parting. There is a
pain, and there is a joy : the first is temporal, and though
great, yet the smallest of the two ; the latter spiritual and
far exceeding the other ; let it prevail. And while I write
this for your sake, I write for my own also : for most
desirous am I to have your sympathies with me in my
course ; and as I shall be but little thinking of turning
back, but rather, I trust, in the midst of all pains and trials,
rejoicing for the goodly heritage which God has bestowed
on me, so I would have you working in spirit with me and
rejoicing also. I am most anxious to be able to cast away
all thoughts of self (though this is difficult to do), and

forgetting all personal matters, to seek only how I may best
do the work allotted to me.   Do you, too, try to cast off all
thoughts for me, in as far as myself alone am concerned,
and look only how I may be most usefully employed, even
if such employment be at the expense of my life ; or, what
is more trying, of my earthly ties while I remain on earth.
St. Paul counted not his life valuable, but spent his days
in perils and trials ; why should not I seek to have the
same spirit ? why should not you have the same thoughts
concerning me ?   Do not fear, from my language, that I am
intending heedlessly to risk my life and strength; no, I
hope to sell my life dearly, not throwing it away, without,
if it please God, buying with it the lives of many souls.

Your affectionate Son,
HENRY W. FOX.

Gravesend : Sunday night, March 7, 1841.

MY DEAR FATHER AND MOTHER AND SISTERS,

I cannot resist the desire of writing a few lines to you
before I leave England : we embark to-morrow morning at
ten o'clock, and sail about mid-day.   We have by this time
had a quiet Sunday, and a more peaceable time for reflection.   We have prayed, and do pray for you all, that the
Comforter may be with you, and supplying you with
stronger faith, enable you to look even through your tears
to the Lord, as a loving Parent who afflicts us according to
His good purposes.   We have enjoyed too many mercies on
late occasions to have any reason for doubting the love of
God towards us, and doubtless we shall hereafter be able to
look on this heavy trial of separation as one of the greatest
of His mercies.   May the blank which it has created in the
daily habits of each, be supplied by a more intimate communion with Jesus Christ !   For ourselves, we feel we are in
a very solemn and responsible situation, for we are commis-
sioned on God's service, and have many prayers poured out

on us ; so that no small spiritual advancement will be a fair
interest for so many talents. My chief source of anxiety is,
lest we fall by weakness of faith, by neglect of prayer, or
yielding to indolence, or some other snare which Satan will
lay before us to keep us from God. So long as we continue
under the shelter of His wings, we are safe : our temptation
is to leave that. We are quite well hitherto, except that
Elizabeth is a good deal tired and worn ; the delicious soft
air and sunny sky of to-day have been very refreshing to us
all. We walked to church about a mile off,— a quiet country
church,—and just now I have been out and have heard the
church-bells ringing for the last time. I cannot tell you
what it has been to part with you ; and I dare scarcely look
back at it. I am thankful the bitter moment of actual
separation is past : still there is much remaining ; but it is
through much tribulation that we must follow the Captain
of our salvation. Again, farewell : I say it differently from
what I have often before said it, for it is heavier ; but let us
remember it is not for ever. The Lord keep you and bless you.

Your affectionate Son and Brother,
HENRY.

To the Rev. H. V. Elliott, Brighton.

Ship "Robarts," off Brighton, 12 o'clock, Friday,
March 12, 1841.

My dear Mr. Elliott,

We are now not more than four or five miles distant from
you, but we cannot see either Brighton or the Square ; we
are lying off the cliffs, a little to the east of Brighton, and as
the air is almost a calm, we have scarcely sufficient.way on
the vessel to stem the tide. The sky is cloudless, the air soft
and warm, and the sea pale blue and smooth as a mirror. I
am writing with my cabin window open, without experienc-
ing any cold. We left London on Saturday afternoon, and
spent a quiet Sunday at Gravesend : the day was very

lovely, and we had the assistance and encouragement of
hearing good and Christian sermons in a chapel-of-ease in
that place. At 9 o'clock on Monday morning we went on
board ; since then we have been gently dropping down the
river and along the coast to our present position, with little
or no wind, with cloudless skies and beautiful weather. The
passengers at present on board are fourteen in number. The
rest, beside our own party, are young men, chiefly cadets ;
three or four of them are interesting and superior young
men, and we have received every civility from them. We
have not as yet seen any traces of religious character among
them, but there may be some ; and we feel that, for a time,
they are our little flock.

To me they are my first charge, and I feel peculiarly interested in them. In your prayers for us, will you pray for a
blessing upon our exertions among them ; for besides the
saving of their own souls, how great a thing it would be if
some half a dozen should be brought to a knowledge of
Christ, receiving them as salt and leaven in India ?

Half-past 2.—We are now much nearer to you, lying just
off St. Mary's Hall, and as the horizon has quite cleared up,
we can make out almost every house with the naked eye.
By aid of the telescope every object is distinct. We have
been looking at St. Mary's Hall, and I have been thinking
of many there aiding us, and praying for Christ's kingdom
among the heathen generally. We have traced every square
and place and house, and thought of our various friends, as
our eyes passed along. Our thoughts have been very much
more drawn towards all there, whom we can all but see ; and
in our meeting to-day, Mr. Noble offered up prayers, especially for you. We have, indeed, the greatest reasons to be
thankful to you, and to pray for you, as you have so much
strengthened our hands by your advice and sympathy and
prayers. On you I look as my missionary father, for your
kind counsel and assistance to me in the winter of 1839 was,

under God, the great means of enabling me to take this
course ; for which I each day find fresh reason to thank
God. * * *

Madras: July 6, 1841.

MY DEAR FATHER AND MOTHER,

You shall have my first letter from this our new home,
whither by God's providence we have been safely and quietly
brought. We made land early on Sunday morning, July 4,
with a very light wind. At daybreak we were off the Sadras'
hills, which are about thirty miles south of this place. We
were about four miles from shore : the appearance of land
was a long flat beach, behind which green wood closed the
prospect at once—the land being the most perfect level that
I ever saw—about five or ten miles inland rose the hills, very
like the Malverns, but about half their height ; we could not
distinguish their colours : on the top of one peak was apparently a hill-fort. After an hour or two's sail, we were off the
seven Pagodas. These are the remains, I believe, of a great
city in Hindu days of glory : two of them now stand in the
sea, which has encroached on the land at that point ; one of
them I saw distinctly through a glass; it was just like Mr.
Thomas's model. We lay becalmed almost all the day. In
the morning one "Catamaran" came alongside : in the evening half a dozen or more sold fish to us : there were large
ones, containing four men, and using a "lateen" sail. A
catamaran of this size consists of four or five logs (*i.e.* rough
trunks of trees) lashed together, about two feet wide at the
front part, which is a little turned up so as to rise more easily
over the water, and about six at the stern ; it floats six inches
above water, and lets the water through the interstices. The
four men paddle along slowly, by means of rude paddles,
which consist of a split bamboo five or six inches wide, quite
straight, and without any blade. Several men came on board ;
their dress does not go so far as "shirt-collar and straps," but

consists of a cap and a piece of native cloth passed between
their legs and fastened before and behind with a string round
their loins : to this string they attach their fishing lines in a
coil, and adroitly throw them out at a single cast the whole
length.   They are mahogany-coloured, and their method of
speaking is, as Mr. Thomas says, like the rattling of pebbles
in an iron pot.   After morning service we had the communion, for the last time that many of us would join in
religious worship until we meet in God's house above.   We
were favoured in being becalmed till sunset, otherwise landing
would have broken up the Sunday.   As it was, it was very
warm, the thermometer standing at 88°, and no air to be
felt.   We anchored at eleven o'clock at night : nothing was
visible but the light-house, the palace of the Nabob of the
Carnatic, with thirty or forty windows, and the lights from
a few houses along shore.   We were up at day-break, and
there lay Madras before us, about sixteen large English
ships (an unusually large number), and two or three times
that number of "dhonies," or small native sloops.   There
was nothing in the appearance of land at two miles distance to distinguish it from England.   To the right it was
almost concealed by shipping ; then appeared a row of
houses, flat-roofed and chimneyless, about six hundred yards
long, and not unlike the middle part of Brighton.   Next, was a
sort of common of equal extent, with some tents pitched upon
it : then came Fort St. George, skirting the shore for half a
mile, and containing within its formidable walls several lofty
houses, a church with a spire (the oldest Protestant church
in India), and a flag-staff.   Further to the left still, was a
line of trees as far as the eye reached, broken by the tops of
a few houses, by one pagoda and an *icehouse !*   The morning
was cool and refreshing, for though the sun shone clearly,
which it had not done before for a fortnight, the land breeze
blew cool and fresh.   Within an hour after daylight, when
we had by signal been made known on shore, a fleet of

" Masulah" boats came off. There is an exact model of one in the Durham Museum,—the only fault of which is, that it is too neat. They are nearly flat-bottomed, and the sides rise up straight from the water about five feet in height : they look very like our life-boats ; they are rowed by six or ten men. Their oars are composed of long poles, at the end of which is tied a heart-shaped blade. The men work hard, but the boat does not move more than three miles an hour : the sides are composed of three broad planks laid one above another, about an inch and a half in thickness, and sewed together ; they are sharp at each end, and steered by an oar. We went ashore with Mr. and Miss C—— : the surf was very low : the waves were not two feet high, and a skiff might almost have crossed it. Our crew had some dress on, viz., a jacket, drawers, and cap of white cotton, edged with dark blue ; they were Roman Catholics, and sang hymns to the Virgin, intermingled with an occasional " Hurrah." Most of the rowers in these boats are like the Catamaran gentry, naked. The better boats, as ours was, are painted red out-side, and over the stern where the passengers sit there is an awning. Immediately on landing we felt the heat to be scorching ; we landed just before the row of houses which I mentioned as lying most to the right hand of Madras, and which contains the custom-house and merchants' and government offices. The sun was reflected from these, and from the pale red sand which composes the road, and was like a furnace. We received a note at once from Mr. G. Arbuthnot, inviting us to his house.

Now I must begin to tell you of the novelties of this land : there is nothing like what we have seen before, except English faces, curs (called Pariah dogs), and sparrows. All is so new that I scarcely know where to begin. The country, as I said before, is a perfect level, and when riding through it you know no more of it than you would in riding along a road cut through a forest. The road is half over-arched

with luxuriant and bushy trees, not high ; many of them are
banians, which have suckers hanging from their branches,
but I saw only one case where they had reached to the
ground and taken root.   The cactus, which we prize so much
in our green-houses, is much valued here as a hedge for a
compound or garden, to keep snakes out : those which I have
seen in blossom have been yellow or rose-coloured, pretty
but not gorgeous.   The soil is not so black as I expected :
sometimes it is quite concealed by the thick foliage of
plantains or young palmyra trees.   One of the most striking
sights is the immense multitude of natives.   Mount Road,
which leads from the fort towards St. Thomas' Mount (ten
miles off), is a fine broad road, with occasional bungalows at
its side, and native villages (or pettahs) branching off from
it.   Each time that I have been in it, it has been crowded
for two or three miles with fully as many pedestrians as
you will find in Regent Street in the gayest hour of the day.
To tell you the style of dress among the people, would be·
like telling you the shape of the clouds ; they are endless in
variety.   The children amuse us much,—little mahogany
creatures running about naked, generally with their heads
bare, and shaven all but the tuft of the crown ; the bigger
boys and men have a roll of cotton-cloth round their loins,
and a turban on their head.   This is the case with some ;
others have fuller and more flowing costumes ; some, a
jacket and trousers, but quite unlike ours in appearance.
The dress of a servant is a white wide turban, a long close
skirt down to the waist and knees, and opening in front, and
a roll of cloth wrapped round the thighs and loins like thick
drawers, causing a protuberance in front.   Almost every
man, and many women, paint their foreheads : some have a
round patch of the size of sixpence between their eyes, others
one, two, or three diverging lines drawn upward from the top
of the nose to the forehead, of white or yellow ochre.   The
men are moderately good-looking, the women and girls are

immoderately ugly; they are always carrying heavier burdens than the men. They bore the lobe of the ear, and occasionally wear ear-rings in the form of a brass ball, as large as a turnip-radish; most commonly they enlarge the hole till you might pass your thumb through it, and then making a roll of betel leaf, which is dark red, they place it in the hole,—which looks very ugly. All living creatures (except the English) are thin; some men are bags of bones, all are slim. The cattle are also thin; there are three kinds of these: 1st, the Brahminee, such as you see in the Zoological Gardens, all milk-white, with humps. 2nd, the common bullocks, exactly like the preceding, only *without* the hump; all draught-work is done by these—two of them abreast, yoked to a " bandy " or cart; the horns of both these are singular looking, more like goats' horns, eighteen inches or two feet long, rising from the top of the head, and keeping the same angle as the face. 3rd, the buffaloes, which are not unlike the preceding, but are grey-black in colour, and the horns, which are long, fall back almost horizontally : all are thin like Pharaoh's kine, and the calves are quite amusing for the length of their legs. The fowls look like plants run to seed, as if their legs were their most important feature : they are all legs. I am obliged to conclude hastily, as this is last post to-day. You shall have another long letter by next month's post.

Your affectionate Son,

HENRY W. FOX.

RESIDENCE OF THE REV. H. W. FOX, MASULIPATAM.

(*From a Talbottype View.*)

CHAPTER IV.

AFTER a short stay at Madras, Mr. Noble, my brother,
and his wife proceeded to their post of destina-
tion, Masulipatam (or Bunder, as it is also called by
the natives), the chief town of the Telugu nation.
Masulipatam contains a population of 80,000, and
lies on the coast, three hundred miles north of Madras,
between the rivers Kistna and Godavery.

The first necessary object for both the missionaries
was to acquire the native language. As soon as
tolerable progress had been made in this, they directed
their attention to different branches of missionary
labour. Mr. Noble undertook the management of a
school for the education of the upper ranks in Masulipatam, where a good English education is given, and
the Bible is made a text-book of instruction. This
school has continued to prosper to the present day,
and Mr. Noble, without intermission, and in the enjoyment of good health, has been able to superintend it.*
This branch of operations might have been greatly

---

* Mr. Noble continued at his post without intermission to the
day of his death, which took place on the 17th of October, 1865, after
the long period of twenty-four years of uninterrupted service in the
mission field.

enlarged, could more suitable teachers have been engaged from England. My brother undertook the office of preaching to the natives, both in Masulipatam and the surrounding country—in other words, the work of an evangelist to a heathen nation. But when it is considered that the nation contained ten millions of people, the idea seems almost preposterous, that one individual should have been suffered to go out single-handed for such a work. Yet such must continue to be the case, whilst we at home remain insensible to the claims of the heathen. We have at length become conscious of the inadequacy of one clergyman to attend to the wants of our own crowded parishes of five or ten thousand professing Christians ; yet how much greater is the destitution, when only one is allotted to millions. But our domestic wants weigh so strongly with many, as to prove a barrier to their advocating the cause of the heathen, because we can ill spare men from home. A short-sighted policy this ; as if we had not an abundant storehouse of material amongst ourselves to supply all vacant places, if only it were moulded by the hand of God's grace, to fit it for its own work : and whether a church that pays heed to His commands, and is zealous in extending the knowledge of His name to the ends of the earth, is likely to enjoy that blessing, or one which turns a deaf ear to the call, and shuts itself up within the narrow limits of its sea-girt isle, is a question easily solved.

Bunder : Sept. 5, 1841. (*Sunday.*)

MY DEAREST SISTER,

I like to give a short time on Sunday to you. I used often to do so of old, and every old thing I like to renew or

continue. It is no sinecure to be a missionary. I do not
mean anything regarding any work I have at present to do,
for my present is just like the work I have had in past years
—language-learning—and our movements and changes have
hitherto prevented this from coming in any sufficient
quantities to prove a weight to me ; but I mean that a
missionary life does not deliver one from spiritual trials,
such as used to beset me of old. There are just the same
temptations to indolence and love of ease which have been
my besetting sins all along ; just the same reluctance to
prayer and reading of the Scriptures : in fact I see nothing
but the grace of God to prevent a missionary from being
as cold and dead a Christian as ever vegetated in an English
parish. Perhaps there are more temptations of this kind,
for all around is ungodly. Probably my work will be
deadening to my spirit, up-hill work with the lowest, most
corrupt, and darkened of any men that I ever met ; but my
Saviour is at my side, He can deliver me ; but we do indeed
need the prayers of fellow-Christians for ourselves as well
as for our people. It is one thing to give up home, country,
friends, etc. : to be a missionary is another—to take up our
cross, forsake all, and follow Christ. For that *all* which is
to be forsaken has followed me here ; it is not without, but
within : a man may travel and yet not bear his cross ; all
this I knew and expected ; now I experience it. It does
not dishearten me. I never expected that the being a
missionary was to work any such wonderful change as
belongs to the work of the Spirit alone. But I have great
cause to thank the Spirit for having made the circumstances
of separation work for good in me. It is my own fault,
my own sin, that they have not worked more, yet I think
I am not forejudging in saying that I have been led to see
and know more of Christ and His kingdom during the last
six months. Absence from home, without hope of ever
seeing it again, of seeing you, my dearest Isabella, and all
whom I have loved very very much, is a daily trial ; it is

not a missionary trial, it is no more than every Englishman
in this land is exposed to, yet it does teach one that there
is no rest on earth for man.   For if ever I feel inclined to
look forward to some plan in the future, it is presently
stopped : for I never plan anything with the idea that it
will be in India, but in England; and immediately a painful
recollection comes across me that I shall never be there
again, or if ever, it must be some years hence, and sorrows
will have come and changes taken place, which will make
each person and scene memorials of pain.   We must rest
only in the hope of heaven ; our reward is not here : now
is the time for work, and blessed be our Lord that He has
given me such a sphere for it, and health and strength to
labour.   I feel that on me, humanly speaking, rest the souls
of thousands yet unborn, for this will naturally be the
fountain for spreading Christianity among the ten millions
of Telugu—in fact, among all the centre of India, and according to our zeal, wisdom, and faith, will the event be.   Pray
for wisdom for us, especially pray for faith.   *   *   *

Your very affectionate Brother,

HENRY.

EXTRACT   OF   A   LETTER   TO   THE   SECRETARY   OF   THE
CHURCH   MISSIONARY   SOCIETY,   DATED   MASULIPATAM,
APRIL 1, 1842.

And now to turn to the various papers which you have
sent me : first about Mr. Humphrey ; I was much grieved
to find that such sad opinions had spread into the missionary
field, and I feel very thankful that our Society has been
enabled to act so decisively.   I have heard of similar
opinions among some Propagation Gospel Society missionaries in Bengal, who go among the native Christians, telling
them they cannot be saved unless baptised by, and living
under the ministry of, apostolically-descended episcopal

clergy; which has often reminded me of those Pharisees who came down to Antioch, requiring the converts to be circumcised. It is evil enough at home, but it appears to me to be even more destructive in missions, to set the form before the spirit; and futile must be the attempt to win souls to Christ by any other means than by Himself. How the movements in Oxford teach one the folly of the idea, that the enlightenment of the present age would prevent men from returning to Romish doctrines. I have traced very many resemblances between actual Romanism and Brahminism, and some of the features of the resemblance would suit our friends in Oxford.

EXTRACTS FROM JOURNAL.

Masulipatam : Tuesday, May 31, 1842.—To-day I have got a new moonshee, son of my old one: he is called Malampilly Subbaroydu; the first is his " house name," *i.e.*, surname, and belongs to his family in common with himself; it is derived from the name of some village. The second is his personal name, answering to a Christian name: it is the name of the great serpent, which, in some of their mythological books, is said to be coiled round the world; like a similar reptile in the Scandinavian mythology. I began reading Genesis in Telugu with him. On coming to the passage where man is said to be made in the image of God, I began to ask him what man was: "Was he mere body?" "Didn't know." "What was the difference between a man and a dog?" "A different shape." "If I were to make an artificial man, would he be the same as a living man?" "He would not speak." "But if by machinery I could make him speak, would there be any difference then?" "No." However, when I told him that man was a soul, a spirit, he generally acknowledged it. I next asked him if God had a body. He could not tell, but he thought He had. I

G

asked him where God was. Was He in the room? He
laughed at this : but when I told him that my body could
not continue its functions without God was present to make
it do so, he allowed His presence, and thence from His not
being visible, that He had not a body. Again, on coming
to the passage, " God sanctified the seventh day," I wanted to
gather his notion of the Telugu expression, which is literally
"to make clean or pure," and accordingly pressed him for
his thoughts ; he could get no further than that it meant
" making it clean ;" but how a day could be made clean, he
could not guess ; when I pressed him to think, his answer
was, " Well, it is enough, let it pass." At last he thought
it meant "make it a good day," which he explained as "a
lucky day," "a day of good omen." On telling him how
ill they treated their women by utterly neglecting to give
them any education (for none of them can read or write, or
know anything beyond menial household duties), I was met
by the general answer, " It is my people's custom ;" which I
believe is to them a stronger motive of action than anything
else, except a rupee.

Masulipatam : June 4, 1842.—To-day I have procured
a new moonshee, a respectable Brahmin who speaks no
English ; but like most of them he shouts his own language.
He is a Neeyogee, which is one of the divisions of the
Brahmin caste ; the subdivisions of caste cause as great a
disunion as the major divisions. A Vaidikee Brahmin will
neither eat nor drink in the presence of a Neeyogee
Brahmin, nor intermarry with him. He is a worshipper
of Vishnu peculiarly, and consequently wears the one
yellow and two white perpendicular streaks on his forehead.
His theory of divinity, as far as I understand him, is new
to me : he says there is one God who has put on a thousand
forms, amongst which forms are Vishnu, and Siva, and
Brahma (a son of Vishnu), and all the train of inferior
deities, besides all Avatarams, or incarnations of Vishnu ;

and that God lives in the heaven without a body. On coming
to the passage in Genesis i. where it is said, "God made the
whales," I asked him the meaning of the Telugu word, and
found that it referred to some large fabulous fish (which he
did not believe to be fabulous) not less than 1,200 coss (a
coss is two and a half miles) in length, and 800 in width,
which he says lives in the depth of the sea.

June 9.—A few days ago my elder moonshee, Markam-
deyooloo, when he came to me, showed me the interpretation of a Sanscrit word used to express a "Brahmin," which
was "one who keeps sin off from himself and from others."
On my expressing my astonishment, and asking who the
persons are who do so, he added, "Oh, priest could do it."
I told him I could not, for that I sinned every day : on
which he drew a comparison between the drunken habits of
some Europeans, and my soberness, to the effect that I thus
kept myself from sin. He asked me what sin I did : I told
him, amongst others, I forgot God, and neglected to worship
Him. "Oh," he said, "if we pray a little time to God in
the morning, that is quite enough : we need not do any
thing more ;" and then asked me, if I knew what things
were sins, why I continued to do them ? I said, it was
because of my sinful nature. He then made a general
assent, and added, it is for this reason the world is increasing
so much. I did not understand what he meant, and asked
him to explain himself ;—he said he would do so, by telling
me what he had learnt from his priest. (N.B.—He is a most
garrulous old man, full of curious nonsensical mythological
stories.) "When God had created the world, He peopled
it with men without sin, and consequently, these, after living
about 100 years or so, had accomplished so much goodness,
that they all ascended to heaven, and the earth was left
without inhabitants ; on this God exclaimed that 'This will
not do ; we must not make men so good.' And so He
created another set of men, but put some sin into them, and

therefore they had not, so many of them, left the earth for heaven, but have multiplied."

My new moonshee has a most scrupulous dread of contamination ; he has not been so much in communication with Europeans as most others with whom I have spoken ; but even amongst them I have observed a shrinking from being touched by a Pariah like myself. This man, however, will not sit within a yard of me, and if my hand accidentally comes near him, he draws back in haste and fear. One day a pocket-handkerchief was lying on the table before us, and the wind accidentally blew it towards us, and it seemed as if it would touch him, but he gave a start of horror and a jump, to escape its unholy touch. I asked him to-day, when I found him at one corner of a small room, where I had put him for a few minutes, at the same time that Ammah (wet nurse) a Pariah, was with baby in the same room, how near a Pariah might come to a Brahmin, he said, "Not nearer than two yards." I asked him if the latter should be touched by the former, what he must do. He said he must bathe. But what till he had bathed? He must not eat, nor make prayers to God, nor do worship.

Monday, June 13, 1842.—Yesterday afternoon as we went out for a walk before church, we met Vencana, a young Brahmin boy, a friend of ours, and a companion of his. I had the day before lent him Draper's "Bible Stories," and he had it in his hand to tell me the story of the part which he had read, which he did very nicely in Telugu. He then asked me rather abruptly, whether among my people, the birth of a female was considered a good thing, or a bad one? I answered, of course, the former : he said, it was not among his people. I told him I knew it was not, but that their opinion was a very bad one. He quoted in defence of it some padyams, *i.e.*, verses, which struck me so much, that this morning I got him to write them out for me ; they were to the following effect :—

" The tree may spring up in the jungle, but a female must not be
    born.
    Mountains and great stones may be formed, but a female must
        not be born.
    Birds and beasts may be produced, but a female must not be
        born."

After a few more words on this subject, Vencana asked
me, what seemed to be another great question, " Whether
riches or learning was best," or rather, how they were considered among my people? After telling him how many
preferred the former, and also their folly, I pointed him to
the true learning and knowledge of God, and how the love
of God could alone bestow happiness : whereon the other
boy asked, in a tone of some surprise, " Can a poor man
love God?" I answered, " Of course he can ; why not?"
" How can he love God," he said, " when he has no rice in
his belly?" * * *

My new moonshee is an intelligent man ; the other day I
was speaking about man's sinfulness, and inability to obtain
heaven by his own works, and he persevered in the doctrine
that " good men did a certain amount of sin, it was true,
but then, they balanced it by a large share of righteousness (punyam) ; so to-day I brought before him in detail,
the argument, that we may know a tree by its fruits, and as
it is evident that a vast number of men sin largely, so their
nature must be also sinful ; this illustration he tried to
answer by a second. " Take a mango-tree," he said ; " the
young fruit when very small is worthless ; even after it is
full-grown it is sour ; but if you wait till it is ripe, it is
delicious ; thus you have a variety of fruit from one tree."
I think he was satisfied by my answer, that these were not
different fruits, but different stages of the same fruit. His
first difficulty was, his disbelief in man's nature being one
only, and not varying according to individuals : we had some
discussion on this point, in which he gave in to what I

advanced ; but whether he was convinced, I am by no means certain :—his second was, he would not believe man's nature to be *only* evil, but evil and good mixed : this point, too, he seemed to yield at last ; but then after all, he said, " God was very merciful, and would take away our sin." When I pressed on him that God is very just, and the case of a prisoner and judge, he at last seemed to have come to a stand-still, and exclaimed, " Well then, how can our sins be taken away ?" Then I was gladly enabled to lay before him Jesus as our Redeemer and our Sacrifice, as bearing our own sins, and suffering our punishment. To all which he listened patiently, but objected, how could one man suffer another's punishment ? such would not be allowed in a court, etc. To which I answered, by the common but very imperfect illustration, of a man having his debts paid by another : and also that He who bore our punishment, was not man only, but God, the Judge Himself. He said no more about it ; presently he began some sentence with the common saying ; " God has made all religions, and therefore," etc. Here, too, I think I succeeded in showing him that these religions were contradictory, and consequently could not all be true, and how could God create a lie ? " Who made them then ?" " Man's evil nature." Thus our conversation ended, and we went on to chant and translate the verses of Vencana.

Masulipatam : Tuesday, June 14, 1842.—Last week I began instruction among my servants. My Maitee, who is my head-servant, is a Mohammedan, and an intelligent fellow, though he is very ignorant of his own religion, and has been cast off by his own people for marrying a Hindu woman ; he speaks a little English. Besides him, I have present, the cook, two horse-keepers, the gardener, occasionally the waterman, an old man rather dull of understanding, baby's Taniketch, or nursery-maid, and sometimes a little inattentive son of hers, Datchmi, *i.e.*, the sweeping-woman, who is very dull, and lastly, the two little girls of Maitee, whom Elizabeth has taken

into the house to instruct, the one eight, the other ten years
of age. They sit down on the ground in a semi-circle before
me. I began with the first two chapters of Genesis, explaining as I went on, and pointing out some of the attributes of
God, the creation, fall, and punishment of man;—the last
few days I have been insisting on our sinful nature, and God's
wrath upon sinners, and going through a list of the most
prominent sins, most of which they assent to, but they seem
astonished at being told of the sin of idolatry. I am also
trying to make them learn the Lord's Prayer, but find them
slow, both at comprehending and remembering it. Three or
four of them seem to understand me pretty fairly ; how far
my words convey, or give rise to correct ideas in their minds,
I cannot well tell ; for if they answer me in any long sentence, or try to explain my words to each other, I only very
imperfectly catch their meaning. I find great difficulty in
expressing myself to them in Telugu ; for very many of the
words which I have been in the habit of using, when conversing with my moonshee on similar subjects, have been of
Sanscrit origin, and like the big Latin words in our language,
are unintelligible to the poor. I have begun it, because I did
not feel it right to let them go on without any instruction,
when I could say a few words to them, but I am a most
incomplete wretched instrument for conveying knowledge to
them. It may be, the Lord may cause light to shine in their
dark understandings through my words, for it is out of weakness that He delights to bring forth strength ; but I cannot
at present look for any such event, according to the ordinary
course of His dealings. I continue to instruct my servants
every morning at 9 o'clock ; after going through the first
two chapters of Genesis loosely and the subjects contained
therein, especially the fall of man, I for several mornings
dwelt upon sin and punishment, and detailed the Ten Commandments, and several other rules whereby we learn what
are particular sins. The servants chimed in with all I told

them, except that idolatry was sin, which was evidently novel
to them.   I then led them to Jesus as the Saviour for sin,
and read to them His birth, as recorded by St. Luke: and
am now going through some of His miracles, *e.g.* casting out
devils, raising the widow's son, healing the centurion's servant
and Jairus' daughter; stilling the tempest; Mary Magdalene
in the house of Simon the Pharisee.   Two or three of them,
viz., Mohammed, one of the horse-keepers, and the gardener,
evidently understand me pretty well, and take an interest in
what I say, but the rest are inattentive, or do not understand
me.   I do not think they have any *system* of belief to be
overcome, but will be willing to believe what master tells
them to be true, the Mussulmans no less than the Hindus.
They can now repeat about half the Lord's Prayer, and
understand its meaning pretty well;—as soon as they know
it all, I shall commence our instruction in the morning with
that prayer.

CHAPTER V.

THOUGH apparently possessed of more robust health than his coadjutor, my brother found the Indian climate much less congenial, and it was not long before the intense heat produced a nervous debility and prostration of strength, which quite disqualified him for work.* It was necessary for him to seek for relief in a change of air ; a short voyage along the coast, and a residence for a few weeks at Vizagapatam were tried without success, and it became needful to have recourse to Madras for medical advice. From thence he was ordered to the Neilgherry hills, which are the nearest sanatory station for Southern India ; rising from the plain to a height of several thousand feet, two hundred miles inland from the coast, they afford a most delight-

---

* It frequently happens that the most vigorous English constitutions suffer most from the heat of a tropical climate, whilst persons of consumptive tendency or sluggish circulation enjoy better health than they would at home. So it proved in my brother's case ; both he and his wife were blessed with strong and vigorous constitutions, and left England in the enjoyment of perfect health ; but the very redundancy and fulness of a healthful temperament seem to have proved a bane in the exciting and enervating climate of India.

ful and refreshing temperature, and abound in scenery
of the wildest and most romantic character. Ootacamund forms the principal residence for invalids on
those hills, and thither, in January, 1843, my brother
proceeded with his wife and little boy, which had been
born previous to their departure from Masulipatam.

A very interesting circumstance occurred about this
time, which rendered their visit to the hills a period
of great usefulness to one young person, who had
previously been sunk in the depths of heathen
degradation.

It so happened that there were two children who
had come down from Masulipatam to Madras, whose
father, a European surgeon, had died when they were
young, leaving them property; but the mother, a
Telugu woman, had brought them up in heathenism:
—after much legal delay, Mr. Tucker was appointed
guardian to these children, a girl fourteen years old,
and a boy thirteen, and he entrusted the former to the
care of my brother and his wife, when they were
proceeding to the hills. The girl was perfectly wild
and ignorant, and it was with difficulty she could be
taught to use a spoon instead of her fingers, to sit on a
chair instead of the ground, or to wear a European dress.
Her notions of religion were of the most debasing
character, and her mind was thoroughly imbued with
the heathen superstitions which she had learnt from
her mother. There was, therefore, a great work to be
done, and that at a somewhat advanced period of
childhood, which threatened to render the task more
hopeless; for there was not only an entire education
to be imparted, a character to be formed, and a mind

developed; but there were counteracting habits and prejudices to be removed, and all the destructive influences of her previous associations to be overcome. My brother and his wife realised the difficulty of the task, but were encouraged by a hope, which God was pleased most abundantly and graciously to fulfil. "We gladly accept her," he wrote, "although the responsibility will be great; the formation of her character will be a great work; assist us in it with your prayers —she may be a chosen one of God, who shall hereafter be for His praise."

After having passed through a preliminary process of breaking in, the character of this girl began rapidly to develope, and greatly to improve.* During a residence of two years on the Neilgherries, so great was the change, that she returned to Madras, where she was sent to a boarding-school, quite a transformed character. This transformation consisted in her having laid aside her heathen ideas, and conformed in all outward customs to those with whom she lived; it was a great struggle for her for some time to dine at table, lest "every one should see her eat." During this period also her mind was improved by the careful instruction which she received, nor did it rest there; for God seemed so to bless the Christian teaching she received, that she gave evident signs of an inward and spiritual transformation of His own gracious working.

The improvement of her character continued after her removal to school, and there was every reason to

* I may mention that from the beginning she was treated by my brother and his wife as one of the family, and was not allowed to associate with the native servants.

believe that she had become a truly converted follower
of our Lord; when, in the year 1848, she was removed
by an early and sudden death, at the age of 19.

My brother took a lively interest in her to the last,
looking upon her as one who should be a crown of his
wife's rejoicing in the presence of our Lord Jesus Christ
at His coming. When on his death-bed, he sent her
an affectionate message, little supposing that Mary
Paterson, whose spiritual welfare he had so tenderly
watched over, had already gone before him to the
mansions of glory.

The following passage relating to Mary Paterson
occurs in a letter dated Nellore, January 5, 1847:—

"Mary Paterson is now more than ever precious to me,
as the crown of rejoicing of my dear wife. I saw her
several times while in Madras, and it was an exceeding
pleasure to have intercourse with so very transparent and
beautiful a mind, which with so great simplicity is resting
and living on Christ. Hers is indeed a wonderful case; the
season of the year reminded us that only four years have
elapsed since she was, in the same month of December,
brought to us at Mr. Tucker's, a heathen child, and now
she is such a beautiful Christian character! yearning and
striving after the conversion of her mother and her heathen
relatives, and desirous of being engaged in making Christ
known to the Telugu women."

Further to illustrate the character of the influence
brought to bear upon this young person's mind, and
its happy effects under the blessing of God, I shall
introduce (after the next), one of the many letters
written to her by Mrs. Fox, whilst she was at school
in Madras; also two from Mary Paterson herself,

which will serve to confirm what has been stated of
her.

Ootacamund, Neilgherry Hills : April 3, 1843.
MY DEAR GEORGE,

You have occasion to be angry with us for so seldom
writing to you, yet you see I do not hesitate to write to
you after so long a silence, braving all your feelings of disappointment or anger. And this is because I am sure of
your brotherly affection and forgiveness ; and yet how backward we are in coming to Christ, who is closer and more
loving than a brother, after we have offended Him ;—is not
this for want of faith in His boundless love ? I find myself
now, after having been devoted to His service these nine
years, with scarcely any knowledge of the love of Christ,
and of course with but very little love for Him. I now
desire to love Him, that is, I do so at times, for at other
times I am indifferent, and have too much regard for my
own ease ; but the desire seems to be almost all that I have.
Do I not seem to be unfit to be a minister of His ? And
may not His present dealings with me, by keeping me back
from ministerial work by ill-health, be intended to prepare
me to make Him known more truly, after learning to know
and to love Him myself ! I can bless God, I think, with all
my heart, for having given me this past year of poor health;
—I have found it healthy for my soul, and it is one of the
tokens of His love. As yet, I cannot see my way before me,
that is, I cannot at all guess at the human probabilities of
my health being so far restored and established as to permit
me to continue in India : to go away now, after I am drawn
by so many ties to the poor heathen, would be a painful
struggle, and my corrupt nature, I fear, would repine at doing
so, and yet I ought to acquiesce and rejoice in the will of
God, whatever it be. Will you make it one of your prayers
for us, that we may be guided to know what is God's will

regarding us, and that we may be quick and ready to follow His guidance? * * * We have under our charge an East Indian girl, a ward of Mr. Tucker's: she was a perfect native, in habits, dress, temper, and mind, when she came to us in December; and now we have daily to wonder how great a change God has wrought in her, and He has done more without our means than by us, forestalling us, as it were, in our plans. When we first knew her, she had the most furious, uncontrolled temper which I ever witnessed; but since we left Madras in January, she has been peaceable and obedient, not once showing the slightest marks of her own fury, but accommodating herself to our dress, habits, and especially that of eating;—she gradually and gently acquiesced, greatly to our wonder, and that of others. She is now English in her outward appearance, has left off chewing that nasty betel-leaf, washes herself pretty clean, wears her clothes tidily, keeps her hair neat like an English girl, though, I am afraid, not quite free from inhabitants;— and eats with us every thing set before her, except beef, which is an abomination to the Hindus, both from super- stition and custom, just as horse or ass-flesh might be to us. She does lessons with Elizabeth, for two or three hours in the afternoon, reads and talks in Telugu with me in St. Luke's gospel, for half or three-quarters of an hour after breakfast; listens to my teaching the servants, works with her needle in the evening, walks out with us in the after- noon; sits quietly at our morning and evening prayer, and says she prays, when I repeat the Lord's Prayer in Telugu; and goes to Church with me. However, she is very slow in her learning, either English, or any other intellectual study, not from want of natural quickness, or of memory, in neither of which does she fail, but from an extraordinary habit of inattention and repulsion to thinking, which I do not think you could believe till you knew a Hindu. I have frequently told her in detail all the great events of Christ's life and

ascension, and their bearing upon us ; but each time she has
listened to them, as novelties she has never heard before ;
notwithstanding I am sure she understood what I said each
time, and could have recollected it if she had taken the
trouble.   She is still the complete heathen : not but that
she seems to have given up, as ridiculous, many heathen
fables and superstitions, but she is still like the other
Hindus, an atheist, "without God in the world," professing,
like many of them, to believe in our God, yet denying Him
His great attributes, or ignorant of them, so that to her
God is but a name.   She leads us continually to the throne
of grace, and there are many Christians here who are
interested in her, and who are interceding for her ; and we
trust that as God has shown to her so great mercies already,
He will not leave her without bringing her to Him.

The three following letters are placed out of the
order of their proper date, to connect them with the
subject of Mary Paterson.

FROM MRS. HENRY FOX TO MARY PATERSON.

Masulipatam : July 16, 1845.

MY DEAR MARY,

I thank you very much for the nice letter which Soobiah
brought me a short time ago.   Mr. Fox and myself were
both much pleased to see how greatly you had improved in
your writing : there were still a few faults in spelling, but
these, if you take pains, will, I hope, soon be corrected.
You will be glad to have a little holiday, and I am sure you
will enjoy the time with so kind a friend as Mrs. S——.
You will also have more time for reading your Bible and for
prayer in your own room alone, than you would have had at
school, and also more quiet, to think of your own soul, and
of God's great goodness to you ; this I hope you will also
enjoy, dear Mary ; for the best knowledge we can have, is

the knowledge of God, both by going to Him in prayer, and
by reading His Word ; just as if we had a dear friend, whom
we wished to know very much of, we should go to him often
to talk with him, and it is just so in our prayer to God,—we
must go to Him, as little children do to their fathers, telling
Him all we want and all we feel, and believing that He is
listening to us, and will give us all He knows will be good
for us. How very good it is of God, is it not, dear Mary,
to allow us to come to Him in this way, and make Him our
Father and our Friend ? All these great blessings, and every
other blessing we have, are given to us through Jesus Christ,
who died for us in our stead, that we might be made the
children of God, and receive all these blessings from our
Father. Jesus is full of love to you, dear Mary, He looks
upon you, I trust, as one of His own dear children ;—how
great His love has been in bringing you out of darkness into
light. Oh, then, seek to know Him more ; go to Him
very often when you are alone, and ask Him to give you
more light, to make you know Him better, and to love Him
more ; He will hear you, for He has said, " Whosoever
cometh to Me, I will in no wise cast out."

In Christ's name, and for His sake alone, you must pray
to God to forgive you your sins, and give you a new heart,
and be assured that He will hear you and answer your prayer.

Give our love to John ; may Jesus bless you both, and
make you His own dear children.

Your affectionate friend,

ELIZABETH FOX.

FROM MARY PATERSON TO MISS TUCKER.

Madras : Jan. 2, 1846.

MY DEAR MISS TUCKER,

It is a long time since I had a letter from you ; it makes
me think that you have been very busy for the last six or
seven months.

This is the third year since we heard about the true God : these three past years, God has been to us very gracious in every thing, and especially that we can read now His most holy Bible ; and how kind He is to put us under the care of such a dear friend as your brother, Mr. Tucker.

I suppose you heard all about the death of my dear friend Mrs. Fox ; though I am sorry for the dear little children, I am glad to think that she is now much happier than before. I had seen her three times before she died ; she was so happy to see me, and spoke to me a long time ; though the doctor told her not to see any one. I am most thankful to have seen her before she left this world (if she had died at Masu-lipatam I should not have seen her), and I hope I may go there also, where she is now, through Jesus Christ.

I think you know very well that I am not confirmed yet, but it was one of my greatest wishes to take the sacrament, but I did not like to tell Mr. Tucker ; and one day he came to the school to see me ; then he spoke to me about it, and asked if I should like to take it. I told him, I will be very glad to do so. Another girl, who is my best friend in the school, wished to take the sacrament with me, and so we did on Christmas-day at Mr. Tucker's. Miss —— gave me a nice little book ; its name is "Companion to the Communion." I like it very much. I am glad to tell you I got a prize again ; if I had not been ill, I would have had the first prize, but this is the second—the name is "Bridges on the 119th Psalm ; " it is a very nice one, and I like to read it.

Will you please tell your sisters that I am very much obliged for the nice little pencil they sent me ;—my best love to them and yourself.

Your affectionate Friend,

A. MARY PATERSON.

H

Madras: April 17, 1847.

MY DEAR MR. FOX,

   *   *   *   I am very happy to tell you that I was confirmed on Easter Monday at Vepery Church : you will be surprised to hear the number of candidates that were confirmed ; there were altogether more than three hundred, and the greater part of them were natives. I was quite surprised to see such a number of native Christians. The Bishop gave us a nice little sermon. You cannot think, dear Mr. Fox, how happy and sorry I felt that day,—happy, because there are many reasons that I should feel so, and it would be a needless thing for me to write and tell you why, for you know just as well as me, and perhaps more too ; and this is the reason why I feel sorry, for all former things come to my mind—what I was, and what I am now ; if it had not been for God's great goodness I should never have known Him, nor His dear Son Jesus ; and I feel that I do not love Him as I ought, nor am I thankful to Him for His great kindness ; will you pray for me, dear Mr. Fox, that He may give me His Holy Spirit to help me to do what I have taken upon myself, that I may hate every kind of sin, and love Him more and more. I must also thank you, too, for you were the first person that taught me about the true God, and also dear Mrs. Fox.

Your affectionate

AGNES MARY PATERSON.

Ootacamund : May 8, 1844.

MY DEAR MOTHER,

   I had intended to have begun a letter to you yesterday, to let you know that I did not forget your birthday ; but various occupations obliged me to postpone writing till to-day. I did not, however, allow the day to pass by without

especially asking blessings for you from our gracious Lord.
It is one of the comforts which we have, in spite of the
distance which we are from each other, that, though our
correspondence takes nearly two months on the road, our
prayers take not so many minutes : what we ask of God this
minute for each other, may be fulfilled by Him the very
next. He is our most rapid, as well as most effectual,
medium of intercourse. My dear mother, may He richly
pour out upon you and my dear father, all His best gifts ;
so much of health and temporal prosperity as may be best
for your souls' health, and to enable you best to glorify His
name. There are no bounds to the spiritual blessings I
desire for you. May you grow daily in Him riper and riper,
till the day when He shall put in the sickle. May you
know Him more and more, in His great love, in His mighty
power, in His wisdom, and goodness, and glory. May He
daily become more precious to you. May you continually
have an increasing communion with Him, and have your
hope of His kingdom grow lighter and lighter as you draw
nearer to it. Though we do not hear from you every mail,
we still have a sort of intercourse in dwelling upon your
affection towards us and in returning it ; and I am often
able to fancy you at your various employments. I was very
glad to hear from Isabella's letters, a few months ago, that
the dining-room was occasionally changed into an evening
school-room. How much might be done in the mass, if
every family would undertake to be teachers of righteousness, not of alphabet only, to a few children or young people.
We shall never see the Church composed exclusively of
godly people, but we may see a larger number of such in
it than at present ; and at least much happiness is gained,
if not an eternal yet a temporal happiness, by increase of
religious instruction. One sees that in this country, religious
education, however slight and however little improved,
humanises the pupils far beyond the common alphabetical

teaching. It was Mrs. Bailey's (of Cottayam) remark, that
the children of her old pupils were much more manageable
at first, than those who came from new families. * * *

From your affectionate Son,

HENRY W. FOX.

During his residence on the hills, he had a daughter
born, and he also made an extensive tour through the
Travancore and Tinnevelly district, in company with
the Rev. Henry Cotterill. He kept a journal of this
tour, which is too voluminous for publication ; but he
derived great advantage from the opportunity thus
afforded him of seeing with his own eyes the most
important field of missionary labours in South India,
and from becoming acquainted with many experienced
and faithful men, whose counsel was of great value—
whose friendship and Christian intercourse were a great
privilege.

He returned with his family to Masulipatam, *viâ*
Madras, in October, 1844, so completely restored in
health, as to give him the most sanguine hope of being
able to labour for Christ in India with fresh vigour ;
but further trials were in store, more severe than he
had yet experienced.

There was, however, a brief season of intermission :
and for more than twelve months he was steadily and
actively employed in his missionary duties : studying
the language, and, as he got more freedom of speech,
going out amongst the people, and preaching to them
Jesus.

Masulipatam : Nov. 10, 1844.

MY DEAR GEORGE,

* * * It is on the good sword of the Word of God
that I have to rely here. I go out among the people, and
get a little talk with them, so lamely and poorly on my part
as to appear wholly inefficient ; and the people either dispute
and oppose, or listen with indifference ; and were it my own
word I had to tell them, I should soon get out of heart ; but
I know the sword of God, clumsily handled though it be,
must reach the hearts of some of them ; so I come away
quite joyfully from the midst of the opposition or the
sluggishness. It is like the Woucali poisoned arrows which
Waterton speaks of ; the Indian blows the arrow, strikes the
prey with a trifling wound, and the arrow falls out again
while the beast runs away as though unscathed ; the hunter,
however, follows, sure of finding the effect of his poison in
the dying animal before it has gone far. So we now sow seed
which we know is good and full of life ; some of it must
spring up, and some one or other will reap the harvest.
Blessed be God for the assurance He gives us, and for the
certain promises He has bestowed upon us in connection
with His work.

Masulipatam : Jan. 15, 1845.

MY DEAR GEORGE,

I begin my letter with a desire to urge upon you to be
very diligent in trying to get some one to come out and join
us here : not that I suppose you are deficient in zeal for us,
or in trying to forward God's work here ; but while I feel
myself so very strongly the want of more missionaries. I
can do nothing else than cry out to you and others to make
known our wants with glowing tongues. I daily feel increasingly my insufficiency here, single-handed among so
many thousands. Our dear brother, Mr. Noble, is tied up
with the management of the English school, in which he
has the head class to himself, and it is a most interesting and

important sphere, to which if he did not give his time, it would be my part to give mine; and this because no one will come out from England to take this work off our hands. Mr. Sharkey and Mr. Taylor, two valuable East Indian young men, are for the present occupied in the same sphere. I am alone in the work of preaching and general evangelising in the town and villages : and what can I do? I am lost and bewildered in the multitude of work : I am yet very imperfect in my knowledge of Telugu, and a considerable portion of my time has to be devoted to the study of it; and when I go among the people, it is with a stammering tongue and a misunderstanding ear. There lies before me the crowded population of this large town of sixty to ninety thousand inhabitants : these are to be preached to, to have an impression made on them. If I go to one part one day, and to another part another day, my time and labour are dissipated. If I keep myself to one portion, my labour is swallowed up in the great flood of heathenism : it is like trying to clear a spot of ground in the centre of a luxuriant jungle,—the roots of the surrounding trees fill up the spot I am at work on, faster than I can clear it. Again, there are the villages in the suburbs : fine populous villages. Again, there are the numerous villages and still more numerous hamlets studding the country all round about. Where I am to begin, I know not. Then there ought to be schools to be looked after, to be established, to be watched and taught : I cannot so much as begin them. And so, though I may be preaching continually to the adults, there is the rising generation growing up in their heathenism ; the most hopeful portion untouched. Besides this, I have my servants to talk to daily,—many cares and calls upon my time,—and, above all, it is only a very limited portion of the day that I can be engaged in out-of-door work. It is not as in England, where you might go from village to village, or spend two or three hours conversing in one village. Here we are

restricted to the short periods before and after sunrise and
sunset : exposure to the mid-day sun is a mere foolhardy
shortening of the time of work, at least to most constitutions.   Besides all this, there comes the work of transla-
tions, as only a portion of the Scriptures has been translated,
and so far as I can judge, a great part of what is done, needs
to be done over again, to render it generally intelligible.
Tracts there are in some numbers ; books are only yet by
ones or twos.   Who is sufficient to unite in his own person
these multifarious duties—preacher, teacher, superintendent
of schools, translator, not for hundreds, but for tens and hundreds of thousands ?   As far as man is concerned, does it not
seem hard that our old school-fellows and fellow-collegians
should refuse to come and share our burden, and make that
easy which is now bewildering and crushing.   Who ever
heard of two or three men being sent to storm a strong fort ?
and I am sure that Masulipatam, with all its idolatries and
wickedness, is a very stronghold of Satan.   I know that our
dear Lord has sent us here about this work of attacking the
town, and we often bless Him that He has done so, but I do
not think that He has intended us to be sent alone.   I cannot
help thinking He is calling others, but they will not hear :
the more so, because it is His revealed plan not to send so
small forces for so large a work.   Our dear Lord sent at first
twelve, and then seventy men through the little country of
Palestine, which is not bigger than this district of Masulipatam by itself.   Paul generally had three or four companions
with him in his missionary work.   Augustine brought no less
than forty monks to evangelise England.   Gideon had his
three hundred men.   God can, if He pleases, magnify Himself by converting many souls, where the instruments are so
very poor and so very few ; but we know that such is not
His ordinary plan, and it can scarcely be that He would do
so, simply to relieve the idleness or *vis inertiæ* of some of
His servants in England from the trouble of getting out of

their snug nests to come here. Pray put this to as many as
you can, young as well as old, that there is a great work to
be done here, and an insufficient number of persons to do it.
God has, however, commenced operations, surely He is even
now calling for fresh labourers ; put it to them whether they
are not the labourers that He is calling. There are, doubtless,
as usual, many young men hanging about Cambridge, taking
private pupils, only because they have got nothing else to do.
Some of them, doubtless, are men of God : I would that these
might feel that God has a greater work for them here in the
villages of Masulipatam, than the getting two or three men
annually through their examination. It is painful to us out
here to think how many young men there are in England in
search of ministerial employment, looking out for curacies
and the like, all the while that there is such a demand for
labourers out here, and no supply of them at all. Do not
take me to be in a complaining mood this month. I have
not a word to say against any one, much less against the
dealings of our blessed Lord in regard to us, who shows
Himself as tender and gentle as He is merciful ; only that I
continually feel that our isolated position here is a great
weight, and the weakness of our force a hindrance to the
Lord's work. Since I wrote to you last, the half-yearly examination of the English schools has taken place ; we issued
invitations to all the Europeans, and many of the more
respectable natives ; almost all the former attended, with a
smaller number of the latter. The examination commenced
at half-past 7 A.M., with prayers as usual, and then the
senior judge, who was in the chair, read a short address in
commendation of the school. The examination began with
the fourth and lowest class, and went upwards. I cannot
recount to you all the lessons of the different classes : suffice
it to say that the first class, consisting of the young men
from eighteen to twenty-nine years of age, have prepared,
during the half-year, eight or nine chapters of St. Luke's

Gospel in English, about half an English grammar, a few chapters of a geography of India, most of the first book of Euclid, and have written short English themes every week. What they know, they know thoroughly, and their minds are rapidly rising above the ordinary style of that of the natives. In the first class are two very nice young men, members of wealthy and most respectable families, whose hearts seem much touched with the Gospel. The elder of the two is much troubled about his sins, and says he has often risen at night and walked about for hours, troubled with the sense of them. He prays, I believe. He is a peculiarly amiable, loving, and lovable young man, and I feel for him much of the affection of a brother. Should it please God to convert him, he would have much to give up in his family and connections. On the last Sunday of the year I baptised our little Johnny by the name of John Arnold. The same morning I baptised our Ayah (*i.e.*, nursery-maid) in the little native congregation meeting at Mr. Noble's house : she walks consistently, and seems to drink in with eagerness all spiritual truth we teach her. My servants, ten or twelve in number, are an interesting congregation every morning : two of them are now baptised ; about two others I feel much interest, hoping the Spirit is working in them, though it is only stirring up the mud. One of them, Harry's bearer, has been hearing me now for eighteen months or more : the other is mother of one of Mr. N.'s servants, who was baptised lately.

* * * Perhaps Tractarianism is not so much the disease of the Church in England, as the chief symptom ; while individually we will not give up our lusts and plans, and submit ourselves in singleness to Christ as our whole Master, the Church as a body won't give up and send out missionaries to India. Those who come out will have to learn, that leaving England, and living in a hot climate, is not their *great trial ;* it is still our sins, our flesh, and the world which it is so hard to give up : if it were not for the

painful struggle against these, and the continual smartings we get by our sins, we should be living a heaven on earth in spite of absence, heat, and the rest.   My own experience, however, is, that I have received more spiritual aid against the devil and my own sins, and a more clear sight of our dear Lord since I came away from England, than I ever did before ; whether this is to be connected with being out here or not, I cannot say ; only, blessed be the Lord for what he has given me, whatever be the occasion.   *   *   *

Your affectionate Brother,

H. W. Fox.

Masulipatam : July 9, 1845

MY DEAR ROBERT,

I have not heard of your return to England, but take it for granted.   *   *   *   What a great blessing is the unanimity and affection which God allows to exist between the members of our family ; for though we are scattered abroad over the face of the world more than most families usually are, yet there are few in which there is more frequent communication and more affection.   I trust that the basis of it is sound upon Christ.   *   *   *   It is no light or shallow matter to be a soldier of Christ ; the cross taken up daily, the sturdy bending of the old man into the one object of the glory of God ; the viewing the unseen world of God (not of philosophy), instead of the visible things of time.   This cannot be a shallow matter, it must be deep or not at all : Christ altogether, or not at all ; no halves, no " dilettante " work in such a business as this ; and yet how many hang about, calling themselves earnest Christians, taking up the profession, and in some measure the approbation of Christ's service, and yet are never heart-worshippers at all : never get beyond the approval of reason, or the likings of the mouth.   Just now you are called to a particular heart-searching concerning your motives in entering into God's ministry, and the sincerity of your purposes, when you shall have entered. I made but little use of my preparatory time before I was ordained. I was wrapt up in Hooker, Butler, etc., to the exclusion of reading my own heart, and frequent prayer. When it pleases God to make you a minister, you must be just like an Oxford eight-oar at the races :—Up till now you have been waiting, training, and are ready to start, but the moment you are started you must be off, straining every nerve in your work *till the end.* A minister is never off duty. I think it would be a good rule to count every day lost in which you have not been at least once engaged in pastoral work, conveying the knowledge of Christ to sinners, or building up His saints : *i.e.*, either visiting people in their houses for religious conversation, cottage lectures, sermons, school, or something of the kind. I have got into such a habit, that if I do not either morning or evening get a distinct preaching of Christ to some poor souls, I count the day a lost one ; this is independent of in-door household teaching. Be a working clergyman. You have been long preparing ; now work, work, work, for the salvation of souls, for the extending of Christ's kingdom. Water your own field first, then everybody else's. If your parish be in a town, I hope you will soon know every alley and court in it; if in the country, every cottage and cottager.

Your affectionate Brother,

H. W. Fox.

TO THE SAME.

I hear you are now very soon going to be ordained ; remember how that before Christ appointed His apostles He spent the night in prayer ; an example to us, how that we should preface so great a work as that of entering on the ministry of God's Church by privacy and prayer. You may find a profitable lesson in the first chapter of Jeremiah, and in those chapters which record the call of Moses. In both,

their exceeding humility is discovered, but it is mingled with
a want of faith, which God reproves, at the same time that
He gives us the blessed instruction, that it is His work His
ministers go about, His word they speak, and that it is He
who guards them frcm evil and from enemies in their work.
May you have such a knowledge of the love of Christ to you
in your own heart, and such a burning love for Him, that
you may long and yearn after the souls committed to you.
It is not men's bodies which are committed to us, it is their
souls, which, while it restricts us in some respects, makes
our charge heavier and more difficult : but then if it was not
difficult we could do it of ourselves ; because it is difficult,
and when we know it to be so, then we are forced to seek
help from God.   May Christ be with you in your ordination
and in your ministry, blessing it to your own soul as well as
that of others.   Our united love to all at home.

Your affectionate Brother,

HENRY W. FOX.

CHAPTER VI.

TOWARDS the latter part of the year 1845 the health
of his wife began to give way, and so rapidly did
it decline that there seemed no other remedy than an
immediate removal to a better clime. In this state of
anxiety he embarked coastwise for Madras, purposing
to send his wife and children to England, and return
to his own duties at Masulipatam; but on reaching
Madras, the advice of his friends and the medical
attendants induced him to accompany her, for indeed
her illness had become so alarming, as to render her
recovery, even in a better climate, a very uncertain
event. She was conveyed on board the barque
"Diana" on the evening of the 30th of October, 1845,
and the vessel was to have sailed the next morning;
but during the night her complaint, hastened probably
by the fatigue of removal, came to a crisis, and she
died the following morning, owing to the bursting of
an abscess in the liver, which produced suffocation.

She was truly in earnest about the work in which
she had engaged, and though it pleased God thus early
to remove her from the scene of earthly labour, the

evidences she had given of devotion to the cause of
Christ, and of her own spiritual union with Him,
furnished the strongest grounds for consolation to her
surviving friends. Though the period of her labours
had been brief, that labour had not been in vain in the
Lord. Others besides Mary Paterson may, at the day
of our Lord's appearing, arise up and call her blessed,
who otherwise had never heard the name of Christ, nor
been admitted to partake of His glory.

She was removed on shore and buried at Madras:
every alleviation which the kind sympathy of Christian
friends could afford, was enjoyed by my brother; and it
certainly was a providential mercy, that the painful
event took place before the vessel had proceeded to
sea, by which he had the satisfaction of having her
committed to the ground by one of his dearest friends,
Mr. Tucker, of Madras. But all the sympathy which
friends can offer at such times, falls far short of
staunching so deep a wound; and unless consolation
be poured in from above, and the soul is capable of
staying itself upon God, of finding comfort in the
sympathy of Jesus, there must remain an aching void,
which nothing can fill—a pain which defies the power
of human remedies.

Shortly after his wife's funeral he was obliged to
embark with his three children, and proceed on his
voyage to England. He had not been many days at
sea before the youngest sickened and died; the vessel
put into Cuddalore, where the child was buried.
There now lay before him a long and dreary voyage,
during which time he was deprived of all the consolations of Christian communion, as there was no one on

board to whom he could open his heart, or who could enter into his sorrows. Although this proved a very painful passage of his life, yet he found the promise hold good, "Whom the Lord loveth He chasteneth," and at no period did he experience the presence and power of God's love so fully, as during this desolate and sorrowful voyage. During it he appears to have made a rapid progress in Christian experience ; the result of his sorrows was to draw him more nearly to his God and Saviour, to wean him more thoroughly from the world, and to confirm him more than ever in his determination to spend and be spent for Christ : so that he set his foot ashore on his native land, with the firm resolve, that by the help of the Lord, he would return to his work in India as speedily as possible. But his own letters will best describe his feelings during this trying period of his life.

To the Rev. R. T. Noble, Masulipatam.

Barque Diana, off Cuddalore : Nov. 6, 1845.

My dear Robert,

Mr. Tucker has told you of God's dealings with me, and of His mercy to me, and to my dear Elizabeth. She came on board to die and to render up her spirit to Christ, and now she is sleeping in Jesus, till the day that He brings His saints with Him. Just this time last year, you and I, with Sharkey, were going over 1 Cor. xv. in Telugu ; now I am called to realise and experience its truth. Blessed be God, His comforts exceed His sorrows, and yet the sorrow is very great ; no man can help me or comfort me in it, nor any creature supply the want created by the loss. You know what it is to be lonely, but you don't know what loneliness is after five years of such close and affectionate intercourse

as I had with my dear wife. It is a terrible gap : nothing
as yet fills it. I trust Christ will, and that I may suffer
nothing earthly to try to fill it. He has repeated His blow,
still in love, in taking little Johnny to Himself : the dear
baby never recovered the attack he had at Bunder,—was
worse on coming on shipboard, and died yesterday afternoon,
after no great pain. His dear mother has been spared the
sorrow, and now has the joy of receiving him. I had no
anticipations of Elizabeth's danger, nor had she, till the day
before she died. I got her on board about mid-day on
Thursday, anticipating rainy weather—she was fatigued with
coming on board, but was not worse all that afternoon or
evening, except that she could take no food. She had a
very bad night with her cough ; about two in the morning
she began to sink and be exhausted ; the doctor, who had
warned me of her danger soon after dark, now spoke of
immediate danger, and seemed to think the hope of surviving was small. The news startled her a good deal, but
her increasing exhaustion, and the fatigue of her cough
allowed her but little to think, and she scarcely spoke. The
abscess seems to have broken about eight in the morning,
when the cough ceased, and she died without pain, quietly
in my arms, on Friday morning. I believe she was spared
the pains of death—exhaustion tried her much, but that was
all. I have nothing to recall of her spiritual state in dying,
she could scarcely speak, nor do I suppose she could collect
her thoughts to pray : but I do not want it. I have much
to remember in days past, and some things which occurred
during the weeks we were at Madras ; and I should have
more, had not my own hard sinful heart given way to the
bustle of packing and preparation, so that I much neglected
reading and prayer with her. The strong assurance and
feeling that she is sleeping in Jesus, and enjoying all His
love, without sin and suffering, is so great a joy, as entirely
to check my desires to have her back again, and very much

to turn my grief into cheerfulness. God is good beyond
my hopes or thoughts, in the abundance of comforts He
supplies me in my thoughts; I want more humbling, and a
broken heart, and more thankfulness for His *redemption* of
me. The thoughts of Bunder I cannot yet dwell on, either
past, or future; but I have confidence, that when it pleases
God to bring me back, He will sustain me under the pain.
I hope He is now preparing me for working for Him better
than I have done, yet. The kindness of our friends at
Madras was extreme, all sympathised with me, and comforted me very much. On board I have no Christian
friends, but much kindness from all, and a nice respectable
gentlemanly captain and doctor—the latter has much that
is hopeful. I have not yet gone to the sailors, I have been
busy myself, and they were engaged in taking in cargo at
Pondicherry and Cuddalore—we hope to sail for good, to-
morrow or next day. I go on shore this afternoon to bury
my dear little baby; the chaplain will bury him—he is a
Christian brother, and very kind to me. The other two
children and I are kept in good health. * * *

Your afflicted and affectionate Brother,

H. W. Fox.

Near the Cape of Good Hope : Jan. 5, 1846.

MY DEAR ISABELLA,

The probability of having an opportunity of sending you
a letter from St. Helena, which will reach you a week or so
before we arrive in England, induces me to begin to write
to you at so early a time : and I am glad I have begun, for
often and often have I wanted to express my thoughts and
feelings to you, and have shrunk from beginning to do so ;
—used, as I have been so long, always to have her to communicate my every thought and wish to, and to receive
from her the kindest and warmest sympathy, I feel very
desolate now that I have no one to tell it to. I cannot

I

write to you at present in a sorrowful tone. I hope that
the bitterest times are over, although as they have hitherto
come at intervals, I do not know but that all my sorrows
may be oftentimes yet renewed before I am able so fully to
rejoice in Christ, so that this loss should not pain me. I
look indeed to a time when my faith shall be so increased
and my affections so weaned, that *all* my thoughts of my
dear Lizzy may be those of gladness and thankfulness.
Now I have many such thoughts of her, and am able at
times heartily to bless our dear Lord for His mercy to her,
and can see her as it were filled with the fulness of His
joy, free from all sin and imperfection, and so happy, and
dear little Johnny with her. However, at times the thoughts
of her are very full of pain. I dare not look back ; for
every pleasant scene is the more agonising because of its
former brightness, and I shrink from looking forward to
think of my desolateness, and how I still have to go through
the rough way and weary land without her affectionate
comfort and presence. However, in regard to those
thoughts, I am convicted before God of having loved her
more than I loved God ; and I very often have ringing in
my ears, "The idols He will utterly abolish." I do thank
Him for my own sake that He has laid this burden upon
me ; in very faithfulness He has afflicted me, and for my
own sake I am unable to wish that this sorrow had not
come, for I could not without it have had such experience
of Christ's tender love, of His powerful support and rich
consolations. I do not know how those who are without Christ
can go through such a sorrow : it seems to me as if it would
have driven me out of my senses at times, if I had not had,
not only the comfort of divine truth in my mind, but the
strength of Christ given me immediately from Himself.
He does appear to me now much more precious than He
ever did before, and at times I have longings after being
with Him, and indifference to this life quite new to me :

nevertheless, at others I am reminded how much the work
of subduing and weaning me from the world has yet to go
on.   It is better to depart and be with Christ, but if He
sees fit to keep me here to accomplish His work in me more
fully, or to use me as an instrument, I am well content.

> " If life be long, I will be glad,
>   That I may long obey;
>   If short, yet why should I be sad,
>   That shall have the same pay?"

says Richard Baxter ; and I often repeat the words with
much meaning.   Again, I have also to use Miss Elliott's
hymn :

> " Oh, teach me from my heart to say,
>   Thy will be done."

So you see there are many fluctuations in my state, but I
think I may say that Christ has triumphed in me and
glorified Himself ; His promises have not one of them failed,
and they have shone out with particular clearness in His
word.

   January 8.—I have been deriving much comfort from
the thought that all the pleasure and happiness which God
gave me in my dear wife was intended to foreshadow and
typify, by very inferior and distant resemblance, the joys I
shall have with Him in heaven.   We are a small party on
board, and all on very good terms, and I receive nothing but
kindness from every one ; but there is no one to whom I can
open my heart, nor any congenial person.   I hope that our
captain, who is a most worthy pleasing character, is a child
of God.   I have got the Doctor to spend half an hour in
the forenoon in reading the Bible with me, and he likes it,
and I think is thoughtful about it.   I have a good demand
for reading religious books, especially among the sailors,
among whom are some very decent, respectable characters,
who listen kindly and thankfully to all my entreaties to
give themselves to Christ.

Jan. 15.—There is one young man among them who has, I hope, been brought to God since we sailed ; the commencement of the change seems to have been occasioned by his reading Baxter's " Call," which I lent him the first Sunday I was on board : his progress in Christian knowledge and experience has been such as to make me very hopeful that the change (for a change there is) is the work of the Holy Ghost. He quite devours the books I lend him, and perseveres in reading the Bible. In one or two others I would hope an impression has been made ; but when I think of the wicked heart within, and the devil and world without, I desire to see tokens that the impression is made, not by me, but by the Holy Ghost. I preach twice on every Sunday ; if the weather is suitable the service is on the quarter-deck in the morning, and about thirty of us are present : at other times, in the cuddy, when we can only muster about fifteen. I have continued to preach extempore, which you will blame me for, and so I should myself, as I am but little satisfied with my sermons ; but for two reasons, the first of which is, the exceeding difficulty of getting a good opportunity of writing on board, as you may observe by the early part of this letter ; and the second the unseemly stiffness, as it seemed to me, in reading a sermon to a congregation such as ours, whether we are sitting in a room round a table, or in the open air on deck, when our ceiling is the awning, our pews, planks supported by a bucket at each end, and when I stand on the top of the booby-hutch, with the capstan covered with the union-jack for my desk. On week-days I usually go forward for half an hour in the evenings among the sailors, after the day's work is over, and get some very interesting opportunities of speaking to them in private ; but if you could see my heart, I think you would wonder and be ashamed at my want of love to the souls about me, and how I have to stir myself to seek their good instead of running to do it : it is the same at Bunder, it was the same at Oxford;—when I would do good, evil is present with me. I trust this lonely time of sorrow on shipboard may be for my soul's growth; but the time is slipping away, and I do not find myself so chastened or weaned from the world as I hoped I should by the grace of God have been: I have learnt some lessons, if I do not forget them, of the evil within me. I wish that you would all join your prayers with mine, that my visit at home may be a blessing and grace to us all, and that our life and conversation may be such, as to stir up every one of us to more devoted and hearty service for Christ. I shall also be very thankful if you will pray with me, that I may be allowed while at home to be the means of getting more missionaries, and in spreading a more real and deep interest in missions. I look on this as my peculiar work while I am at home. I could have wished for another year of such experience as my last at Bunder was, but God may use my poor instrumentality for "driving out labourers" into the distant vineyard. If you can devise or plan any means to aid me, I shall be most thankful. I come home confident that all of you who so heartily bid me God speed at first going out, will not attempt to delay my return to my work. As for my own present wishes, I have not a desire except to be at Bunder again; but I know so far regarding the law of sin within me, as to be aware that my desires may change, and try to lead me from my duty. I shall look, therefore, to you, my dear sister, to uphold me, should I give way; the parting with my dear children, probably for life, will be a sore trial, and now all the more bitter since God has taken my dear Lizzy from me. I cannot tell, nor are you likely to know, what she was to me, and how entirely we were one;—there was not a plan, a thought, I believe scarcely a wish, but we had it in common: no sort of reserve existed between us. You know how much we were permitted to be together, and this enabled us to live in the closer unity; to love her was almost like loving myself, and I knew and was persuaded that I had her entire affection. You know that her affections were warm, even as your own are; and now there is this great separation of communion. I doubt not but that she loves me now, even more than she could while with me, and her love is more hallowed in Christ; and I know that I do not love her one whit the less, though the yearnings after and longing for her at times make my very heart sore. At such times I have no resource but to lay up my sorrows with Christ, the Man of sorrows, and He gives me comfort and even joy: "the oil of gladness for ashes." The world and life seem as if they could never be bright to me again; but if so, I may have the same brightness in the knowledge and love of Christ, and nothing shall prevent our joy when we sleep in Jesus, and when we rise in our renewed bodies to meet Him as He comes down to earth. What a precious treasure is accumulating for us in the presence of God; how many are waiting to rejoice with us, and yet I desire to look forward, not so much to the rejoicing in meeting them again, as to the joy of beholding the King in His beauty. What an all-absorbing splendour and glory must that of God be! The poor heathen have not even these prospects among those of their heaven: to meet again in the life to come, is a thought which has not entered into their heads, and when they lose their dear ones, they part with them for ever. Blessed be God for His Gospel, and blessed also be His name that He has made us to know it: and I add, Blessed be God for those years of happiness which He allowed me to spend with my dear, dear wife, and for the dear children He has given me, one of whom, as a sort of first-fruits, He has already taken home: I have a strong assurance that He will hear our prayers for the conversion of the other two.

Your affectionate Brother,

HENRY W. FOX.

CHAPTER VII.

MY brother remained in England about six months, and embarked in the steamer "Ripon," on his return to India in October. During his residence in England, his time was principally taken up by attending missionary meetings in various parts of the country; and in the month of May he was present at the anniversary meeting of the Church Missionary Society in London, where he seconded a resolution, " in a speech," to use the words of Mr. Venn, "which is remembered by many who heard it, as singularly effective in the simplicity and ability with which he described his missionary labours."

The step which he had now to take was one of the most painful in his life. The loss of his wife called for submission—that trial was passive, it was suffering the will of God; but he had now to encounter a trial which called for action, the tearing himself away from his dear children, and going out once more to his work—not, as before, with a companion to cheer him on his way, and to share his joys and sorrows, but alone—

leaving behind all he held dear on earth, and returning to scenes that would remind him at every turn of his former ties and his present desolation. But there was no hesitancy in making this sacrifice, for a more powerful principle than human love had possession of his heart, and formed the ruling passion of his soul: instead of being sickened of his work by the losses he had sustained whilst prosecuting it—instead of turning from it with disgust, or returning to it from a stern sense of duty alone—his heart was wholly bent on prosecuting his labours; the one purpose for which he desired to live was "that he might preach among the Gentiles the unsearchable riches of Christ." Such was the sanctifying influence of affliction upon his heart, such the peaceable fruits of righteousness, such the increased devotion and oneness of purpose that pervaded his soul.

The following letters and journal illustrate this portion of his life.

To the Rev. R. T. Noble, Masulipatam.

Durham : June 15, 1846.

My dear Robert,

I scarcely know where to begin my letter to you; ever since I wrote in April, I have been moving about in scenes full of interest to you, as well as to myself; but I fear I shall but ill succeed in conveying to you a description of them all. My visits have been chiefly of a missionary character, and I have often wished that you could be with me, to have been cheered and encouraged by what I witnessed. It has seemed to me, that a more decided and warmer interest, and a higher tone is taken in reference to missions than used to be formerly. Men speak now of the duty and call that God is making upon us, and do not dwell so much in a self-congratulatory spirit upon successes : at every meeting which I have attended, our Society has seemed the nucleus for assembling the really pious and evangelical clergy of the neighbourhood. I may take a somewhat exaggerated view, because I now see things in a different position, as a deputation and missionary, from what I used to do before we went out ; nevertheless, I think that there is much for which to thank God, in the truer missionary spirit that is abroad among those who are really His children. Still the interest has not come up to the point of men giving *themselves* up to be missionaries. I have never neglected to press the call as a personal question upon all the younger clergymen whom I have met with in my journeyings, but the result has been the same. " They all with one consent began to make excuse." I have been downcast at times, but I acknowledge that this is through want of faith ; God may yet press the matter home on the consciences of some to whom I have spoken. I have been struck with the circumstance that so many men apparently suitable, and who take much interest in missionary matters, confess that they never yet put it as a practical question to their own consciences, " Am I called to go ? " There exists a very serious obstacle to getting men, in the great demand which there is everywhere for curates ; this is much increased of late years, and both presents itself as an argument for staying at home, and also prevents young men from looking about them before taking orders. I have pressed the matter upon —— and he is evidently uneasy in his mind about it, but is kept back by the view that he is now in a position of importance where God has placed him, and which, if he were to leave it, would, as far as man can see, not be well filled up : so he does not see his way in leaving it ; nevertheless, it is *our* part to think of Gideon, and of the glory of God displayed in saving by few. * * *

To THE REV. R. T. NOBLE, MASULIPATAM.

Harrow: Aug. 27, 1846.

MY DEAR ROBERT,

* * * About the time of your receiving this, I shall
be parting with my children, and all : will you remember
me before God?—it will be a struggle to flesh and blood. I
scarcely dare to look forward to it now : will you ask of our
Father that He will be with me in that hour, and that I may
glorify Him by entire submission to His will? This life is
not for enjoyment but for work, and discipline, and humiliation; hereafter, how greatly shall we rejoice in the full presence of our blessed Lord, which those dear ones who have
gone before are ever now enjoying : blessed be His name!
both for their sake and for ours! All you have said in your
letter about more missionaries, more and more fills me with
an anxious and a painful yearning to see them move; perhaps
I too much strain after an object of my own heart, and yet
it is God's will that they should go out, and I am quite
convinced that the lack does not arise from want of God's
command, but from man's disobedience.

EXTRACTS FROM JOURNAL OF A JOURNEY TO INDIA BY
THE OVERLAND ROUTE.

On Tuesday afternoon, Oct. 20, 1846, the mails were
brought alongside the "Ripon" steamer, which was lying out
in the middle of Southampton Water. This was the last visit
which the steam-tug was to pay us, and therefore all the
friends of passengers who had lingered to see the last of them,
had now to return : they quite crowded the deck of the
smaller vessel, while the side of our huge steamer was also
studded with those bidding their friends their last farewell. Each party exchanged huzzas as we separated, and sore
hearts as there must have been in each vessel, I did not notice
many sad countenances : in my own case the bitterest scenes
had occurred at a distance, and I now had to part with my

faithful and dear friend E., who had continued by me to the last. At length the hawser, which held us tight to the buoy— our last link to dear old England—was loosened, our head swung heavily round, the order of "Go a-head, full speed," was given, and we rushed down Southampton Water at ten miles an hour. It was now about four o'clock, and the approach of dinner took us all down into the saloon to prepare for it. We were a crowded party, of above a hundred passengers, occu- pying every available seat at the two tables, which ran the whole length of the saloon. There were old Indian officers and civilians returning to the tropics, after a year or two of renovation of health in England : there were young cadets and writers about to launch into life, and enter a new world at a very early age, full of spirits and bright prospects : there were planters and merchants, young and old, bound for Bengal, or Ceylon, or China. There were two other mission- aries, Scotchmen, beside myself, and a young clergyman, who, with a party of merry young men, was going to spend the winter, touring through Egypt and Syria. There were two or three married ladies, with daughters, returning to join their husbands in India, and one with two or three little children. There were middle-aged Indians, who had been home to recruit and to marry, and were returning with their young and newly-married wives; and there was a troop of young ladies (some almost girls), accompanying relatives, or going out to join them. I could not help thinking how soon their fresh English faces would be blanched, and their lively health and spirits become dull beneath a tropical sun. Long before dinner was over it was quite dark, and we had passed the Needles, and were steaming away in the open channel, with a slight motion in the vessel, scarcely enough to injure the most delicate of our party. I had the privilege of a nice light and airy cabin all to myself, situated on the upper deck, so that I had the prospect of much comfort during the first half of our voyage. The captain of the ship, a fine old sailor, had installed me in the position of chaplain, and expressed his desire for regular religious services,—a desire which, as it afterwards proved, proceeded from a sincere and religious heart. Next morning, Wednesday, we found ourselves labouring against a heavy, short, but not high sea, and a blustering foul wind. On coming into the saloon I heard all sorts of complaints, how that in the middle of the night the engines had been stopped for an hour, to allow time for cooling one of the cranks, which had become almost red-hot; how, that the engine would make only six revolutions in a minute instead of sixteen, and how that the lower-deck cabins were all full of water, which had dashed in through the ports; almost every one had had their beds wetted, together with their carpet bags and portmanteaus. The steamer, a very fine vessel, was on her first trip, and had been hurried prematurely out of dock, so that everything went wrong about her. We continued in this way, steaming slowly down the channel, with the head sea rising, and the wind increasing to a gale : she rode it out well, however, but in consequence of the state of her engines, at twelve o'clock the officer in charge of the mails ordered that her helm should be put up, and that she should be run into some port on the nearest coast. We now lay broadside to the sea, which occasionally gave us some heavy blows and made us roll, and also washed over the fore-part of the vessel, and poured down into the hold through the open hatchways, which, in the hurry of departure had no covering whatever over them. About an hour after, the head of the rudder broke off, so that the wheel was useless, and the ship unmanageable. We were now for several hours in the most imminent danger of going to the bottom, and it was only the goodness of God which preserved us. The water which poured down her hatchways was gradually rising up to the level of the fires, and there being no command over the vessel, the sea washed over her, more and more. The captain, as he

afterwards told me, gave us all up for lost, and retired several
times to his cabin, and there kneeling down, prayed to God
to deliver us from the danger. The only hope consisted in
our being able to make the land and get into smooth water
before the water gained on us. About four o'clock the
boatswain very gallantly volunteered to be let down over
the stern and hook on two chains to the rings on each side
of the rudder itself : this he did, plunged under water every
other second as the waves dashed up ; by this means we
again had power of steering, by bringing the chains round
the capstan, and steering by men at the capstan bars. By
half-past four we saw land right a-head, and also on the
weather-bow. It was five or six miles distant, high, and
dimly seen through the haze. Up to this time I had been
lying quietly in my cabin, reading and dozing, and utterly
ignorant that there was anything the matter, for we did not
roll or pitch much, and there was not nearly so much noise
on deck, as there would have been in bad weather in a
sailing vessel. When I came to dinner I was much startled
by one of our party saying, with a gloomy face, " It will be
well if we get ashore at all ; the rudder is gone, and we are
in the greatest danger." I was glad to go to my own cabin,
to commend us all to God, and to seek for His presence and
strength in the hour of fear, and He mercifully granted it :
for though some natural shrinking from death remained, I
felt happy and confident in reunion with Christ, after all
should be over, and meeting those dear ones who have passed
through the river of death before me. It was growing dusk
as we neared the shore, but some on board recognised the
coast, and we found ourselves running into Torbay, a secure
and sheltered anchorage. By half-past seven we had
anchored in smooth water, and all our danger was over : had
we been out at sea, in the Bay of Biscay, for instance, or
had the ship's head not been turned towards the land before
the rudder broke, it would have been barely possible that

we should have escaped. As it is, our deliverance has been one conspicuously from God. When all was over, and about forty of the passengers were waiting in the saloon for tea, our captain sent for me, and asked me to return thanks to Almighty God for our great deliverance, which I did ; all knelt, and I hope many joined sincerely. There has been since then a return to usual thoughts and feelings on the part of most of us, at least, so far as is observable, although there is a general expression of thankfulness and acknowledgment of God's hand in the escape, from most of us. Seldom, perhaps, has there been so much danger with so little suffering or inconvenience. We have in no ways suffered any thing, except the wetting of some of the luggage in the cabins and in the hold.

Thursday Morning, Oct. 22.—At sunrise we found ourselves lying in Torbay, a fine semi-circular bay, with bluff cliffs, and green hills surrounding it : on the right was Torquay with its white houses perched up on the hill, about four miles off; in the centre was another pretty town, and towards the left, lying snugly under the shelter of the western horn of the bay, was the small fishing town of Brixham. Four or five small ships lay in shore of us, and a fishing smack soon paid us a visit. By eight o'clock the purser of the ship started for the shore to convey the news of our disaster to London. He reached town by four the same afternoon, and a telegraphic express was immediately sent down to Southampton to order the Oriental steamer round to our assistance : he returned himself on board about one o'clock on Friday, to announce the result of his expedition. Meanwhile we lay perfectly quiet, as steady as if we were on shore, all Thursday and Friday, with a fine bright sea and clear sky the greater part of the time, and with a fine view of the beautiful coast around us : numerous fishing and other boats perpetually in motion enlivened the scene. A few of the passengers landed at Brixham or Torquay for some hours, and some even ran up to London and back. Late on Friday night the light of the Oriental steamer, and another smaller vessel were seen, and they soon ran alongside and anchored near us. The whole of Saturday was a day of bustle and confusion, baggage and cargo were being transhipped into the smaller steamer or into boats, and thence into the Oriental. By four o'clock they carried the passengers over in smaller vessels, the weather being all the while very favourable, and while we were dining on board our new home, they finished all the carrying process, and we expected to start the same night. We did not do so, however, till daylight the next morning.

Sunday, Oct. 25.—On coming on deck I found that we were running along the Devonshire coast about a mile off the shore : the coast was fine, precipitous and hilly : the cliffs often tinged with a ruddy colour, mingled with the greenness of the grass which clung to their face. Many little combs and valleys appeared, in which lay hid a clump of trees and a cottage ; we passed on beyond the Start Point, sighted Dartmouth, lying in its little rocky cleft in the hills, and gradually edging away to the southward, lost sight of land in a few hours. Although the wind blew fresh, the sky was bright, and the sea was smooth. Eleven o'clock was the hour for morning. prayers ; but as the time drew on, those ladies who were able to leave their cabins, together with most of the gentlemen, were assembled on deck, lying along the seats which were fixed there : most of them declared their inability to descend into the saloon through fear of sea-sickness, and so it was arranged that we should have service on deck. I was glad to find that many were really anxious to have the service, and did not make their sickness an excuse. Accordingly I read prayers on deck : the ladies lying at full length, the gentlemen sitting or standing as they could with their hats on, my hair blowing in the wind, and my voice going everywhere. I had

to strain my voice, and found afterwards that I was heard,
but at the time thought otherwise.   I, however, preached,
or rather made a short address, on Rom. xii. 1, drawing
attention to the call which God had made on us by His
late deliverance, and then to His great *mercy* in Christ.
The party, about forty in number, were attentive, but cold.
All the afternoon I was qualmish and sleepy; I had several
walks and conversations with fellow-passengers on deck, and
in the evening we had service again in the saloon, with
about twenty present, and I preached from Luke x. 25—27,
the obligation of the law.   The day was to my own soul
very lifeless and cold, and my preaching was similar.
Towards evening the wind became light and the sea fell.

The journal is continued, giving a lively description
of first impressions at Gibraltar, Malta, Alexandria,
Cairo, and the Desert; but this is a journey so frequently performed in the present day, and possessing
so little novelty, that the remainder is omitted.   He
reached Ceylon on the 6th, and Madras on the 10th of
December, 1846.

Madras : Dec. 12, 1846.

My dearest Sister,

Here I am at last, by God's mercy, surrounded by much
kindness, and attended by gracious marks of God's love on
all sides.   I looked forward with many painful anticipations
to my arrival here, and I have found them fully realized.
Every sound and sight recalls my dear Lizzy to mind; there
is not a spot in Madras which is not associated with her;
many houses and rooms remind me of her presence, and I
cannot go about the streets without remembering the last
time I did so, when I had left her for an hour or two only.
The children also continually come to my mind, and I feel

that I am very desolate. Last evening I went as usual to the Friday evening meeting at the Browns', and how empty did the house seem; for when last there, she was lying in one of the rooms below, and the dear little children's voices were scarcely hushed before the hour of meeting : every one there looked just as they did a year ago—husbands and wives still preserved to each other—but to me how great the change ! Do not think I am complaining ; I can call God to witness, I do heartily bless Him for the change, both for her sake and for my own. I would not have it otherwise, but yet it is full of sorrow for the present. I do not want you to grieve with me, for I cannot think of giving you sorrow ; but I want you to pray for me that I may glorify God in this land, and time of trial, by looking beyond this life, and rejoicing in His promises. I have had many sorrows of late, and I feel I am going to have more, but I think I have learnt to look on sorrows with a welcome eye as God's best gifts. I have been thinking of God's tenderness in His dealings with me ever since my dearest wife died. If I had had to go back to Bunder, and let the children go away at once, how almost insupportable would have been the trial : but He allowed me to come home to you all, and be comforted by your affection and love ; and in England I visited but few places which were closely associated with her : and now, after I have had thirteen months of teaching, He has brought me back to Madras, first to break, as it were, the greatness of the pain of revisiting the scenes of our happy days at Bunder. The sea voyage home was indeed a time of great trial ; but then to make up for that He made it a time of much converse with Him, and of many consolations. * * *

Your affectionate Brother,

HENRY W. FOX.

K

Cullapilly : Feb. 13, 1847.—I am now out on my first excursion to the villages, since my return to India. I have commenced by coming here to the great annual bathing-festival, which occurs on " Siva-rátri," or the Siva-night. It is a large village about twelve miles due south of Masulipatam, situated on the most northerly branch of the river Kistna, and containing a considerable pagoda, devoted to the god Siva, under his common name of Nagesvara-swami, or the Lord of Snakes. It is curious that the bathing in the river Kistna, a personification of Vishnu, should be held in connection with, and in honour of the rival god. It is a festival of three days' continuance, the main features of which are the religious bathing by thou-sands in the river, and their repairing to the temple of Siva to make their obeisance and offerings to the idol. I left my house at four o'clock in the morning, and proceeded through the entire length of the native town on to the open country beyond it. In consequence of the many showers which had fallen rather heavily a few days previously, I found the wet portions of the plain filled with water ; in crossing the first, the water reached my horse's girths, and in the second he began to sink so deep in the treacherous mire, that I was obliged to leap off and lead him through the mud and water for two hundred yards, knee-deep. A great part of the rest of the country (for there was no road) was of a miry and treacherous character ; so that when the sun rose I had still three or four miles of my journey before me. By this time I had no longer any difficulty in discerning my way, for I found crowds of people streaming in from all directions along the main path ; and for the last two miles I was continually passing a string of people trudging to the festival, the majority on foot, and a few in common bullock-carts. There were old and young, the tottering and bent figure of the old

GOPARAM, OR GATEWAY OF THE TEMPLE AT CULLAPILLY,
WITH IDOL CAR.
(*From a Talbottype View.*)

woman, and little children toddling alongside their parents, or carried on their sides. There was about an equal number of men and women, but nearly all were of a poor and shabby appearance. On reaching Cullapilly, I found the pagoda very prettily situated, on the side of a tank full of water-lilies, both red and white, and the whole place alive with the visitors to the festival. After giving directions about the pitching of my tent on the bund of the tank, about a quarter of a mile from the pagoda, I rode down towards the river, which lies at about half a mile distance from the village. There was a solid stream of people the whole distance — a few returning from the waterside — but the majority on their way thither; and already I could hear the roar of the voices of the multitude engaged in their ablutions, and the occasional screechings and drummings of music, proceeding from them. As we drew near to the river we passed several small raree shows, consisting each of a box gaily painted with mythological figures, and opening with folding-doors so as to display inside the tawdry image of either Vishnu or Siva ; these were placed in the road by their owners, who stood by begging for money, and reaping a rich harvest from the piety of the people. When I asked some of them why they provided mere toys for worship, instead of serving God, they made the common answer of patting their stomach, to show that it was their livelihood. There was also a large number of clamorous beggars, lining one side of the road for the distance of about a quarter of a mile : each beggar spread out a long cloth or mat by the road-side, and as the people came back from the river they threw a few grains of rice, or now and then a single chili, or less frequently a cowrie shell (in value about one-fiftieth of a farthing) on each cloth : so that there was a prospect of two or three handfuls of rice being gathered from each cloth. I found the crowd of bathers lining the river-side for a distance of 600 yards or

half a mile : the river here, though the smallest of the main
branches of the Kistna, varies from a quarter to half a
mile wide, and at present is about seven or eight feet below
its banks : on the higher bank were collected the crowds of
visitors ; some sitting, some standing idle, some engaged in
preparing their food, but the majority were changing their
wet clothes, or rubbing their coloured powders on their
foreheads, or preparing their diminutive amount of alms :
in the river itself stood hundreds in the act of bathing.
The process appeared to be generally of this kind : the party
after scrambling down the steep and slippery bank, proceeded into the water, till a little beyond the knees, of course
without removing any part of their dress.   Some friend
commenced by pouring a number of pots full of water over
their head and back ; then there was the raising of a little
of the water to the mouth in the two hands, and drinking
it, then the throwing two or three handfuls of water upwards, by way of libation ; and then some over the head
backwards, and then plunging the whole body several times
in the water.   Men and women were mingled together pro-
miscuously.   I stood watching them for a considerable time ;
the noise of so many voices was sufficiently great to render
conversation of scarcely any use ; so I was a silent observer
of many hundreds going through a ceremony which they all
believe to acquire for them a great amount of religious
merit, and which they believe removes their sin.   I saw
two or three men with little baskets, which they took into
the water with them, and dipped in the water.   On inquiry
I found that the basket contained the little household god
of the party, an image a few inches long.

On my return I found a boy going about chanting and
begging, with a long piece of wire run through both his
cheeks.   Siva is the bloody deity, and it is in honour of him
or his wife that cuttings or mutilations are made ; this is
the only one I have seen to-day, but I am told this evening

that near the temple there are some men cutting themselves, and piercing their flesh.

As I returned, I found the same close streams of people
still moving down to the river : there could not have been less
than four or five thousand in all, either on the river-banks or
on the way thither, during the three-quarters of an hour that
I was there.   There were about twenty bullock-carts covered
with mats, in which women of the wealthier class changed
their dress, and about a dozen palanquins, in which those
who could afford the expense had come to the festival ; but
the mass were on foot.   Before I left Masulipatam I was told
that not many people of wealth came out to this festival, on
account of the sums they are expected to expend in case
they do so.   I found this to be the case ; the majority of the
visitors seem to be of the lower classes.   On coming back I
found a considerable part of the road leading to the temple
lined with temporary booths, for the sale of toys, bangles,
ornaments, or simple articles of food.   The booths reminded
me much, as indeed did most of the scene besides, of the
outskirts of an English race-course : of course the booths
had no table or anything to raise them from the ground ;
they consisted of a few sticks, so arranged as to allow a
cloth or mat to be stretched on them, which sheltered the
seller and his goods from the sun.   I was glad to take rest
and get my breakfast in my tent ; it was not long before all
the neighbourhood was covered with groups of people cook-
ing their food, eating it, or lying down to sleep after it : for
out of the six or seven thousand strangers who have come
for this occasion, none seem to have any place to lodge in —
the open field is their parlour and their bed-room.   The
continual noise of their talking, and the unceasing hummings
of the large drums at the pagoda, have been far from agreeable
all day.   In the afternoon, finding that no one came to my
tent for conversation, I went out into the crowd, and wended
my way to the temple, after two or three conversations by

the way. The people were loitering about, with no other occupation than that of a few jugglers and mountebanks to amuse them. While waiting about the temple-gateway, watching the continual passing of the crowds in and out, there came forth a bridal palanquin, in which was placed a small brazen trident, eight or nine inches high, half wrapped up in cloth. This is the " Trishúlam," and is, I believe, a representative of the god : by the side walked a man with a horse-hair flapper, to drive away the flies from the god. Before the palanquin went a Brahmin, who lay down on the ground, every here and there, a large leaf, and on it placed a handful of boiled rice : he was followed by a boy who gathered the leaves and rice into his basket. I found that nearly every one that went into the pagoda purchased as he went a little earthenware saucer, such as is used for a lamp, with a wick and a few drops of oil to offer to the idol inside. There was no uproar, or riot, or excitement, only a large crowd; I obtained a good many opportunities of speaking to groups of people, and two or three times went over the history of Christ, as the only Saviour from sin. I had no opposition, for which I was thankful. On returning, after about a couple of hours' ramble, I brought with me to my tent a crowd of people, and sitting there I continued for two hours more to talk to successive groups who sat on the ground, until I was quite tired. A good many asked for tracts, which I supplied : I was glad there was none of that eagerness for tracts which I read of, as sometimes occurring ; for on such occasions I feel that the consumption is not repaid by the number who read them ; the desire being, not that of reading, but of possession. I have had many good listeners, no positive opposition : my only annoyance has been that of two or three people, who were so fond of hearing their own tongues speak, as not to allow me to finish a sentence.

It is a serious reflection that I am here alone in the midst

of Satan's kingdom : here he is rampant and triumphant;
not a soul out of the thousands here but is a sworn servant
of his; he has all his own way with them, and would do
his worst towards me; it is a consideration to make me
run to Christ more lovingly and earnestly, as my only
defence against the powerful and Evil One.

Cullapilly : Monday, Feb. 15.—The noise on Saturday
night of the crowds of people who were bivouacking in
the open air all round about, and of the beating of the
drums at the pagoda, continued till a late hour : and I was
awakened about four in the morning by the same drumming, and by the voices of the crowds, who were beginning
to wake up.   During the night there had been a minor
procession of the idol in a little car : the great procession
in the great car was to take place on Sunday afternoon.
When I went out for a morning walk, soon after day-break,
I found the people streaming away to their villages just as
they had been crowding from them the previous morning ;
though the festival is one of three days' duration, yet the
greater number are content with the first day, and before
mid-day about two-thirds had left the village for their
homes. ·There was some bathing again in the morning, I
was told, but the number of bathers could not be great.
I had all the forenoon to myself in quiet, but from the
middle of the day I had a quick succession of visitors, some
boys, some grown-up men, who came to hold a conversation,
but most of them to ask for tracts, I had again many
favourable opportunities of telling them of Christ as their
only way of salvation.   Their continual struggle is for works
of their own; I as continually press upon them the impossibility of bringing out of the unclean man anything
which can cleanse him.   I had a long and very interesting
conversation with a well-behaved and intelligent Mussul-
man, who with every appearance of lively interest, honestly
confessed, when it was pressed upon him, that a forgiveness

of sins from without was necessary, and that he could not find any such in his religion. In the afternoon I went to the pagoda, where the crowd was great as well as the noise : I could not hold much conversation in consequence, but I was remarkably enabled, as to-day also, in giving such ready answers to those who put foolish, captious questions, as quite to silence them. About half an hour after dusk they began to prepare for the car procession. The car, a lofty frame-work of wood, of a pyramidical form, strongly tied together with a net-work of ropes, was covered over with dingy red cloth, and adorned with long strings of leaves, on which were suspended pumpkins and gourds. No fewer than three " Zemindars," or wealthy land-holders (they call them " princes ") attended the festival, and added to its splendour, such as it was, by their own bejewelled persons, their match-lock and spearmen, and three or four elephants and camels. I stood near the car, to see the idol brought from the pagoda, in order to be placed in the car ; the crowd was great, but a number of lighted torches made every object distinctly visible. Just then several Brahmins came forward in a rude manner, and told me to move out of the way, for the god was coming ; at least their gestures told me so, for the sound of the drums prevented me from hearing more than a word or so. I took it to be merely a piece of impudence on their part to require me to do that which they had not the slightest right to do in the public street, and so I stood my ground. Several with vehement gestures told me again, and one of the Zemindars talked at me with words inaudible from the great noise. As I thought it better not to oppose their wishes, I moved on a few yards ; but that would not content them, and presently I found that the spearmen and others who were pushing the people about, began to push them against me, and others began to hustle me. I fancy that had it been right to do so, I might easily enough have stood my ground against them ; but as I had no reason to irritate them, but the contrary, I moved down the street; and as I went, I found three or four people throw dust upon me. I was more astonished than annoyed at this rudeness, which is so unusual towards an European; I presume that the excitement of the festival, the concealment which the darkness afforded, and the presence of the Zemindars, emboldened them to forsake their usual submissive conduct. I stood in a side street, and saw the cumbrous car dragged slowly on, and when it had passed I looked down the street, filled with a dense crowd, upon whom the light of the torches streamed. I returned home to the quiet of my tent, to reflect on the contrast of a quiet English Sunday, with the singular, profane, and idolatrous scenes I had witnessed.

To-day I have had numerous visitors in my tent. One man much interested me : he stayed more than an hour, spelling out, for he could not read well, first, the Ten Commandments, and afterwards a little tract of eight pages. It was a laborious task for him, as well as tiresome to me ; but he persevered through it, asking me questions as he went on about what he did not understand. I told him all the way of salvation ; he seemed cordially to approve of all, and to be pleased with the good news he heard ; he was not of those dull men who chime in with any new thing which they hear, but an intelligent, lively person. I have had no great opposition or discussion, or any new subjects started. Several have harped on the trite topics, that all things are God, and that He is materially the substance of all : others again, that our bodies are created by Him, but He is the soul of all men ; that there is but one Spirit, ours and His being the same ; others, that God is the author of sin, " for if He is not," they say, " who is ?" Others, that the way to purify the soul is to restrain and keep under the senses ; others, that believing in or serving God is necessarily connected with the ascetic life of a hermit.

It is quite remarkable how readily they fly off from the subject ; pretending to answer some questions I have asked, they will go on with a long rigmarole about what has no more to do with it than the man in the moon.

All these three days God has very mercifully kept me from the adversary, by keeping me from those noisy and difficult discussions which, from my imperfect knowledge of the language, I so much dread. He has also kept me in great peace, and made me feel much enjoyment in this sort of life.

I have given away about 150 tracts, rather withholding them than offering them to the people. Most of my visitors have been from Masulipatam ; of the rest, not above half a dozen are inhabitants of this village.

Sallapilly : Feb. 16, 1847.—This forenoon was spent like several others ; in the early morning I took a walk, and on my return through the village I wanted to find out the school. It is curious what falsehoods they unblushingly tell : from not less than eight or nine people I have had an answer to my question of where the school was, to the effect that there was no school at all in the village, while some of them, on my charging them with the falsehood, have pointed out to me where it was. In my tent I had visitors for two or three hours ; among others, a man came and sat down outside (he would not come in) and conversed for about an hour : he had the usual appearance of a " Sanyási," a mendicant friar, but was not one of the filthiest and worst class. The marks by which I discovered his character were his greater quantity of hair on his face, the larger amount of ashes on his forehead, and particularly his strings of beads on his neck and arm, his cloth of the sacred yellow, and the tiger's skin carried on his back. He was not strictly a Sanyási, but was employing himself in going about to beg money to build a pagoda in his native village ; he had collected, he said, 400 rupees (£40), but

200 rupees more were needed; for some weeks past he had not got a farthing. He was a cheerful, good-natured fellow; had no objections to make to what I urged upon him, both in regard to his sins, and to Christ's redemption, and appeared an ordinary sort of man, unable to read. Though I had dwelt for some time on their sin in taking God's name in vain, at last he went off in a jovial mood, chanting "Bhagavan! Bhagavan! Narâyana!" (names of God). This, they think, purges the sins away. He, like other religious characters I have seen among them, seemed to be totally devoid of anything like seriousness or devotion. As I sent off my tent, about 2 o'clock, I walked into the village, to get into the shade of the houses, and went to a street full of Brahmins, where I had been treated somewhat rudely in the morning. In a few minutes I had the whole horde upon me, and there ensued a discussion most utterly profitless, except to myself, to whom it served as a grindstone to sharpen me for further contests. About 2 o'clock, Brahmins, old and young, with pride and impudence strongly marked in their faces, surrounded me, and sometimes one, but more commonly three or four at once assailed me with childish and ludicrous questions; many of them of a quite unanswerable character: "Why were some men born rich and others poor?" "How was it that my caste (which they confound with religion) had denied the divisions of caste?" On my telling them of the evidence we had to the truth of Christ's life from enemies as well as friends, one of them answered me, in a thoroughly Hindu fashion, "Probably," he said, "these were only sham enemies, pretended for the occasion; for instance (pointing to two men) if I want to get possession of this man's house, I persuade the other, who is a friend of mine, to pretend to be my enemy, and then I bring him into court to swear that the house is mine, and the circumstance of his being my enemy adds much to the weight of his evidence." Sometimes they were

so eager to beset me with what they thought flooring questions, that one would pull the other by the arm to stop him, in order that he might get his word in; and then they would ask me a series of questions one after another, giving me no time to answer. "Is there any difference between God and your body?" "Who knows the difference between right and wrong?" "Is your God the God of the whole world, or only of your country?" I turned the tables on them, by laughing at their hot eagerness to assail me, and at their unfair dealing. I could only feel at the end that God had graciously delivered me out of the hand of the enemy, and also I felt sorry at these poor men's wilfully refusing the light and the treasure. But I rejoiced to find Satan alive to the fact of his kingdom being disturbed; anything is better than the deadness of some places; I had not expected such decided opposition as I have found here: they are quite alive to the fact that Christianity will not allow idolatry, and fight shy of this subject. On leaving Cullapilly I took a Brahmin village in my way here, intending to leave a few tracts in it. I found a boy to whom I had given a book at Cullapilly: he first told me that he had read and understood it all, but immediately after he said he had not looked into it, but had placed it upon one of the rafters of his house: when he went in to look for it he came out again, and said it was gone—some one had thrown it away; but when he was urged to produce it, he presently pulled it out, and that without any marks of shame at his falsehood. When I had offered the tracts I had brought, the Brahmins would not have them; they said, "We believe our religion, and don't want to hear anything against it. I had a ten minutes' fruitless discussion on horseback with five or six of them; they were so silly and captious that I could tell them nothing valuable. If I asked them, "Have you not committed many sins?" they answered me, "What difference is there between sin and righteousness?

who can tell?" Here, however, I made them look foolish,
by obliging them to answer their own questions, by further
asking them whether lying, stealing, etc., were not sins?
Nevertheless, they shuffled, as well as they could, by mentioning cases in which, according to their views, it was
necessary, if not right, to lie and steal. If I incidentally
spoke of God, immediately they interposed, "Who is God?
what God do you mean? what form has He got?" When I
illustrated the sure punishment of sin by the case of an
English judge punishing a convicted felon, they tried to be
off at a tangent, by appending the statement : "Yes, one of
your judges will punish the felon, but if he was open to
bribes he would perhaps let him off"—although this was
nothing to the point, for I had distinctly stated the pre-
sumption that the judge would act justly.   I was glad
during the discussion that a couple of women were standing
listening in the door-way of the house where we were
talking : to have a female listener, is to me, as yet, a very
rare occurrence.

I have changed my quarters by coming to this village
about five miles north of Cullapilly ; it is a considerable
village, the capital of the country, and the residence of a
Zemindar, or land-holder, who has quite a grand palace, far
superior to any thing I have seen elsewhere.

Masulipatam: March 27.—I have been here rather more
than a fortnight since my return from the villages.   My
employment is to go out before sunrise into the town, which
is close to my house, and there spend an hour or so in conversing, preaching, and disputing with a crowd of people in
some corner of a street.   I get ready listeners, though not
so favourable ones as in the villages.   Nevertheless, I make
the name of Christ known to many, and give away a few
tracts.   Nearly the whole day I am engaged with visitors
in my house : many boys from the English school come
and spend hours with me ; many grown-up natives pay me

visits, with whom I have long and interesting conversations. I have adorned the walls of my principal rooms with pictures; some, portraits and views, others, of birds and animals, and on my tables I have placed a variety of nick-nacks and curiosities—little mummy figures from Egypt, chimney ornaments from England, a small globe, and these form grand attractions to my visitors, who are as delighted to see these things as a child is to see a raree-show. Besides this, fame has noised abroad that I possess some magnetic fish and ducks, and a camera obscura, and other wonderful things from Europe; and I often find, after a long conversation on other matters of a higher kind, that I have been honoured with the visit in consequence of my visitor's curiosity to see the wonderful things I possess. I, of course, gladly exhibit them, and so I hope I prepare the way for more confidence and kindly acquaintance with my native neighbours, besides conveying to them as full statements as I can of the way of salvation through Christ. With the younger part of my visitors I find that so simple a thing as a magnetic toy goes to shake their confidence in their heathen miracles, as exhibiting to them the existence of natural wonders greater than those which their people tell them regarding the gods. The fish and the duck that will come when they are called, and have the semblance of life, although they are manifestly only tin toys, afford a ready comparison with the idols, which can neither stand nor walk, nor hear, nor see, and yet are said to be alive.

A few days ago while conversing with a crowd of people in the street, and when some of them were asking me the common question, " Suppose we join your religion, how shall we get our livelihood?" and while I was endeavouring to show them that those who committed their souls to God, would be found far from losers in regard to their bodies, I used the illustration of the prodigal son : " Suppose," I said, " a little boy was to leave his father's house, and go to

a far country, surely he would soon find himself in want :
then, half-starved as he was, if he was to return home, and
humbly ask for food, would not his father most joyfully
receive him, feed him and clothe him, as a recovered lost
one ? " " No," said the man I spoke to, " the father would
have nothing to do with the lad ; how could he tell what
he had *eaten*, while he had been absent from home "—meaning, that as the father could not tell whether the boy had not
eaten food prepared by people of inferior caste, and consequently lost his caste, he would count him as unclean, and
drive him away.   I was scarcely prepared to hear so
unblushing a statement of the hard-heartedness to which the
system of caste reduced people.   The speaker was not a
Brahmin, nor apparently any thing more than an ordinary
Sudra working man.

On several occasions of late I have had the low morality
of the Hindu religious books brought out in common conversation.   Pressing on the people the fact of their having
sinned, which some deny, but which they commonly evade
by asking, " Who knows the difference between right and
wrong ? what is sin ? " I asked them " What is lying ? what
is theft ? Are they right or wrong ? are they sins or not ? "
I have been answered several times, " Why that depends
on the occasion ! if a man lies or steals to satisfy hunger, of
course there is no harm in it." Sometimes they say, " Of
course everybody tells lies ; how could the world go on
without lying ? "

I was much shocked one morning by that old wicked statement made to me by a farmer just come out of the country.
I was asking him, as above mentioned, whether he had not
sinned ; whether, for instance, he had not told many lies.
" And if I have," said he, " who is it that made me to tell
them ; who else but God ? It is not my fault." I told him
that thus he was charging God with being a liar ; for if I
were to send my servant into the bazaar and make him steal,

I should be just as much a thief as he was. " Well, what then," said the man, " God *is* a thief and a liar ; if not, how does it happen that some men are born rich and others poor." I turned away from him, saying, I dared to speak no longer with such a blasphemer, and began to express to the bystanders my horror and grief at these expressions : they only laughed, but the man seemed a little ashamed, for he came back presently to justify himself, saying that, in .his religion, his god (Krishna) was related to have committed thefts and told lies, and as he believed all this, he was surely right in saying what he did. The worst of it is, that it was not the man's own idea, but the systematic doctrine maintained by a large proportion of the Hindus ; that men are mere puppets, and God is the immediate instigator of all their actions, both good and bad.

TENT OF THE REV. H. W. FOX, PITCHED NEAR SALLAPILLY.
(*From a Talbotype View.*)

CHAPTER VIII.

Sallapilly : Feb. 17, 1847.

MY DEAR GEORGE,

I have no one to disturb me here, but the natives who come to my tent, and this in the way of business ; the intervals between their going and coming, and my evenings, are all my own for reading and writing. I thus combine more active employment in real evangelisation, with improvement in Telugu, and leisure for my own use. I am more and more inclined to carry out Mr. Venn's proposed plans, so far as the seasons allow me ; about six months I must be under cover of a roof, but the rest of my time I hope to spend in my snug tent. I wish some of the Cantabs knew what a happy life it is—to have it not as a πάρεργον, but as actually one's business to be preaching Christ to those who have never heard of Him, is very joyful. When I have been to a village and told the people there of Him, and left tracts with them, I come away joyfully, recollecting that there is one more obstacle to Christ's coming removed : whether they will hear, or whether they will forbear, He has been preached among them, and so the end is coming all more quickly. Besides this, the seed is sown, and some will spring up to bear fruit, and Christ shall see of the travail of His soul in that village. * * * I look back to my visit to England with much thankfulness and

L

pleasure; perhaps with more than if it had been made under more outwardly happy circumstances. I feel so thankful for all the happy intercourse we had together, and the interchange of affection between all the members of the family, and especially for the love you have all shown to my dear little children. But I cannot say I look with satisfaction on my missionary work there. I look indeed with exceeding pleasure upon all the meetings in the North : I enjoyed them thoroughly—but what I considered my more important season in the South, I regard with less satisfaction. It is, perhaps, because I expected to see results in the shape of men, and saw none, nor any prospects of any. This is want of faith, but it also arises from feeling that I might have said and done more.

Your affectionate Brother,
HENRY W. FOX.

TO THE REV. J. Y. NICHOLSON, EMMANUEL COLLEGE, CAMBRIDGE.

Masulipatam : Feb. 25, 1847.

MY DEAR FRIEND,

I have been purposing some time to fulfil my promise of writing a long letter to you. I promised Ragland that I would try and do so on my journey up here from Madras, but that journey is over, and I have got myself settled in my new house, and I am out in my tent in the villages, and yet my promise is unfulfilled; so I take advantage of a forenoon in which I am staying in a traveller's bungalow, and therefore have no native visitors as I have when I am in my tent. I wish that you and all your missionary circle could be with me, either in my house at Masulipatam, or in my tent in some of the villages, that you might yourselves see how free from personal hardship a missionary's life in

India is. I have a large new house, one end of which lies
empty for want of some brother missionary to come and
occupy it. In it I have every comfort and convenience I
could wish : I have my drawing-room and dining-room, my
bed-room and bathing-room adjoining, and my study besides ; so that I live like a prince. Then I have the society
of my dear brother Noble, and of two Christian families,
and sometimes of one or two others like-minded, among our
European residents : so that I am really without any outward want. When I come out in my tent, my servants
pitch it for me in an eligible situation, in or near a village ;
it is just twelve feet square inside, and has double walls and
top, separated the one from the other by a space of two feet
wide, and here I have my tables, my chair, my bed, my
books, and a great part of the day long I have an audience
of black faces, and turbáned or shaven heads, inside and
outside the door. I say, that I wish you could see how
free from outward hardships we are ; for I fear that it is the
dread of them which keeps so many men from coming out
to us ; and yet, supposing a missionary's life was one of
hardship, surely we have no right to shrink from it on that
account. Our dear Lord's life was one of hardship, and we
are not to be above walking in His steps : as Christians we
are born to hardships, and blessed is the man who receives
them from the Lord. Through much tribulation must we
enter into the kingdom of heaven ; why, then, should we
shrink from our allotted tribulation ? All the way as I came
along the road from Madras, I was thinking how I could
tell you of my journey. It is scarcely worth while to
describe to you the journey itself in detail ; it is enough to
say I was on horseback, and travelled a stage from ten to
fifteen miles every morning and evening, halting at comfort-
able bungalows, or houses built by the Government for the
use of travellers. There is no inn-keeper in them, but the

people attached to them are always ready to procure me milk, and boil my kettle, and for dinner kill me a chicken and curry it. I enjoyed my journey greatly, as the season (the beginning of January) was cool and bright, and the crops on the ground made the boundless plain through which I rode greener and prettier than I had ever seen it before. In the loneliness of my journey,—for I had no one to speak English to, except in two or three towns where I stopped for a few days,—I had much enjoyment. But the subject about which I was continually thinking I would write to you, was that of the desolation of the country in a spiritual point of view. I rode 250 miles in a straight line, through a populous country, passing through villages every three or four miles, and seeing many others in all directions, and occasionally coming to considerable towns; but in all that district there was not a single Christian missionary, not one person from whom a heathen might hear the Word of Life. My road lay parallel to the sea-coast, at no great distance from it, but I might have gone inland for 100 or 200, or 300 miles, and except in one place have found the whole land equally wanting in Christian teachers. On Sunday evening I went into a village and had a long conversation with some Brahmins; the discussion coming to no satisfactory conclusion, the chief speaker said, " Well, come to-morrow, and we will have a full talk on the subject : you shall bring your books, and I will bring mine, and we will see which is true." I could only tell him that by the next morning I must be on my journey again, and I thought of the almost impossibility of a Christian preacher ever reaching him, as the village lay 200 miles from Madras, and 150 from Guntoor, the next missionary station. And now that I am moving to my own district, I often think of you and the missionary collectors who assemble in your rooms. I pass from one large village to another, I see the intermediate

distances broken by smaller villages,—the country as distinguished from the town is, I think, more closely peopled
than that in England,—and yet I am alone in visiting the
people ; I find generally the very name of Christ unknown,
and perfect ignorance as to either the sin or folly of idolatry.   The whole district, without another missionary in it,
is nearly 100 miles each way ; it is impossible that I can
visit even the chief villages for two or three days each,
during the six months in the year in which the weather
allows me to be out.

And now, my dear friend, in regard to these wants, which I
feel a hundred times more than I express, and which you would
feel similarly if you were here ; I wish you would try and
impress upon your missionary circle, that in reference to this
heathen country, thus destitute of the preaching of the Gospel,
God has given England the great commission to evangelise it.
And in all Cambridge, to whom has that commission come so
markedly and surely, as to the members of that little body,
into whose hearts it has pleased God to put the desire of
collecting subscriptions for missions, and to assemble for
information on the subject ?   I do not think that you ought
to be content, if two or three out of your number go out
annually as missionaries, but rather expect that every one
should do so, unless some one or two may have peculiar
indications that they are not to go.   It appears to me, that
in the case of those whom God has called to missionary
work, by having given them an interest in the subject, the
peculiar indications for the guiding of their course, are not to
be sought on the side of going, but on that of staying.   If
no extraordinary indication of God's will regarding them
hereafter occurs, their course is to come abroad, as the called
of God.   You will remember in that vision of Isaiah which
Mr. Carus read to us, when assembled in his room on the
Sunday evening of the missionary week last year ; Isaiah's

call consisted simply in his standing near and hearing God ask, " Whom shall I send, and who will go for us?" If your friends will be content with a call like Isaiah's, they have had it already. I wish, however, that they had it ever ringing in their ears, that God has given Christian England one peculiar mission, which is—not to stay at home and work among her own ignorant and poor, but to go abroad and evangelise India first, as most closely united in social and political ties ; then Africa, China, and all other countries which have become our neighbours " by commercial relation." We are all daily longing and praying for the speedy coming of our blessed Lord to restore all things ; and sometimes we are apt to wonder why He delays His coming ; but it is not *He*, but *we* who are the cause of the delay. He cannot come, as He said, until the Gospel has been preached in all nations for a witness, and He has ordered His faithful people to go and preach it. But we don't go, and ·the Gospel is not yet preached, and so His return is delayed. When I have been in a village preaching the Gospel of the kingdom, I feel " Now there is one more obstacle to Christ's return removed." This is the joy of a missionary, which I suppose you in England do not feel ; for there is no promise connected with pastoral work in England in reference to His second coming. It is not said, " All the souls in Barnwell parish shall be converted, and then will the end come," but, " The Gospel is to be preached unto all nations, and then shall the end come." The Gospel has been preached in all England ten times over—in India not yet once. He who wishes to have a peculiar part assigned to him in hastening the return of his Lord, let him pray to be made a missionary. The excuse I used to hear in England about our large towns and their neglected state and their heathen population, and so on, often occurs to my mind ; I call it an excuse, because, except in two or three cases, I have observed it to be

palpably no better. Young men say they can't come out
to Masulipatam, because the heathen thousands of Manchester or St. Giles' have a prior claim on their labours, and
so having pacified their consciences, they take a nice curacy
in a village or country town. Any one who urges this
ground for staying at home, ought, as it appears to me,
in more consistency to go to St. Giles' or Manchester, or
some such place, and be content with nothing else than such
a heathenish demoralised sphere ; if he gets tired of it and
leaves it, he must then come out to us, or else find some new
reason for remaining in England. And now having given
you a long talk, which I hope you will make use of to those
whom it may most concern, it is but fair that I should give
you some Indian information, and not make this letter a
mere sermon. So I will tell you what is daily coming
before me—the notions and views of the respectable classes
of the heathen in this part of the country. The first point
then is idolatry ; they believe, and that without shame, that
the idol is indeed very God. For instance, at a great
bathing-festival which I witnessed ten days ago, I asked the
people what they came to do ; their answer was universally,
" I came to bathe in the sacred river Kistna, and when that
was done I went to the temple to see the god." " And what
sort of god is he?" " He is of the lingam (φαλλος) shape."
And then they told me how the idol lingam had been self-
born out of the earth generations ago, to the truth of which
an old inscription bore witness. This is not strange : for the
universal notion is that God has a material form, and one
object of their religious worship is, to be permitted to have a
sight of that form. This is a view I have daily to argue
against, by the simple proof,—If he had a material form,
wherever God is, there would that form be visible ; all
acknowledge that He is omnipresent,—that He is now near
us ; how then, if He has a form, does it not appear to us
here ? Connected with this is their saying, " He is the all-

pervader—He is in everything." By which they mean that
everything is materially made of Him, and is a part of His
substance. So low are their usual views of the Godhead;
but they yet descend further, by both incidentally and
positively charging God with being the author and perpe-
trator of sin. "Is He not the Creator of all things? If He
did not originate sin, who did? If God made me a sinful
being, He is to blame, and my faults can't be laid to my
charge. I am not an independent being; I have no choice
of good or evil; I only do as He wrote at the time of my
birth. Men are but puppets, God pulls the strings, and for
His amusement sometimes makes us commit sin, sometimes
perform righteousness." This is the common language I
meet with daily; it is what they have received from their
fathers, and I can only answer it by an indirect appeal to
their moral sense, which I always find existing in them, and
bearing witness to the truth of God, although it lies half
dormant behind a tissue of blasphemous dogmas. When
I charge them with sin, the commonest answer I receive is,
"Who knows the difference between right and wrong? I
do not know whether I have ever sinned or not; how can
I remember?" And when in answer to this I take the
practical course of enumerating a variety of sins, and asking
them if so and so is good or bad, and beginning usually with
falsehood and theft, I receive not unfrequently these answers,
"Why! lying is necessary, how could the world go on
without it;" or, "If I steal to satisfy my hunger, there is
no harm in it." Of course, when I press them further, their
moral sense speaks out, and they usually with a laugh
acknowledge the sin; and yet these subterfuges are not
merely made for the occasion, in order to parry my questions,
but they are the self-deceits by which Satan has hardened
and set to sleep their consciences. They have no thought
of the judgment to come: they all acknowledge, at least
after a little disputing, that there is a hell, and that God

will punish sinners in it; but it is manifest that the idea
has no living existence in their minds. No doubt the
universal belief has gone far to produce this end; fatalism
has added to it. One man said to me yesterday, "If we
join the Christian religion, shall we obtain absorption by
it," meaning of course, that union of the soul which dwells
for a while in the human body, with its great Divine origin,
so as to lose all individuality, as a drop of water in the sea.
Now it is to these people that I invite—no, not I, but God
calls—some of your circle to come and preach the free salvation of the soul and body through the sacrifice of Christ.
I preach this to them continually : the need of a remission
of sins ; Christ's suffering the only remission ; His resurrection and ascension ; His coming again, and the great
resurrection and judgment. It is indeed a happy work to be
so employed ; would that there were more to enjoy its
happiness. How gladly should I welcome some one or two
of you, who might come out overland by July or August,
when the worst of the hot season is over : a couple of
months spent in Masulipatam would give the bare rudiments
of the language, and then we could go out together into the
villages for six months and hear nothing but Telugu all
day long. I would suggest, in answer to any one who might
say, " I have not qualifications for a missionary life," that
so various are the spheres of missionary life, requiring such
very different kinds and degrees of talent, that if a man is
not fit for any of them, he is certainly not fit for any
ministerial sphere in England. Some have great difficulties
in regard to opposition on the part of their parents : I
would suggest, in such cases, that they should get some
friend, whose age, character, and position has weight with
their parents, to open the subject to them. The subject
which, coming from a young man, a father might at once
treat as visionary and absurd, may, when quietly brought
forward by one of riper years and judgment, at least claim

a calm consideration.   My paper obliges me to conclude by
assuring you of my being,

Your very sincere Friend,
HENRY W. FOX.

Mangalagherry : Sunday Evening, Feb. 28, 1847.

MY DEAREST ISABELLA,

I have been thinking about you often to-day, and so I
think I will spend half an hour this evening in writing to
you.   The cause of my thoughts recurring to you so often, I
believe is, that I have been reading Newton's " Cardiphonia,"
which I used to read at Rugby, and have scarcely ever
looked into since.   Newton is much mixed up with my
recollections of Rugby, and that brings to my mind the
time when I used to receive from you a long letter regularly
every Sunday morning, which served as my food during
the following week.   I believe those letters of yours were,
under God, among the chief means of fanning into a flame
the smoking flax, and bringing the full light of Christ's
sun to break through my twilight.   I was then, as I am
now, lonely : I had friends and companions, but none in
Christ, for it was before —— was touched by the Spirit of
God ; and I used to look to you as my chief, and indeed
only Christian companion, though so far off : and now it
is the same, my heart flies to you as the dearest companion
on earth, and distant as we are, I seem to have more and
closer communion with you than with any other alive.
While I am writing (nine o'clock at night) the roar of the
devil's festival is going on, about a quarter of a mile off ;
the crack of the fireworks, the braying of harsh trumpets,
the screeching of clarionets, and the hammering of tom-toms,
rise above the confused sound of a thousand or two of people,
and tell me that the procession of the god has set out from
the temple.   I have only just come back from the town to
the bungalow ; crowds of poor beings worn out with the

excitement of the day were lying asleep in all directions on
the ground ; vast crowds fill the streets and neighbourhood
of the temple, in the midst of whom are several men like
madmen, dancing about with two lighted torches (made of
cotton rags) in their hands, which they dash together till the
sparks fly out, and almost cover their naked bodies ; or they
beat themselves with the lighted ends, or they hold them, so
that the flame scorches their chests or their faces ; and one
man was walking about on stilts, with four long wooden
skewers run through the skin of his arms and back, and the
further ends of them on fire : and all this is not for devotion
or religion's sake, but to get two or three pence by it.   This,
for the time being, is Satan's seat, where he sits triumphant ;
but I trust the time has come, when the Lord Jesus is going
to turn him out of it.   After a long talk in the morning, for
an hour and a half, till I was quite hoarse, about idols and
the true way of salvation, I had been spending a quiet
Sunday in the travellers' bungalow, reading the first nine or
ten chapters of the Acts, which I thought was a good preparation for going to the people again, when the heat of the
day was over.   However, I shrunk a good deal from going
into the noisy crowd of devil's servants, all alone ; not that
I had anything personally to fear, but the contest seemed
great.   I was able to remember, and take courage from the
remembrance, that the one Lord of heaven and earth was
on my side, and would be with me in the midst of them ;
and when I went, I had about an hour of remarkably quiet
satisfactory preaching, to attentive and assenting listeners,
many of whom were Brahmins, and one or two learned ones ;
so that Christ has prevailed, and would not let Satan have
his way.   In this work of mine, going about disturbing Satan's
snug nests, the thought is hourly pressed upon me with
exceeding vividness, that I am in the midst of a battle with
the powers of darkness : it much helps to keep me watchful
and prayerful, for how can I stand against them one moment,

if Jesus does not uphold me? As a man I may contend with
the Brahmins, who are but men, but how can I in my own
strength contend with Satan and his busy hosts? It is just
like going into some of the dark recesses of a pagoda with a
torch; out fly the unclean bats by hundreds: so the torch
of Christ's Gospel will bring out the evil spirits to try and
flutter it out; but, blessed be God, it shall scorch their
wings instead. During the fortnight's tour, in which, like a
knight-errant, I have had to meet all comers, whatsoever
they be, I have been wonderfully preserved. Again and
again to my astonishment, have I come out of discussions
victorious, where I am sure that nothing but God's hand
shut up the mouths of opponents: not once has He let me be
put down, or vanquished; and this is the more markedly
His doing, because my imperfect ability of speaking and
understanding, renders me so very liable to be crushed or
confounded by a noisy Brahmin: but He would not let it be
so. "He has made His saints victorious," and on the very
head of language He has loosed my tongue to an extent I
certainly did not expect in so short a time; and I can begin
to expostulate, to urge the horrors of hell, the certainty of
punishment, the love of God in dying for us, upon my
hearers' consciences. He is a wonderful God, full of kindness, and bearing with our sins, and short-comings, and cold
hearts. Leaving the noise and crowd of the town, I walked
up the silent and lonely steps on the side of the hill which
led to the pagoda of the idol, which is so fond of sugar and
water, and there looked down on the town, half hid among
the trees, and the tall goparam, a tower rising above all, and
the milk-white buildings inside the pagoda, gleaming in the
bright moonlight, and the many lights down the street,
reaching far away; and as the roar and drumming came up
to me, I remembered how at that hour (eight o'clock) our
friends at Guntoor, only thirteen miles off, were met together
for evening worship, and how at the same time, the thou-

sands of congregations in quiet happy England, were just
assembling for afternoon service ; while here, the thousands
assembled to worship a dirty stone were indulging in dissi-
pation and devilry.   Blessed day ! when Jesus shall come to
set all things to rights ; "the times of refreshing from the
presence of the Lord ; " poor souls, now taking it all easy,
but then shrinking with horror from the sight of Him coming on the clouds of heaven.   Oh, dear sister, what a joyful
day for us ! to rise with dear Lizzy and little Johnny, and
our dear brother and sister, and the other loved ones in
Hove Churchyard, to meet Him in the air, and so we shall
ever be with the Lord.   We may well work on with
patience, as long as He has work for us to do, with such a
joy set before us.   May it please God early to make my
darling Harry and Mary rejoice in this prospect through
their love to Christ.   I do greatly long and pray, that they
may be spared the uneasy pantings after the world, and from
the dishonour done to Christ by most in their youth, and
that they may early, even from now, know what is the
settled joy and peace of real believers.

Your very affectionate Brother,

HENRY W. FOX.

Masulipatam : March 22, 1847.

MY DEAR FATHER AND MOTHER,

I cannot sufficiently thank you for the letters which I
have received from you so regularly every mail since my
arrival.   I received my mother's letter of January 29,
yesterday.   The receipt of them is a great relief to my soli-
tude : at times I feel downcast by my loneliness, and at such
times it is an inexpressible relief to look across the water, and
feel your affection and your sympathy.   Your love towards,
and care of, my dear children, is a fresh source of love to
you, and most thankful do I feel to you for your kindness

to them. You may say that they are your grand-children, but it is not all grand-children that receive such parental love. Christ has emptied me of earthly sources of satisfaction, in order to fill me with His fulness ; and when I am suffering from a sense of my earthly emptiness, I can sometimes pray that He would empty me still more, in order that I may have more room for Him. I do sometimes feel weary, and ready to faint ; but He reassures me, and He never lets me have those heavy thoughts about the future, which I used to entertain. I have returned from my village tour, as the weather was becoming too hot to live in my tent : the last day it was up to 98° for some hours. On my return the weather feels cool enough, but it is beginning to warm up; the season, however, is favourable as yet, and we have had several cloudy days—very unusual at this season, and I am in excellent health and strength. I am too busy at present. I cannot get my work done : as my house is near the town, I have visitors half the day long, occupying all my leisure time, and a good deal more. I also go into the town itself morning and evening, and have long and animated discussions. You remember that till now I had kept to the outskirts and villages in the suburbs ; now I am able, by Christ's help, to go into the streets and bazaars, and meet all comers : so that I am able to attack the stronghold of Satan. The English school is also beginning to receive its visible blessing ; there are two dear little boys in it—one fourteen, and the other almost sixteen—very desirous of being baptised, and showing marks, as we think, of the work of the Holy Spirit in them. One is a very respectable Brahmin, and the other a respectable Sudra. We must wait a little time before we take the step; they come to Mr. Noble or to me every day. I see also a good many other boys in private : the magnetic fishes, ducks, etc., and other toys and pictures, are a great attraction, and make my house quite a show-room ; and as I generally get an opportunity

of telling my visitors of Christ before they ask to see the
curiosities, it all works for good.   *   *   *
Your very affectionate Son,

H. W. Fox.

EXTRACTS FROM JOURNAL.

Masulipatam: July 8, 1847.—In my usual morning visit
to the streets of the town, I fell in with a boy who had
lately left Mr. Noble's English school. After an interesting
conversation, in which it appeared what a consent of the
understanding there might be to the truth, without any
inclination of the heart towards God, he began to speak
about my going regularly into the streets to preach and
converse about religion. He said, "The people crowd round
you, not because they care to hear what you have to say,
but they think you are mad, and so they come for mere
curiosity's sake." I was struck with the remark, which was
made in great simplicity, and I believe that there is a great
deal of truth in it. Indeed, this regular street-preaching
quite puzzles them ; they do not know what to make of it,
and from the remarks I hear about it, many of them don't
like it, for it seems like a systematic attack upon their
religion in their homes. They are, on the whole, however, very civil and attentive, though often very silly.

A few days ago a Brahmin, with whom I have been long
and intimately acquainted, lost his only child, a little boy
about two and a half years old. Added to the natural feeling of a parent, a Brahmin has an additional source of grief,
in the thought that it is only by the ceremonies and prayers
of his son after the father's death, that he can be delivered
out of the pains of purgatory ; and so he who dies without
leaving a son behind him is especially cursed. How far
this feeling affected the individual in question, I cannot say :
for he is a believer in nothing, save money ; but it is probable that superstitious feelings may have remained even

when belief has ceased. However, his natural feelings were roused, and when he came to see me next day he told me it was no use staying in his house : if he sat down to do anything, he could not do it, and that he got up and wandered restlessly about ; and besides, there was the baby's poor mother crying without stopping. I felt much for him, knowing that in all the ranges of his thoughts, and in all heathenism, there was not one word that could afford him any comfort. I pointed this out to him, telling him how much I felt for him, and begging him, as I knew he placed no belief in heathenism, to look and see if the comfort during sorrow which we Christians receive, and of which I gave him assurance from my own experience, was not a most forcible evidence of its Divine authority. " You *are now* in sorrow," I said, "and feel what it is ; and you find that neither in yourself nor in that which is around you, have you the slightest alleviation of it ; surely that religion which does what man cannot do, must be from God." He acknowledged with much heartiness that it was so, and said that this was an undoubted proof, much stronger than external proofs. I asked him then where he believed his child was ; he said he believed it was with Jesus Christ, but he should never go there, nor see it any more. I asked him if he had a word of comfort to give to his poor weeping wife. He acknowledged that he had none ; nor indeed could he have, for if he did believe in his father's religion he must suppose that he would never meet his child again, for already it was probably wandering about in some other transmigration. Nor could he look to the sorrow as being from a Father's hand, but only that it was a curse incurred by sins during some former state of being. However, having learnt from me before, he now said, " God has given me two blows,—the death of my relation a week ago, and now the death of my child ; my sin must be very great." These were ideas he had gained from me, and were not indigenous ones. He promised to consider the Christian religion closer than he had ever done, and took away a Gospel of St. Luke, with the promise of reading it carefully.

Masulipatam: July 15, 1847.—Yesterday morning I went to a collection of huts, inhabited by Chuklus, and lying on the outskirts of the town, half a mile distant from my house. These people are shoemakers and workers in leather, and are consequently considered the most unclean of all the most despised of the Pariah class : their habits have not indeed much to recommend them. As soon as I entered the thick cluster of huts, I was surrounded by twenty-five or thirty of them ; half were men, half women and boys. After a while I asked where their god was ; they pointed out a square hut in the middle of the cluster, with mud walls four feet high, and a sloping roof of palmyra-leaf thatch. There, they said, was their Ammaváru, or village goddess. On asking what was inside, they said, "A stone." Reproaching them for worshipping a stone, I said, "Go and fetch it to me." They made excuses first, "It is too heavy to carry ;" and when I said, "Let two or three carry it," they next said, "It is planted in the ground." After ten minutes' conversation with them, telling them of Christ, and His love and death, I went up to the hut and crept in at the low door-way, and at once detected the lies they had told me. On a little raised dais of dry clay, reclined, first, a slip of wood two feet long, on which was cut very imperfectly a rude figure of a man, four or five inches long, and in the style a school-boy might carve with his knife ; next to it was an old worm-eaten piece of wood, ten inches long, resembling nothing so much as an old tent-peg, or a withered root of mangel-wurzel : these two, they said, were the husband or husbands of the goddess : next was a misshapen rough stone, about a foot square,—this was the Ammaváru herself : further on lay three stones, about the size and shape of small paving-stones, these were her children. It is difficult to conceive

M

that state of mind which could believe such coarse and common materials to possess a divine nature ; yet many, if not all the people about me, seemed quite serious in believing these stones to be their deity. They did not regard them as the creator or creators of the world, but simply as their gods, whom if they were to forsake, they would pay their lives in forfeit.

After leaving the hut again, I returned to the subject of Christ, and called on them to forsake these miserable stones, and to come to Him as their dying but living Saviour. One man said quite seriously, "But if we all turn Christians, what will become of the dead cattle?" For the Chuklus are the privileged consumers of all bullocks, cows, and buffaloes which die of disease or old age. "Suppose," he added, "some of us join your religion, and we will leave some behind to eat the cattle."

I suppose that, so long as the human heart can escape having to humble itself before God, as worthless and unprofitable, and to accept the righteousness of another and not its own, there is nothing too vile or degrading to which it will not descend. For indeed, what difference is there between these worm-eaten stumps of wood and shapeless stones of the Chuklus, and the silver and marble bejewelled figures of the Virgin and saints which I saw the people adoring at Malta, except a few degrees of civilisation and elegance ? Religiously and morally viewed, the one worship is just as degraded and humiliating as the other.

Masulipatam: July 31, 1847.—Ten days ago, Mr. Sharkey and I went out to the public bungalow at the village of Neddamole, ten miles from here ; our object was partly to preach to the people in the neighbouring villages, but chiefly to obtain in the quiet of the bungalow that seclusion which we cannot obtain in our houses here, where native visitors are coming and going all day long : for we wanted to make progress in revising and preparing some Telugu manuscripts

for the press. We stayed three days, visiting the villages
morning and evening, and having some interesting opportunities of making Christ known.

Last Sunday, July 25th, we baptised in our little congregation, Sitapàti, a young man of a respectable Sudra
caste, and about twenty-one years of age. The way in
which he was brought to us, encourages us in the hope that
God has many other hidden ones, whom He will in due
time bring out from among the heathen. About six
months ago he became acquinted with David, a young
man of about his own age, who was baptised last autumn,
and who had once been of the same caste as Sitapàti. I
do not know that the acquaintance led to anything about
that time, but two or three months ago, Sitapàti speaks of
himself as beginning to think about his sins, and to feel
anxious concerning them : in this state of feeling he asked
his acquaintance, David, what was the cure for his sins?
David told him of Christ ; and it seems that almost immediately the young man was led to desire to be a Christian.
When in this state, David one day informed me of him,
and at my request brought him to me. I found him very
ignorant, yet desirous of being taught, and professing a
desire to be baptised. He came to me several times for
instruction, and read a little of St. Matthew's Gospel.
However, his relatives seem to have found out the turn his
mind was taking, and he told me he was afraid of their
locking him up in the house and not letting him go out.
This led him to spend a great part of his time at the
school-house, where David lives, as it was then the holidays : and during that time, of his own accord, he broke his
caste by eating of David's supper, prepared by a Pariah
cook. His father and elder brother,—the former, an old
man who had once been a gardener ; the latter, a strong,
stout, and violent young man,—at last, finding that Sitapàti
absented himself much from home, came one Sunday after-

noon to the school-house to seek for him. This led to two
or three interviews between him and these relatives, in the
presence of Mr. Noble or myself : in which they endeavoured
by threats and enticements to induce him to come home with
them ; but he steadily resisted, and said he wished to become
a Christian ; and told them their efforts were useless, for he
had already broken caste.

On the Monday morning, when they came to my house,
the brother used all sorts of entreaties, urging how he had
fed him, and taken care of him from a child, and taught him
to read, etc., and would he now leave them ?   All this while
his face quivered with passion ; and had not the interview
been in my presence, I am sure he would have endeavoured
to drag his brother off by force. Next day, when Sitapàti
was in Mr. Noble's compound, his brother and another
person, who apparently had been lying hid on purpose,
sprang out and seized him, and taking him head and feet,
dragged him out of the compound, and some little distance
towards the place where they lived.   However, the alarm
was given, and Mr. N. and two or three servants ran out
and overtook them, and insisted on the young man being
released, which, after a short while, was done.   Mr. N. then
asked him where he wished to go—with him, or with his
brothers ?   It did not require much for the poor young man,
whose face was bleeding from a blow received from his
brother, to decide to return with Mr. Noble.   Next day,
with the too ordinary barefaced falsehood of a Hindu, the
brother laid a complaint before the magistrate, that Mr. N.
was detaining his brother by force.   The collector sent for
the young man, and in public court examined him for a long
time concerning the correctness of his brother's complaint :
Sitapàti publicly declared that it was of his own free will
that he had gone to, and was living with Mr. N., and as
publicly declared his purpose of becoming a Christian.   This
was truly making a good confession ; for all round about

were crowds of Brahmins and others, whose enmity against
the Gospel is not small : some of them said among themselves, as I was afterwards told by one who said he heard
the words, " I wish I could get hold of that young man, I
would murder him." The magistrate of course dismissed
the complaint, with a warning to the brother. Since then
Sitapàti has been going on steadily, and daily receiving
instruction in the knowledge of the leading truths of the
Gospel, till last Sunday, when having assurance of his
sincerity, and being satisfied that he knew what it was into
which he was to be baptised, he was received into Christ's
visible Church. His coming over to us, and the publicity
which was given to it by his examination before the collector,
made a much greater sensation in the town than I could have
expected : it was added, however, to a recent baptism of a
young Brahmin at Vizagapatam, which caused great sensation here, and was well known there ; the effect was, that
nearly half the boys in Mr. Noble's English school were
withdrawn. After a while many of them came back, but in
all he lost fifteen, among whom were some of the most
hopeful and interesting youths. The school, however, was
not left empty, for the vacancies were rapidly filled up by
new applicants, who crowded to gain admission, among
whom were the sons of the principal Sudra Ameen,
and the Sheristadar of his court. The story which was
current here, as it has been elsewhere on similar occasions,
was that we had given the young man a potion, the effect of
which was to attach him to us ; the way in which they
supposed it was done, was to sprinkle a powder on his
head. The parents of some boys feared, or pretended to
fear, that we should do so to their boys, if they remained
in school : not considering that it would have been easy for
us to have done so any time these last three years past, or
when the boys come to our houses, which they freely do.
But the fact is that, like the Jews of old, they cannot but

acknowledge that a wonderful thing has happened, an influence has been produced on a man's mind, to induce him to deny himself, and give up his family and his caste ; and not knowing whence it proceeds, they attribute it to magic or medicine. I do not think the Hindu system knows anything of an influence of Divine power on the heart or feelings of man : it is more conversant with mere outward ceremonies, or at least with a mere intellectual theorising on Deity.

Neddamole : Aug. 11, 1847.—Mr. Sharkey and I have started for a month's tour through the villages, being desirous of taking advantage of the continuance of cloudy weather, which enables us to be out much during the day-time. There is so much rain, however, that we are not able to take our tents with us, but keep ourselves on the line of road on which there are public bungalows, and from them visit the numerous villages which lie within two or three miles of our resting-place.

Weyoor : Aug. 13, 1847.—After visiting two or three villages from Neddamole, we started at an early hour yesterday morning for this bungalow, which is fifteen miles further on. I did not, however, like to pass by the large village of Prámarru, where I had been so well received on my two visits in February and March. It lies nearly half-way, and so on our arriving there about eight o'clock in the morning, we left our horses with our horse-keepers and entered the village. We soon met the Naick, or head Sudra of the place, with whom I had formed an acquaintance before, and he led us to the chief school—the friendship of the master of which I had purchased by putting the Naick's little boy to his school, and paying for him for four months. The school-master was not there, but was away getting shaved, as it was a lucky day for that rare operation, and an old blind superannuated master was keeping in order about twenty boys. Here we spent more than an hour sheltered

from the sun—Mr. S. in one part, and I in another, of the
spacious room where the school was held : he was speaking
to and reading with some adults and a few boys. I had a
small congregation, varying from six to a dozen of the elder
boys, to whom I acted as school-master, sitting down and
making them sit, and then making them read the Ten
Commandments, and explaining them to them. Afterwards,
when I began to speak of the forgiveness of sin, and asked,
" Who can take away sins ? " one quiet little lad gave me a nice
answer, " Only God," he said, " can take away sin." When
I praised him for his answer, the other lads, who were
several of them Brahmins, looked rather contemptuously at
him, and said, " Oh ! he is only a barber ! " for the barber
caste is an inferior one. When we had tired the patience
of the school-master, who had meanwhile arrived, with his
new-shaven head shining like an egg, and who ought to
have dismissed the school nearly an hour before, we went
out, and crossing the narrow street, entered the house or
shop of the village carpenter. He is not paid as such an
one would be in England, by the job, or for the article he
makes or mends, but is a regular village servant. Every
villager who possesses a plough pays him (in grain) about
half a rupee annually for each plough, that is about four or
five days' pay, and for this the carpenter has to make, if
need be, or keep in repair, the farmer's ploughs and sledges
on which the straw is carried from the field. Carts are a
separate charge ; perhaps because they scarcely existed in
the days of old when this village custom was established.
Sitting down on some logs of wood, we had more than a
dozen men and four or five women as listeners. Mr. S. had
a long discussion with a Brahmin, who was a Vedantist,
and maintained, first, that " all is God, and God is all ; "
then, that he himself was God ; and lastly, that God
was the author and agent of all sin. He was no stray
infidel ; the same doctrines meet us on all sides, and it

is difficult to say whether such men are better or worse than atheists.

It is one of the painful parts of our dealings with the people, and particularly with the Brahmins, that their mouths are so full of lies; it is scarcely possible to speak five minutes with one of them, but he utters two or three palpable falsehoods. When rebuked for them, all they have to say is, " It is the custom of the country; " or, " How could the world go on without lying? "

On leaving Prámarru, about 11 A.M., we had a sunny ride for nearly two hours; rather warmer than we had hoped for, but a cool breeze in our faces prevented our feeling it oppressive. Each time I pass through this part of the country I am struck with its numerous population. The villages lie round in all directions in clusters : from one spot 1 counted no less than fifteen in sight within a circle, the radius of which was about three miles, and probably I overlooked some, for the low thatched huts which compose them are not very conspicuous in that flat country.

Yesterday evening in this village, and this afternoon in the large village of Walloor, about four miles distant, we had crowded audiences, from twenty to thirty persons standing round one or both of us, and generally listening very quietly. The burden of one man's argument yesterday was, " All our gods are one and the same ; whomsoever we worship, we shall go to heaven." Not only is this absolutely false, and contradicted by almost every popular book, but I have little doubt but that the speaker knew it to be so, just as well as I did : and it was not difficult to point out his mistake. This afternoon one clever old man would consent to everything that was said : " It is all right, this is just what our book says," etc.,—except the way of deliverance from sin ; and, as usual, he was slow in discerning the fact of Christ's atonement, however clearly stated. " You expect to be saved by believing in your Gooroo (teacher,

meaning Christ), and we expect to be saved by believing in
ours ; the only difference is that of language ; you in English
give Him one name, we give Him another." When, however,
pressed to state his way of forgiveness of sin, it was the
old story, " You must live purely, and pray to God, and
this will be your deliverance." It was easy to point out to
him by the usual illustrations the folly of trying to purge
away the sin of an unclean heart, by that which comes forth
from that heart, and is consequently itself unclean.

Weyoor : Aug. 15.—Yesterday, in the middle of the day,
I went into the village, to the parts of it inhabited by the
toddy-drawers and the cowherds : for the different castes,
especially such as these, generally cluster together in a distinct spot. After addressing a few Pariahs and toddy-
drawers, in the locality of the latter, I went in quest of a
cowherd's house, where Pèrentalu, the village goddess, is
kept. Her little temple lies about a quarter of a mile from
the village, and she is famous all the country round for the
swinging festival which takes place here in February
annually ; but for some reason or other, she (that is the
image) is kept in a house in the village belonging to one of
the cowherds, who are her patrons and priests. On mentioning my wish to see the image, the man I spoke to
offered at once to show me the way, and, to my astonishment, led me to the house, and took me inside the little
court of the house, and pointed out the door of the room
where the goddess and her husband Chintanna are kept. I
sat down, and had half-an-hour's opportunity of addressing
about a dozen common people on the subject of idolatry
and of Christ's death and sacrifice for sin. When I rose up,
I found that while my back was turned a lock had been
put on the door where the idols are kept, which had been
unlocked when I first entered : on my noticing this, they
all said, " Oh, the old man who has got the key is not
here ; " and when I pointed out to them that the lock had

been put on during the last few minutes, they pretended not
to know of it, though every one in the place but myself,
who had my back turned, must have seen it done.   Oh
lying, lying! it seems to be the very meat and drink of
the people.   While talking of this goddess, I said I had
witnessed a swinging at Peddana (near Masulipatam), and
that then the victim had shown considerable symptoms of
pain when the hooks entered his flesh, contrary to the
usual story, that the goddess preserves him from pain, and
I asked if the same ever occurred here.   "Oh no," said the
man, "this goddess has great power!"   "But has not the
goddess of Peddana also great power?"   "No, *she* was only
made by men, *this one* is not so, but was a gift from Siva."
I was here amused with a nice little girl about five years
old, who came feeling my clothes, and with much curiosity
asked her father what I was : she had never seen a white
man, or English clothes before, and seemed scarcely to know
what sort of animal I was.   In most of the villages off the
road which we visit, the people, particularly the women,
look at us with wonder, being probably the first of the
species whom they have ever seen.
    Both yesterday, and this morning, I visited a small
Pariah hamlet, half a mile distant, and containing seven or
eight huts : the people do not engage in agriculture, but are
weavers of the coarse cotton cloths worn by the lowest
classes.   I had good audiences each time, of ten or twelve
men and women, who were much interested in all I said.
I spoke of sin, read the Ten Commandments, and enlarged
on them; I dwelt much on heaven and hell, and the
deliverance from fear of death, and the joyful prospect of
the day of release which Christians enjoy ; and then went
through the history of Christ, and showed how His atonement removed our sin, and set us free to serve God with
thankfulness.   They had no opposition to offer, and seemed
to like all I told them, and to accept it : they asked several

SWINGING FESTIVAL, PEDDANA.

questions, and wished to know if I would come and see
them again. This work among the Pariahs is so entirely
different from our conversation with Brahmins, as to remind
me much of missionary labours in lands where caste, civilisation, and a *system* of heathenism are all unknown. To
the natural eye it looks more hopeful and pleasant, but we
have never room to forget that the whole work of converting and fixing the truth in the heart, is the work of
the Holy Ghost.

In this village this evening, during a long conversation
with some Brahmins, the chief of them asked me the
identical question which was put to me a few days ago.
"All you say seems very good, but how is it that the
Company have been eighty years in this country, and yet
have never till now sent to tell us of these things?" I
again acknowledged that it was a grievous sin and culpa-
bility of the Government to have so neglected them, in
which view he seemed to acquiesce : I then corrected a
mistake he entertained, in supposing that *we* were sent by the
Company, and told him that my authority was, first, God's
commission, and next, that of the Queen of England, whose
servant I, as well as the Company, was. It was with some
difficulty that the bystanders could be persuaded we were
not sent and maintained by the East India Company.

Beizwarah : Aug. 17, 1847.—We made a short ride from
Weyoor yesterday morning, to the next bungalow at Kan-
kepad. On the way we entered a village of middling size in
order to speak with the people, but though we stayed more
than a quarter of an hour there, and walked about the little
lanes in it, we could not find a single man ; they were all
Brahmins and Sudras, out ploughing, for a village has only
a tiny Pariah hamlet of three huts under it, and so the
inhabitants have to labour in the fields themselves.

On the way we again stopped at a considerable village
named Parunky, and walked into it ; near a pagoda (in better

order than usual), we found two or three people, and others
joined us as soon as we stopped to speak to them. They of
course received us with profound respect : there was one, an
old Brahmin, who had a musical instrument a good deal
like a guitar, with three metal strings of similar size and
tone. He was a " singer of songs," they said, so we asked
him for a song, and sitting down on the mud ledge against
a mud wall, he began to sing a song in praise of Ràma.
Unlike Hindu instrumental music, their songs are by no
means tuneless, and on the whole, the song, accompanied by
a little twanging of his instrument, was not unpleasant,
though his voice was not musical, and his time poor and
monotonous. When he had done, Mr. Sharkey began to
tell them that he knew of a better person to praise than
Ráma, and went on to tell them about Christ. This led us
into a general talk about Him which lasted more than half-
an-hour ; they were quiet people and had no serious objections to make, or at least made none : the few they made
were at once answered without difficulty, and they had no
reply to make. They were such as these : " Nay, but we
have always hitherto believed these images to be gods ; "
" Our fathers believed them ; " or, " This is all related in
our books." " But are your Shasters true or false ? " " Of
course they are true." " How do you know them to be
true ? " " Are they not *books* ? " " But what support have
you for them, what evidence ? " " They are their own
support, their own evidence." In this village, as in many
others, on our producing tracts, the question was put to us,
" Is this your own hand-writing, or is it printed ? " For in
most places the majority, nay, rather the whole of the people
have never seen a printed paper. Of course, in all these
villages, the very name of Christ is utterly unknown, and to
be told that there is sin in idolatry is as great a novelty to
the people, as the names of their gods are to the most
ignorant of our English villagers. And this is in a district

which has been in quiet peaceful possession of the East India Company for eighty years; and nearly three generations have gone down to the grave, and another is rapidly descending, in utter ignorance of those truths and that light, for the spread of which alone God has been pleased to give the country to our nation. How great is the blood-guiltiness on the head of the East India Company, for not having sent missionaries, and established Christian Bible-schools; and how great is the sin of our whole nation, and of our Established Church in particular, for having left these people in utter darkness; and how great is the guilt of our universities and other places of education in England, in having sent but two men, and during the six years we have been here, in having sent us no help or addition to our number, to go to those hundreds of villages which we can never hope to visit; how great a weight of sin and guilt thus hangs over us, thus clings to us, God alone knows, who in the day of judgment will require the blood of these men at our hands. There are thousands in England, who talk of these things, but we who move among the people, and see them, *we feel* them; and then we are at once reminded of the priest and the Levite, who looked at the wounded man, doubtless pitied him, but "passed by on the other side." May our long-suffering God have mercy on them and on us.

We have fallen in, two or three times, with a party of "Medicine people,"—*Rasayogulu*, as they call themselves. They live, that is, they have houses, in Masulipatam, but seem to spend a large part of the year in wandering about the country. They seem to be wandering village quack-doctors, and like the apothecary of old, they adorn both themselves and their families with strings of uncouth beads and nuts, to acquire a sort of mysterious character. Their little encampment was the exact counterpart of a set of gipsy huts on an English common; only instead of cloth, the covering of the low oval tent consisted of a coarse sort of

mat. Each tent was about seven feet long, five feet wide at
the ground, and three-and-a-half feet high. Inside was a
low rude cot, upon which sometimes a child was lying :
before the doors were plenty of ugly black sows with their
young ones, all grubbing up the ground; snarling pariah
dogs were near them, and at a little distance was a crowd of
forty or fifty donkeys grazing. Whenever near a town or
village we see donkeys, we may be sure that there are either
washermen (who use the poor creatures to carry bundles of
dirty clothes), or basket-makers (a wild curious race), or
jugglers, or some similar wandering low class. There is no
animal so deeply despised as the poor donkey, and to speak
of riding on one excites a sort of derision and amusement.

Beizwarah : Aug. 19, 1847.—This place is a small town,
if it deserves the name, of 3,000 or 4,000 inhabitants, and
lies at the crossing of the great north road from Madras to
Calcutta, with the great road from the coast at Masulipatam to Hyderabad. It is close on the edge of the sacred
river Kistna, now a full mile wide, rolling its muddy, yet
sweet water, rapidly to the sea. From these two reasons it
is both a place for travellers and the abode of many Brahmins,—for all places on this river are sacred,—and where-
ever any pickings or stealings are to be had, either from
festivals or from visitors to sacred spots, there are large numbers of lazy vicious Brahmins to be found. It presents to us
all the signs of a bad place, and what we have seen of the
Brahmins tells us this too plainly.

On the afternoon of the day of our arrival, we went into
a street inhabited by Brahmins, and fell into conversation
with a man squatting on the mud ledge beside his house-
door. Not many minutes had elapsed before there was a
crowd of thirty or forty people, chiefly Brahmins, many of
them sitting along the same ledge as the first man was on ;
others, who could not find room, standing in the street
like ourselves. For some time Mr. Sharkey had a very

IDOL CAR AND PART OF SIVA'S PAGODA, BEIZWARAH.
(*From a Talbottype View.*)

interesting conversation with a very old intelligent man, who said he was eighty-four years old, and who did not speak for the sake of controversy, but, as he said, in order to acquire information.   He began by saying he rejected and disbelieved all Hindu systems : "The Adwai system (or the wild pantheistic creed, which is so common, "all is God, God is all, I am God, you are God ; there is no distinction between right and wrong, truth and untruth ") is false ; the Dwaitam system (or the Gnostic doctrine of the eternity of two principles, good and bad, of which *matter* is the evil one) is false ; the Vasishta Adwaitam (a mixture of the other two) is also false and nonsensical."   But though the old gentleman went on in a garrulous manner to tell us what his system was, and though he greatly approved of the Christian scheme which Mr. S. set before him, yet it was not very clear that he had any distinct system at all, but rambled into loose metaphysics ; and as for including the subject of the remission of sins in his system, he never seemed to think of it.   All this while the other people kept very quiet, and listened ; but finding the old man did nothing but ramble in the fields of most unprofitable metaphysics, we began to speak to the rest of the crowd, and then we discerned their want of manners and of virtue.   They showed no personal rudeness or insult towards us, but as soon as we began to talk, half a dozen at once began to talk also, either to one of us or to one another, and no peaceable opportunity of speaking to more than two or three at a time could be obtained.   They stood up for the worship of idols,—they denied the existence of sin,— they mocked the idea of anything spiritual, anything which which was not productive of vice, money, or bodily pleasure. At last I drew near to one man to speak to him ; he said, " I want none of your books, not I."   I answered, " I have no intention of giving you any, I force my books on no one ; but listen to me for a few moments."   And I then began to speak seriously of his sins and of the coming judgment; but his continual remark was in this strain, "What care I? I don't know whether I have sinned or not; I never saw the hell you speak of." I said to him, "Now answer me one question: Which do you count of most value, your soul or your body,—things present, or things to come?" His answer was, "Of course things present: of course my body is most important to me." It was the bold bad acknowledgment of, and glorying in, the principle which is the chief feature of the " body of sin " within us, and which every unconverted man steadily acts on; but the shameless boasting about it marks a hardness and a deadness of conscience which is very painful to the hearer.

As we walked away from this painful conversation we took our course down to the river side: it was now a little after sunset, and several of those with whom we had been speaking, followed us to perform their evening devotions. Stepping a yard into the river, or squatting down at the edge of the water, they began to mutter some Sanscrit verses or charms; presently the man would take up a little water in his hand, and carry a few drops to his mouth three times in succession, then he went on with his mutterings, then he threw up three or four libations of the water with his right hand, then he turned to the west, then to the east, then he made crossings on his breast, not to be distinguished from Romish crossings, and so went on with a variety of signs and symbols, and gesticulations and mutterings. There was something ludicrous in seeing some of the men going through this unmeaning child's play (to them it is neither more nor less) with all gravity; but it was also painful to look at these, or at others who were smiling at us from time to time, and to remember that all this was a pretence of religion on the part of evil men, who had only a few minutes before been uttering blas-

phemy, negations of all religion, professions of utter un-
godliness, and viciousness. I could not help being much
reminded by this scene, of the inside of a Romish church :
the same muttering and running over of charms and
prayers in an unknown tongue, the same cycle of bodily
gesticulations, and then the rising and going away with
the same appearance of self-satisfaction, with the same
deceived conscience and unforgiven soul.

Next morning we had one of those strong contrasts which
add greatly to the variety and interest of missionary work.
We went to the Malapalam, or Pariah hamlet, which lies a
quarter of a mile away from the town, and consists of about
thirty houses : the work of all the inhabitants is farm-
labour under the farmers, except that of two or three who
are weavers. As we drew near we saw a crowd of persons
just outside the bushes and mud-walls which bound the
hamlet, and found there a Sepoy, two or three peons (or
constables), and the cutwal of the town, driving and
pushing and thrusting about twenty men, who showed
great unwillingness to go where they were wanted. We
inquired of the peons what was the matter, and were told
that a number of carts, laden with Government treasure,
were crossing the river in boats, and that these Pariahs
were being sent down to the river-side to work all day at
unlading and lading the boxes of treasure. "What pay do
they get for this work?" we asked. "Oh, no pay at all;
they have to do the work for nothing." We exclaimed
against the injustice of this compulsory labour ; the peons
appealed to custom. We inquired, "If men are to be
forced to labour without pay, why do you not go and com-
pel some of those lazy Brahmins, who are doing nothing, to
go and do the work?" "What! make the Brahmins work!
they would at once make a petition to the collector, and get
us turned out of our places." On our still pressing the
injustice of the proceeding, the peons assured us it was not

N

unjust as we thought, for, said they, " This is an old custom, that the village work is to be done without pay by the Vetti people among the Pariahs, and they have a piece of freehold land by way of reward." We found afterwards that this piece of land is very small, and that the Vettis only get one-third of the produce, for they are not allowed to cultivate it themselves, and one-third goes to the farmer who cultivates it, and another third to Government. We asked, however, of the peons, how many Vetti people there were in the village who thus owed this free service, and they told us about a dozen men. " But here you are carrying away nearly twenty men ; what right have you to take these others ? " " We want all this number, and Vettis or not, we must have them."

We visited these poor people twice, and Mr. Sharkey *at length preached Christ* to them : they received the doctrine very readily, and expressed themselves willing to follow it ; they had no objections to make, but only asked a few questions about their stone goddess, whether they ought to worship it or not. It is much more pleasant thus to find people acquiescing in the truth, and the work among them looks more hopeful, yet all these appearances are merely marks of the natural mind consenting to what is manifestly true ; and these poor people were the more ready to receive our words, as we appeared to them in the light of persons who abhorred the oppression they suffered. What we long to see is some sign of the Spirit at work, some anxious inquiring, some honest persevering in well-doing, some crying out for sin : all else is deceptive.

Condapilly: Aug. 20, 1847.—At an early hour this morning we left Beizwarah, and passing by the northern pillar of Hercules, by a road cut out of its foot and overhanging the river, we again found ourselves in a plain, bounded by another and somewhat loftier range of hills at the distance of nine or ten miles. In striking contrast with all the

country from Masulipatam to Beizwarah, this plain, ten
miles wide, and reaching northwards for many miles more, is
very thinly inhabited, and only half cultivated. From the
top of the hill above Beizwarah, which I ascended yesterday,
I saw only four or five villages. The range towards which
we were proceeding across the plain was about 800 or 900
feet high, rather falling off at either end : under the centre
part of it lies the little town, or rather village, of Condapilly. We were both of us laid up all day with headache :
in the afternoon Mr. Sharkey had an interesting conversation
with two young natives who came to see him, and in the
evening we spent half-an-hour in the bazaar, speaking of
Christ to a crowd of people. The hill which is immediately
above our heads is very beautiful; it is composed of a fine pur-
plish rock, of which many massive projections stand out pre-
cipitously, but it is otherwise pretty plentifully covered with
bushes and small trees, which at this season are beautifully
green and refreshing. A slight valley or hollow just behind
the house, reminded me for a few moments of Nightingale
valley at Clifton ; but it has not its depths, nor its richness
of wood, still more, it has not the attendant softness and
moisture of air, and the gentler light of an English sky.
There are a few leopards among the jungle, and one was
killed quite close to this house a short while ago, but I
believe they seldom or never attack men. The greenness
of all around and the abundance of trees make me almost
forget I am in India.

As we were leaving the fort this evening we found one of
the Sepoys busy adorning a little stone image of Hanuman
(the monkey-god who helped Ráma to conquer Ceylon) ; he
was daubing red paint over it, and lighting lamps before it.
We stopped to speak to him, and tried to point out to him
the absurdity and the thousand contradictions involved in
supposing the dirty stone to be a god. His answers and his
manner greatly struck us, for he really *seemed serious* in

what he was doing : he really seemed to believe the thing
to be a god, and to be hurt at the contrary being stated ;
this is a rare occurrence. Lightness of mind, half-belief,
want of seriousness, are the almost universal characteristics
of the people regarding the idols, and were exhibited in
another Hindu who stood by, and laughed at the absurdi-
ties of the idol.

Beizwarah : Aug. 23, 1847.—Saturday was a very interesting day to me. As Mr. Sharkey was poorly, I sallied
out by myself at sunrise, and passed right through the
village to the adjoining hamlets of Pariahs. Here, as usual,
I found more women than men ; yet after half-an-hour conversing with these former, I had also an audience of about
six or seven of the latter for a similar length of time. They
have, as it were, no religion to give up, having only a loose
attachment to a shapeless stone lying in the adjoining field,
and no system of priesthood or books to keep up superstition. They listened, therefore, and as far as the natural man
goes, consented to all I told them of our dear Lord's suffering and sacrifice for them, and some promised to pray to
Him. These poor folk are always delighted when I tell
them we are all brothers and sisters, and that the distinctions
of caste are human and false : the whole burden of the evil
system bears down on them who are (not outcasts, or people
without caste according to European notions, but) at the
bottom of the list, and are trodden underfoot by all.
Leaving them and returning to the town, I fell in with two
or three Brahmins settling accounts with some farmers ; and
had a conversation of some length with them : one of the
Brahmins expressed himself dissatisfied with idolatry, and
professed to be desirous of learning something better. The
roguish cast of his countenance made me suspect that there
was little sincerity in what he said. Walking down the
street with him we stopped beside where the schoolmaster,
and another man with great daubs of Vishnu's mark on his

forehead, and who was said to be a Gooroo, or learned teacher, were sitting. I did not intend to stay, but soon found myself sitting down in the verandah, and having an amicable discussion with the latter of the two men, in the presence of twenty or thirty other persons.

Though said to be learned (Hindu learning is about as much as that of a schoolboy who can construe Ovid's Metamorphoses, and knows a little of Lemprière's Dictionary), he was not a very acute man, and I found no great difficulty both in answering his objections and overthrowing his defences. After some little time spent in pointing out the inconsistencies of the existing system of religion with the original Hindu books, in which I exhibited my little acquaintance with those books,—which, though little, is great in comparison with that professed by Brahmins, which is none at all,—then quoted to them the ever sacred *Gayatri Mantram*, the very sound of which, from unhallowed lips, astounded them ; and, having thus acquired a character of being learned, I was led naturally to unfold the Christian system, Christ crucified, and man saved and renewed through faith in His blood. After this the discussion kept harping on this great topic, in which I had to answer a variety of objections and difficulties, chiefly of a trifling, childish, character, such as, "How can a man save others, who could not save himself?"—although I had particularly dwelt on the fact that Christ's sacrifice was a voluntary one, and that He was born in order to be slain. I was also led to the subject of evidences, and this is a very difficult one. With the Hindus, as with some Oxford doctors, the harder a doctrine is to swallow, and the less evidence there is of its truth,—the truer and greater is the exercise of faith in believing it ; that is to say, if the doctrine is one of their own. Consequently, in regard to religious and moral questions, the Hindus generally do not seem to understand what is meant by the word *Evidence*. "The book" is evidence,

not only for the doctrine, but for itself also. Again, the
utter ignorance not only of history, but of the very existence
of such a thing as *history*, prevents a Hindu from at all
appreciating the value of external evidence. The proofs I
made use of on this occasion, as being at least the most
handy, were two. First, if a book contains within it
doctrines which are in accordance with the character of
God, so far as our moral sense enables us to know it,
that book has probability in its favour that it is a Divine
revelation. This principle they are willing to admit, as
well as the reverse one, that a book which contains statements and doctrines contrary to the Divine character, is
not of Divine origin. With these two I was able utterly to
overthrow their abominably vicious books, and to give some
authority to the Gospel. Secondly, I brought forward the
case of Josephus, as an enemy living in that time and
country, uniting his evidence to that of the Apostles, who,
although friendly, were yet eye-witnesses. Coming further
to the question of the evidence of my friend's books, he
asserted the Vedas to have sprung incarnate from the mouth
of Brahma, far back in the depths of eternity. I asked
him for the proof of this fact, "for," said I, "in your
authoritative commentaries (for they also have "fathers,"
whose word on religious subjects is counted to be as good as
their god's, and whose interpretations alone are to be received
as expressing the meaning of their scriptures) on the Vedas
there are mentioned the names of the very men who wrote
the different hymns, and yet you say the books were never
written at all, but are born from Brahma." He appealed to
the Puránas, a set of books holding very much the position
of the semi-fabulous monkish tales and lives of the saints.
"Very good," said I, "let us then see what weight is to be
rested on the word of these same Puránas;" and so I went
on to remind him of some of the monstrous fables contained
in them : *e.g.*, the length of India being said to be 90,000

miles; Mount Meru, in the centre of the earth, being 800,000
miles in height above the earth, and 160,000 below it ; the
seven concentric rings of land and seas, the latter of sugar,
water, butter-milk, spirits, etc., and to assert on my own
experience and that of eye-witnesses that these statements
were false.   He could not deny my statements, but said,
" Never mind the Puránas ; what have they to do with the
subject?"   He had already forgotten that he had himself
mentioned them a few minutes before, as his authority for
the divinity of the Vedas.   I now pressed him for some
evidence.   " What sort of evidence do you want ? " he said.
I answered, " Any will do, so long as it is good ; please to
say what you believe about your books, and give me evidence
for your statements."   So he began : " The Vedas are the
personification of God, that is the Word of God."   " Now,"
said I, " please to tell me what proofs you can give me for
that fact."   He was nonplussed, and had not a word to say.
So before I went away I said, " This is always the way ; I
have asked the most learned men in Masulipatam the same
question, and they, like you, have not a word to say : how is it
possible for you to allege a proof, seeing that none exists ?"

About the middle of the day, the persons who had visited
Mr. S. the day before, made their appearance again, bringing
with them three or four others, among whom was one particularly sensible, well-behaved Brahmin, who had received a
little English education at Vizagapatam, and knew the out-
lines of Christian truth, and greatly approved what he knew.
They stayed with us about two hours, and came the next
day also while we were at morning service, and afterwards
remained with us about an hour and a half, and even came
for an hour more in the afternoon.   The most interesting
questions were put, and the difficulties started by this
Brahmin were just such as we might expect to come to the
mind of such a man : points of evidence both Hindu and
Christian, the nature of sin, man's corruption, the work of

Christ, how it was to be applied, how it was satisfactory, the new birth, and many other subjects were discussed. I was thankful, not only that we were able to give answers, but that our hearers were satisfied, and went away apparently (especially the above-mentioned Brahmin) convinced of the truth of Christ, but exclaiming, " How can a man forsake all ?"

We spent Sunday at Condapilly, and were joined in our morning service by the apothecary and his wife, and the wife of the drummer,—the drummer himself being unwell, and the commanding officer absent.

The same evening, as I was returning to our bungalow, I fell in with a most interesting character ; he was a Sepoy, who, I found, after a few words of conversation, was there on leave of absence, and was about to start to join his regiment (the 16th Madras Native Infantry) in a few minutes. I discovered that though he was a stranger to me personally, yet by his gallant exploits he was well known, not to me only, but to thousands more. In the war in the Sawun Warre, in 1845, he had been taken one day as an orderly by a Lieutenant Campbell, of the Bombay European Infantry, who with a party of thirty or forty of his own men, had been ordered to dislodge a party of the enemy from the dense jungle close at hand. This Sepoy, Kótappa by name, was the only native of the party, all the rest were European soldiers. When they had advanced a little way into the forest, they were fired on by an unseen enemy with deadly aim, and nearly half the soldiers were struck down dead. He described here the wounds of several of them : among others the officer was shot in the forehead, and fell dead. The soldiers retreated ; Kótappa, who was thus left alone, threw himself flat on the body of the officer, and after a few minutes discovered that the enemy had retreated, as well as his friends ; so, rising up, he took the dead body on his shoulder, and carried it some little distance to the rear, where he laid it down, to return for the cap, sword, and double-barrelled gun of Lieutenant Campbell. While he was returning with these, five of the enemy made their appearance, armed with matchlocks; one of them fired at him, and wounded him in the fleshy part of the arm. He said that he was in a great fright himself, expecting that his last hour was come, but he knelt down and took deliberate aim with the officer's gun, which was in his hand, and shot one of the five men in the knee; the others seeing him fall, took to their heels; and some of our officers. hearing the firing, concluded that there must be some of the party who had advanced into the jungle, yet alive, and sent forward some troops to bring them off: these brought back Kótappa, the wounded enemy, and the dead body. For this gallant action Kótappa has been rewarded by the Madras Government with a star of merit, to be worn on the breast, and with promotion to the rank of Naick (corporal) : but the circumstance which led to my being familiar with this story was this :—Some of the inhabitants of Perth, in Scotland, of which town Lieutenant Campbell was a native, had struck a large and beautiful gold medal, on which was recorded both pictorially, and in Hindustani and English, the event which drew forth this mark of their gratitude ; and sent the medal to Kótappa. He brought us the medal to the bungalow, to show it to us, and seemed to be justly proud of the distinction conferred on him, though at the same time he was a man of quiet and humble manner. He was very grateful to the East India Company for the rewards which he had received from them. He is a native of Conda-pilly, and of the Golla or cowherd caste. I was reminded of David, the shepherd, who went up against the lion and the bear and slew them, and I grieved at the difference of this poor man and the Bethlehemite; for the former knew not how to "go up in the strength of the Lord." We took the opportunity of telling him of a yet better Master than the Company, and of yet more glorious deeds done for him than he had done for his officer, and gave him a couple of tracts to read on the way.

To Mrs. SYMONDS, WADHAM COLLEGE, OXFORD.

Masulipatam, South India: Aug. 26, 1847.

MY DEAR MRS. SYMONDS,

I trust you will not think me presuming, in thus beginning a letter to you, almost from the other side of the globe. The strong interest which I know you take in missions, and your desire to promote our dear Lord's kingdom, have induced me to write to you, hoping that you may be able to effect that movement among the elders of the university which I have endeavoured to stir among the juniors by letters to A—— and others. I sent home, a few months ago, copies of the first journal of my tour in this district; one of which I directed to be forwarded to Mr. Golightly, who perhaps will be good enough to let you see it, in case you should think it would be interesting to you, as I am at this moment on a similar tour among the villages. I could give many interesting details of the work in the benighted districts, but my desire is rather to ask you to consider, and if your thoughts agree with mine, to set before others, as you will have opportunity of doing, a subject which I think is altogether lost sight of in England, and particularly in our universities,—I mean the duty of men, of some considerable standing and experience in the ministry, or in education, to come out as missionaries. I was particularly interested in seeing Dr. Jeune's name among the speakers at the Church Missionary Meeting at Exeter Hall in May, and still more so with the hearty, truly missionary tone of his speech; yet, when I laid down the paper, it was with a sigh, that he, and others in similar positions, are content to remain at home and talk over the subject, but will not come out here to India or to China to *act* in it. The importance of men of high standing and known ability becoming missionaries,

will, I think, appear to you to be very great, if you consider it in the following lights :—1st. Such a step would be
a noble instance of self-sacrifice for Christ's sake, and would
redound more to the praise of His name in England, than
the departure of ten men unknown or of ordinary abilities.
Every one would be compelled to say, that in such an act
there was no worldly motive at work ; the most thoughtless
and worldly would have an instance brought home to them
of the power of God. The sufferings of Cranmer and his
companions in Broad Street, would scarcely be more effectual,
under God, in fanning the flame of love to Christ in lukewarm hearts, than such a martyrdom as this would be.
2ndly. By this means the missionary cause would be not
only brought into much wider notice (there are tens of
thousands of intelligent people, and even many good people
in England, who can be said to know little more of missions
than the name), but it would be placed in the eyes of the
godly members of the Church, and particularly of the young
men in the universities, in its rightly exalted position.
It would no longer be the too true reproach of the scoffer :
" You talk very greatly about missions, but you won't send
any men to be missionaries but the refuse ; if you do really
mean that it is the most, or one among the most honourable
causes you can engage in, then, let us see some of your
leading men engage in it themselves : or else you will never
persuade us that you consider it anything else than a mean,
unimportant sphere of work." Such a step would open the
eyes of well-meaning parents, who regard a son's wish to be
a missionary as a mere wild romantic scheme, which none
but a boy would embark in. 3rdly. Any one godly man of
some standing in the university would doubtless carry along
with him, in his movement, several younger members. I
believe there are several not unwilling to move, but they
want to be led ; and who so fit to lead them in so holy a
cause as the head of their college, a tutor, or a senior fellow ?

If we pull a large stone out of a wall, it is sure to carry
along with it a number of smaller ones, which would never
have moved without it.   The above reasons alone are surely
enough to justify a senior man leaving Oxford for India,
even if he had not the slightest prospect of utility on this
side the ocean : the glorifying the name of Christ, the
honour paid to missions (the one great work of God's
church), the encouragement given to those who wish to go,
the favour created in the eyes of those who wish to keep
them from going, and the almost certain carrying away
from England some young and efficient missionaries ; these
are motives, for much less than which good men and great
men have been content to lay down their lives.   4thly,
however, the value of such a man in an Indian Mission is
greater than I can tell you : we are often mere young
men without experience, and we want an elder of sober
judgment to guide us : we have most of us left England as
soon as our college career was over, and plunged into such
a vortex of unceasing work, as entirely prevents us from
extensive reading.   Oh, how profitable to us and to the
whole mission, would be the presence of an earnest-minded
man of God, who could decide for us at once doubtful
questions in the Hebrew or Greek, as we labour at transla-
tions of the Scriptures ; who could guide us by his deeper
insight into the principles of language ; who would con-
descend to lend his stores of learning, and his trained powers
of mind to the composition of books suited to the native
mind.   Or again, how invaluable would such a man be,
by undertaking a large English school among the natives.
Arnold himself would have found a boundless field for the
exercise of his great powers of giving a Christian education
among the hundreds of young Hindus, who, in every town
are seeking for an English education.   Again, such an one,
even though he never learnt one word of the native tongue,
would be of vast value, by taking upon him many of the

affairs of the mission which need sober judgment, and by
doing which, he would set his younger companions free to
give their undivided energies and undisturbed time, to
direct intercourse with the natives. There are many places
where he would find important work to be done among the
English and half-caste residents in the place. And these
are not mere theoretical untried plans : in Mr. Tucker, who
came to India about the age of forty, and who never learnt
a sentence of any native language, we have had one who
has (to the eye of man) done more for the work of missions
than any man since Buchanan's and David Brown's time.
He possessed a sphere, and obtained an influence, which
the hardest-working Bishop in England might envy ; and
has done a work, the effect of which will not, I trust,
cease to be seen until Christ comes. Nevertheless, men of
forty or even fifty years of age need not despair of acquiring
a useful knowledge of a foreign language : doubtless, the
difficulty increases annually from the age of childhood, but
the Bishop of St. David's and the Bishop of New Zealand
are instances to encourage any one inclined to despond. I
know how difficult it is, even for self-denying Christian
men, to remove out of a sphere which seems very important,
and betake themselves to another ; and I suppose that at
first sight, at least the head of a house, and perhaps even a
college tutor, or the rector of a large parish, would throw
aside the idea of personally engaging in missionary work,
because, as they say, they are already engaged in a more
important sphere, being placed there by God Himself. I
wish that you might be permitted to dissolve such a
fallacious obstacle in the mind of some in high places.
1. For the argument that God has placed a man in such or
such a position is no proof that He intends to keep him
there all his life ; indeed, this first post may be intended
in God's wisdom *only* as a place of preparation for a second
and more important one, such as a missionary field. 2. It

sounds strange in my ears—though I dare not affirm that what jars in mine ought to jar in the ears of other men also— to hear of any place or post in the wide earth spoken of as greater in importance, more honourable or glorious, than that of a missionary. St. Paul, I think, felt as I did. His apostleship to the Gentiles, or mission to the heathen, was, in his eyes, a larger office than that of either a bishop or a king : and to me it seems that there is not a bishop who might not doff his lawn sleeves, and take to the white jacket of a missionary, and acknowledge, that though lowered in the eyes of the world, he was set in a more prominent and important post than that which he held before. Before he was but a pastor, or pastor of pastors, in a land where Christ's parting command has long been fulfilled ; now he stands at the head of Christ's army, going forth to conquer fresh kingdoms for his Lord. Now, he is an apostle, a father of a nation, the first herald of truth and light in a dark land, the remover of the reproach on Christ's Church, that though 1,800 years have past since He went up on high, she has not yet a tenth part accomplished His *one* last parting command. Now, he is a successor of Peter and of Paul, whereas before he could only count back as far as Timothy and Titus. On this point I am borne out by a very striking passage in Archdeacon Hare's Sermons, on the Victory of Faith—where he unhesitatingly states, that missionaries, not bishops, are the true successors of the apostles, whose office was only accidentally episcopal, but essentially evangelistic. In old days, a missionary sphere was not despised by men in high and important posts. I think it was in the second century that Pantænus, the head of the University of Alexandria (I suppose we might call him vice-chancellor), did not hesitate to resign that post, in order to engage in the (to him) more important work of a missionary in India. 3. Connected with this, is a subject

yet more painful to a missionary, viz., to see men in
England, good and worthy men, who have long been
interested in missionary work, and who yet have refused
to engage in it themselves (often on the score of the importance of their present position), at once accepting the
appointment of bishop to some of our colonies. It tells
us, who are at work out here, how low after all they
regarded the missionary cause; that while the office of
apostle could not draw them from England, that of colonial
bishop could move them at once—as if it were really more
important to be superintending the clergy of the Cape of
Good Hope, or some place out in Australia or the Canadas,
than to be planting a Church in a land where Christ's name
was not yet known.

I dare not undertake to say that I am right: but for
several months past I have come to the conclusion that
missionary work obtains, not only a peculiar interest, but
also draws its chief importance from its close connection
with our Lord's second coming. The prophecy that "the
Gospel of the kingdom must first be preached among all
nations, and *then shall the end come*," appears to me to have
reference, not only to our Lord's coming at the destruction of
Jerusalem, but to His greater and final coming; if so, all
delay in missionary work is delay of that blessed day, towards
which our eyes are bent in eager expectation: all increase of
activity and speed in preaching the Gospel hastens its glorious
approach. And considering that no promise, of which I am
aware, leads us to expect that at that day England will be
more holy, or the Gospel more fully preached, or the people
more spiritually provided for than at present,—then the
conclusion is forced upon us, that every godly minister who
remains in England, while he *might* go abroad to heathen
countries, is by this step delaying our Lord's coming. For
myself it is a subject of frequent joy, that with all my
imperfections and inability, which render me rather fit for

some unimportant post in England, than for the glorious
and difficult one in which I am placed, I am yet an instrument in hastening the great day. Whether the people will
hear or not, yet the Gospel is being, by my poor means,
preached in a district where the name of Christ is utterly
unkno'wn. There are many who speak of our Lord's coming
as being very near, but unless missionary work and zeal, and
the number of missionaries be increased many fold more than
they have these last fifty years, a hundred years or more must
elapse before the Gospel is known in all nations. There are
many nations in British India who have not been preached
to at all yet : still more among whom the work is but commencing. All China, except a tiny fringe of a few feeble
missions along the coast ; all Siberia, the enormous district
of Tartary, Thibet, Nepaul, Ava, Cochin China, the endless
yet large islands of the Chinese seas, Persia, and the adjoining
countries, Arabia and Asia Minor, fourth-fifths of Africa,—
indeed, without over-stating the want, something like three-
fourths of the whole world are still without the preaching of
the Gospel. In India, which is the fairest specimen of all,
and which has been open to all missionaries for exactly
thirty years, and where Germans (who put us to shame) and
Americans, and Scotch and English of all denominations,
have been at work,—years and years must elapse, at the
present rate, before the Gospel can be said to be *fairly preached*
among the nations. I speak here, not of conversion, but of
preaching. During the present missionary tour into the
villages, I have twice been challenged on this subject of the
spiritual neglect of the people on the part of the English.
In the last case it was by a respectable Brahmin, with whom
I had been having a long conversation concerning the Gospel
and his false religion : he was silenced and half convinced,
but added, " If all you say be true, and our way leads only
to hell, and yours to heaven, how is it that the English
Government has had possession of these parts about eighty

years, and yet never till now has sent to tell us of these
things ?" Consider what tens and thousands of thousands, in
this neighbourhood alone, have during this time "gone down
to the grave in sorrow." I do not know what you might be
able to effect : yet as one of our Lord's servants, who, being on
the spot, is able to feel intensely our national sin in the
spiritual neglect of India, I would exhort you to endeavour
to do something towards the increase of missionaries from
Oxford. As the Church of England is the chief and the
established body of Christians in England, she is specially
bound to undertake those spiritual duties which fall to the
nation : and as our universities are the acknowledged and
most exclusive nurseries for the clergy of our Church, it is of
course from them that missionaries are to be sought, and not
from other quarters. Under these circumstances, is the
subject of missions at all alien to the studies of those, who
in our colleges are preparing for the ministry of our Church ?
If not so, then, neither is it out of place, as it appears to me,
for those who direct their studies to bring this great subject
in its various bearings, historical and otherwise, systematically
before the students. I scarcely dare suggest the method ;
yet if the warden would take the subject into his consideration, I think he might find some way, whether by weekly
lectures or terminal essays, or as his experience might direct,
in which either personally or through the tutors of his
college, the whole subject of missions might take its rightful
position in the education of young men. Again, the Professor of Ecclesiastical History will surely make a curious
anomaly of his whole lectures, if he does not in turn direct a
course of them to the subject of missions. A man would be
considered little better than a pedant who should be familiar
with all ancient history, yet have never heard more than a
vague rumour of Napoleon, nor be acquainted with the
existence of a Reform Bill, a Corn Law, or a famine in
Ireland : and that ecclesiastical history may be classed as

much of the same character, which is content to dwell on
the growth of the Church of Christ 1500 years ago, on the
quarrels and heresies within it, and the separation of its
members, but shall be altogether silent concerning the spread
of the same Church during our own and our father's life-time,
and the intensely interesting prospect of its further advance.
What an admirable subject for one of Dr. Hampden's course
of lectures, or for the lectures of the Professor of Pastoral
Theology; for he can scarcely omit (if I do not mistake his
sphere) the subject of introducing the whole question of
missions to a parish.   Or again, how often might the pulpit
of St. Mary's be made the source of most interesting and
profitable missionary sermons.   It seems hard, both for the
members of the university and for the cause of missions, that
it should have to hide itself in little informal meetings
in private rooms, instead of being perpetually presented
by those who rule or direct the studies of the university to
the attention of all members of it, as the *one* great work of
the Church of God, of which they desire to be ministers.
For as in an individual case every Christian man has greatly
to labour in the mortification of sin and in the growth of his
own spiritual-mindedness, yet still his *great work* for God in
the world is the doing good to others : so in regard to the
Church of God, her work within herself, her pastoral and
episcopal and collegiate functions, of vast importance as they
are, must be reckoned to be second to those which she has
to perform to others,—that is, to heathen nations.   Can it
be that the heavy judgments which have come upon our
nation at large, and on Oxford in particular, in having been
these last sixteen years the mother and nest of a very grievous
and noisome heresy, are to be traced as punishments for the
especial neglect of the missionary duty, which lies on both
nation and university particularly ? Cambridge is not so guilty
as Oxford : from the former there are at least five missionaries
now in South India,—from the latter, I am the only one.

I must ask your forbearance in thus occupying so large a portion of my letter with subjects which are probably not personally very interesting to you, but I have supposed that you possess an influence in high quarters, which no one else to whom I am able to write, possesses. May I ask of you to stir up your own prayers and those of your friends, to entreat God to have mercy on the heathen. 1st. That He would send a missionary, self-devoting spirit upon our universities, and raise up missionaries both in England and in heathen lands. 2ndly. That missionaries may be filled with the Spirit of God, may be faithful, laborious, patient, and humble. Satan attacks us very fiercely, knowing that if he can undo us and bring us down into a low worldly frame, he has most effectually put an obstacle in the way of Christ's work. 3rdly. That the young Christian churches and converts may be built up and strengthened, to know Christ spiritually, and to walk purely and holily. 4thly. That the Holy Spirit may be poured out abundantly upon the thirsty heathen lands, and thousands on thousands be brought willing captives to Christ's footstool. Again, let me entreat of you, by the love you bear to our dear Lord Christ, and by all the compassion you feel for the myriads of poor hell-travelling ignorant heathen, whose quick-coming judgment and torments we dare not dwell on, even in thought, that you would endeavour, by whatever means God puts in your power, to stir up men to be missionaries. The field is almost boundless, the work, with all its privations, is a joyous one ; and the bright crown of glory awaiting us in common with all who love Christ's appearing, is enough to make us sing and be glad, in the midst of all outward sorrows and discouragements.

Will you be so kind as to remember me with all respect, and with the strongest feeling of Christian regard to the warden. May he be abundantly blessed in his high position. Also to the subwarden. I often think, with great

pleasure, and with much thankfulness both to them and to
the fellows, of the kindness with which I was received in
Wadham last year, and the opportunity they gave me of
speaking of missions in the Hall. I hope Mr. Tucker may
be permitted to have a similar opportunity if he should visit
Oxford this autumn. And now again begging you to
forgive me for troubling you with this long letter,

Very truly and sincerely yours in Christ,
H. W. Fox.

To the Rev. J. Tucker (late of Madras), Church
Missionary Society, London.

Ramachandra Apparaupettah Bungalow : Sept. 2, 1847.

My dear Friend,

You see by the above line that I am in a φιλτατῷ βυγγαλῷ,
the very name will remind you of dear India, which I know
is as dear to you (or more so) as it is to me, in spite of its
hot sun and dry dull plains. I am out now on another
tour ; but as we are in the middle of the monsoon, I cannot
bring my tent, and consequently keep myself to the high
roads, and the bungalows on them. We have only two
high roads, or I may say roads of any kind in the district,
running at right angles to each other, viz., that from Bunder,
towards Secunderabad, 100 miles of which are in our
Zillah, and the Calcutta road, of which about the same
length runs through the Collectorate. I am now on the
latter, one stage short of Ellore, from which I returned
yesterday, after staying there four days with Major ——
and Captain ——, two Christian officers in the 47th Native
Infantry. Sharkey started with me from Bunder nearly a
month ago, and we travelled together for a fortnight as far
as Condapilly and back to Beizwarah : when, as he was not
very well, he returned to Bunder. We visited a great

many villages together, and in most of them found the
Gospel a new subject, and the name of Christ quite unknown :
printed characters have never been seen by the majority of
the village readers, though the villages we have visited have
all been within two or three miles of the high road. No
less than four times has the question been put to me, twice
by Sudras, and twice by Brahmins : "If all you say is
true, how is it that during these eighty years that the
Company have ruled this country, they have never till
now, sent to tell us of these things? Since then, what
millions have perished in ignorance." This, coupled with
the fact, that until undeceived, the people, both in Bunder
and in the villages, supposed us to be the Company's
missionaries, most practically refutes the foolish cry, that
if the Government were to attempt to preach the Gospel,
the people would rise in arms against us. The Hindus
have the perception, as we have, of the simple principle, that
if a man believes a thing to be true, he is right in making it
known to those who are ignorant of it. Sharkey's power
of speaking greatly astonishes the people, and no one is
able to answer him ; for by adroitly expressing his argument in clear forcible language, he places the truth in fair
contrast with the gross falsehood of Hinduism, and they
are compelled to acknowledge the truth of what he says.
However, I am thankful also to say that he preaches
Christ, and is anxiously desirous of making Him known.
He will have told you of Mrs. Sharkey's little girl's school ;
it has increased in numbers since we came out, and will
increase yet more. We have sent David (who was baptised
last August) down to Madras for a wife out of Mrs.
Peter's school, so that I hope we shall soon have a really
native Christian sister in our congregation, which I cannot
say we have had hitherto. Jacob has gone to Vizagapatam
to fetch his two little daughters, Maria and Anna, and his
heathen wife, if she will come. About five weeks ago we

baptised Sitapati, a young Sudra, who joined us at the end
of May. He was quite unconverted and unknown to us
before he came to seek for baptism ; nevertheless, his
coming being known through the town, in consequence of
his having to witness a good confession in the public
Cutchery, was the cause of a good many scholars leaving the
English school : their places were filled up immediately by
crowds of applicants, and the school is now larger (about
sixty), and in better order than formerly. I and Sharkey go
on in the town, quietly preaching and discussing in the
streets ; of late I have decided to go more among the Pariahs
and Chuklus than I used to do, both because it is to the poor
that the Gospel is peculiarly to be preached, and also they
are less bound by prejudice and priestcraft than the upper
classes. I have been spending a very interesting afternoon
to-day. In the early morning when I was talking in the
village here, I had for one of my hearers an old man of
respectable appearance, who took an interest in what I said,
and asked for a book ; he turned out to be the landholder
of a neighbouring village, and begged that I would pay him
a visit at his own house. I went, therefore, about four
o'clock to his village, which is a very small one about a
mile distant, and consisting of Sudras, most of whom are
farmers of his land. He spread a little cotton carpet (you
know the striped blue and white tent carpets) before his
door, and when I had squatted down on it, he sat down
beside me, and about a dozen of the Sudras of the village
came around us ; the conversation soon turned to religion,
and I had a good opportunity of telling them of Christ's
history and His redemption of man, to which they listened
with much interest, and consented to it all. After half-an-
hour thus spent, the old man sent for the tract I had given
him in the morning, and asked me to read it to them. It
was a very clever and pointed tract, on the follies and wickedness of caste, and they all listened with delight, and often

repeated expressions of admiration at the exposé, and particularly at the hits against the Brahmins. In the middle a Brahmin came past, one of the learned class, so they stopped him to ask him some questions ; and I had half-an-hour's discussion with him, exposing the wickedness of their gods, to which he could make no answer. All the other hearers chimed in with what I said. After he was gone, and I had read enough of the tract, I opened St. Luke's Gospel, and read the parable of the prodigal son : they were delighted with the story, but not so much so with the explanation of it. It grew quite late before I had done, when I left them with a warning of the responsibility they had now incurred by having heard of Christ. In many places we find a strong dislike of the Brahmins among the Sudras, arising, I think, from all the power of the country being in the hands of the former, who occupy almost every magisterial and revenue post, and from the consequent tyranny they exercise. I am continually forced to feel that our present work is that of preparation : if there is to be any extensive conversion of the people in this neighbourhood, it will be in the days of our successors, but whether those days will ever come or not I cannot tell ; at all events the Gospel has been preached among the Telugu nation, and that is enough to satisfy God's prophecy. * * *

Your affectionate Friend,
HENRY W. FOX.

To THE REV. T. G. RAGLAND, MADRAS.
Masulipatam : Sept. 7, 1847.
MY DEAR FRIEND,

I returned into Bunder to-day, after a month and a day's absence. Sharkey was my companion for the first fortnight : his society I greatly enjoyed. I rejoiced to see the power which he has over the natives through his admirable

Telugu, and to find him desirous and striving to preach
Christ crucified. I am more practically convinced than ever
that the preaching the wonderful, endless, boundless love
of our dear Saviour, is the doctrine both for the sceptic and
the low worldling; but how hard it is to do so, when the
heart that should speak is itself cold, and when the tongue
itself is still cramped and confined to commonplaces as
mine is. I trust the Lord will gradually loosen my tongue
to speak His Gospel freely : and as St. Paul sought of the
Ephesians to pray for him, that "utterance might be given
to him to open his mouth *boldly*," so I would ask of you,
dear friend, and of all who will pray for a poor weak
brother, to entreat the Lord for me, that I also may have
the same utterance given me to speak clearly, and distinctly, and fully, the Gospel of Christ. My trial and difficulty is not that of fear or danger, as St. Paul's was, but
first, of sluggishness in going to work, and then inability,
dulness, and a tied tongue when in my work. Still I thank
God that, though imperfectly, He has permitted me this
month past to preach His dear Son in many villages
where He was not before known : if it be His will to spare
and to prosper us, I trust that we may be able to preach
Him in most of the large villages through the district.
After returning to Beizwarah, I struck off along the great
Calcutta road, which turns north as far as Ellore, forty miles.
This is the only other town in all our large collectorate
(which is nearly a hundred miles each way), and contains, I
should suppose, about 20,000 or 30,000 inhabitants. In
due time I hope it will be a missionary seat. I have
returned almost all the way by the same road as I went,
speaking a second time in the villages I visited before.
Almost everywhere the people listen willingly : the novelty
and the strangeness of a *dora* coming into their village
probably accounts for this. We have been a good deal
among the Pariahs, who are a very poor, oppressed people,

yet seem not to have that superstition or those religious lies
and priestcraft to restrain them from a profession of the
Gospel which the upper classes have ; for many of them say
they will turn Christians, though their words are spoken only
half seriously. But the other people do not even say so
much. The whole class of Sudras and Komatis (Banyans)
listen much more willingly than the Brahmins. From what
this journey has shown me, I am inclined to suppose that
the population is much the thickest within thirty miles of the
coast. I do not know any reason to account for this, except
that this year at least much more rain falls near the sea than
at a distance from it. But the change is very marked, from
the numerous and clustered villages, and the generally cultivated state of the country within that distance, and the
villages few and far between, and the country half over-
grown with bushes and low jungle beyond that distance.
Still my experience is very limited. I purpose, if it please
God, to keep moving about to short distances from home till
the middle of November, by which time our rain will
have cleared up, and I hope to go out in tents, with
Darling as my companion, and stretch right across the
district to the north as far as Rajahmundry. We have heard
nothing more of my butler's son, except that he is at Rajahmundry, and whether that information is true or not, I do
not know. I have great confidence that he is a child of God,
and that therefore he will be kept safe, though for a while
removed from all means of grace. There were in him the
strongest marks of a tender conscience, of a sense of sin, and
love to Jesus, arising from our Lord's great sacrifice for him.
The Brahmin boy has for months past quite gone back. I
do not doubt that his coming forward arose from some stings
of conscience and desire to be saved : whether we were right
in delaying to baptise him, I do not know. Unless the Lord
works with a strong hand in him, I see no hope for him :
in him there never appeared the marks of a humbled heart.

The young Sudra, Sitapati, who broke caste, and was afterwards brought before the collector, was baptised by the name
of Andrew about six weeks ago. There is everything to
make us hope well of him. *   *   *

Affectionately yours,

HENRY W. FOX.

CHAPTER IX.

Towards the close of the year 1847 my brother's health again failed, not as before, from the nervous irritation produced by the heat upon his system, but from repeated attacks of dysentery, which so weakened him as to render a voyage to sea essential for his restoration. After a short voyage along the coast, he was obliged to resort to Madras for medical aid, and it was there that, after mature deliberation, the professional men in that place declared that his constitution was not suited for India, and that he must proceed home immediately, for ever renouncing the hope of being able to return.

This decision was too plainly in accordance with his own experience to allow of its being disputed, and it was with a heavy heart that he bade adieu to India's shores: after his return home he frequently expressed his lively sorrow on this account, and said he found it more difficult to submit to the will of God in this trial, than in any other he had ever experienced. He returned home by the overland route, and arrived in

England in the month of March, just in time to have
the painful satisfaction of closing his beloved father's
eyes, and ministering to him in his last hours. He
reached Durham on the 15th of April; and on the
18th his father died.

Masulipatam : Oct. 2, 1847.

MY DEAR FATHER AND MOTHER,

I very much wished to write to you yesterday, but was
quite unable to do so : not as usual, because I was too busy,
for I have had time enough on my hands for some days
past ; but I was not strong enough, as I am only recovering from a sharp, though not severe, attack of illness,
which has laid me up for a fortnight. I trust that now,
by God's continued mercy, I shall go on improving, and
be about my work in another week. My ailment was a
slight dysentery, arising from and accompanied by bilious-
ness. The depressing and weakening nature of the disease
itself, added to the remedies used, brought me low enough.
* * * I am thankful, however, that the attack was
checked at once, and I do not suppose I shall be any the
worse for it when it is over. Among the other mercies
I received was that of the unremitting and kind attention
of the doctor of the station, who visited me every morning
and night. My servants also were very kind, and my
butler waited on me with the attention which one might
expect from an old attached servant, rather than what I
should look for from a man not ten months in my service :
so that my illness has been full of marks of my Father's
tenderness, just as the stars shine brightest in the darkest
night. In this, the sharpest attack of illness I remember
to have had, as well as in other slighter illnesses, I have
found my mind and spirit greatly fail me : for two or three
days when suffering from weakness, I was unable to collect

my thoughts to pray, or my desires to have any longing after
God. I was, however, kept resting on Him peacefully, without doubts or anxieties, or those temptations which Satan
likes to bring against an enfeebled child of God. Though
I knew I was in no danger, yet my mind often ran on my
death, as this was just such a shadowy valley as leads to it,
and I desired rather to go to the end of it than to turn back.
I could desire to have more lively sights of Christ during
illness; I know not whether the absence of such does not
mark a too dull looking at Him while in health, or it may be
greatly the physical depression of the soul which hides Him
from me. I can see, however, that my various little illnesses
are all given me by way of training and preparing me for
the last struggle : from my late experience of the *pain of
weakness* I could almost shrink from the dark valley, but
that were to mistrust my Saviour : David says, *I will fear no
evil.* And He can, if it is good for me and for His glory,
make the valley shorter even than the few days of weakness
I this time suffered, as indeed is common in India ; or what
is best, He can make His presence to shine in the darkest
part of the valley, and in " His presence is fulness of joy,"
whether in sickness or in health, on earth or in heaven. I
am thankful now to be raised up again, to be allowed to go
on in my poor way with the glorious work which He permits
me to be engaged in. Yesterday, thirty years ago, I was
born to you : the round number of thirty seems to make
this birth-day one of the stages of life, and I feel all the
older for having passed out of my twenties, though I suppose
to you the age seems a little one after all. What an unspeakable mercy it is to be quite freed from all those uneasi-
nesses of growing older, and so nearer the end of life, with
which the men of the world are troubled at every memorial
of the passing away of their years ? The poor heathen are
terribly afraid of death : to mention the subject to them is
almost a piece of bad manners, and to speak, however inci-

dentally, of any man's death with whom we may be conversing is an evil omen, and causes a shudder of pain in the
poor listener.   What a bondage is this to be freed from !
They are astonished to hear me speak of death as a thing
greatly to be longed for.   I knew that you would all be
thinking of me yesterday, and especially I knew my dear
children would pray for me.

October 6.—I have had a letter from each of you since I
wrote last : very many thanks for them.   I am very thankful to hear by the last, that you are both so well again after
having been both tried by illness : it is like the bright, clear
shining after rain ; nevertheless, we must look for the return
of the rain again and again as long as we are in this stormy,
sinful world.   Your account of Seaton meeting interested
me much.   I have heard very little of the meetings of the
Church Missionary Society this year ; I should like to have
heard more, as I feel strongly interested in the places I
visited as "deputation" last year.   I wrote a long letter to
Mr. Dixon, to be in time for the September meeting at
Shields, which I think was the meeting I liked best of all
I was at.   *   *   *

Your very affectionate Son,

HENRY W. FOX.

MY DEAR MR. T——,

I have put off writing till to-day, hoping that I might
advance enough in health to be able to officiate at your
marriage : but I am now obliged to give up all hopes of it.
I am thankful to say I am better, but my progress is so slow
that it may be a week or more before I shall be able to leave
the house.   It is a great disappointment to me, I assure
you, and I am sorry to disappoint you ; but we must rest
content with what is ordered for us by One wiser and
greater than we are.   I have asked Mr. Noble to take my

place, to which he has kindly consented. * * * May I request of you, and also extend the same request to Miss J——, that you would very carefully read over the marriage service. The time of marriage is usually and naturally one of great excitement and gaiety, and the danger is great of the really solemn character of the act being forgotten at the moment. I am sure also it will be a benefit to each of you to consider calmly and in private, the importance and the religious character of the union you are about to enter on, and to which your attention will be drawn by the language and the prayers of our beautiful marriage-service. For it is not a light matter, nor is it a tie merely for furthering your present happiness, which you are about to form ; but it will especially affect your interests for eternity. Should either husband or wife be forward in pressing on into Christ's kingdom, how great is the assistance heavenward received by the other ; or should one be opposed to a close and fervent serving of God, how deadening is the effect on the desires and efforts of the other. Permit me to advise you with all earnestness to cement your union by commencing from *the first* to read the Bible, and to join in prayer together. I can tell you that when it shall please God to remove one of you, such hours will form the brightest spots in the recollection of the survivor. Forgive me for giving you a sermon on your wedding ; that you may both be, not only rendered the happier by your union, but also be abundantly blessed in it by Him who is the giver of all good gifts, and by our Lord Jesus Christ, who purchased gifts for men by His death and resurrection, is the earnest desire and prayer of

Your sincere Friend,

HENRY W. FOX.

To the Rev. H. V. Elliott, Brighton.

At Sea : Nov. 13, 1847.

My very dear Friend,

My last letter to you was from my tent ; this is from the cabin of a small coasting-vessel. I was then endeavouring to do God's work by preaching Him to the villagers ; I trust I am now also about His work by suffering His will, though it is much less agreeable to the flesh, and is not in accordance with my hopes. But what are my hopes or my will, when different from His, but rebellious motions of the heart ? After a month in the villages in August and September, I was attacked, soon after my return, by a lingering, though not acute disease ; and after being confined to my arm-chair for nearly two months, and being much reduced, the doctor who attended on me recommended change of air and a sea-voyage, as the best cure ; and this accounts for my writing to you, rolling about in the Bay of Bengal. I hope, but I dare not plan, lest I fight against God's will—to be able to return to my work in about six weeks, and take advantage of the two or three remaining months of cold weather. A day or two before I fell ill, I commenced the enclosed letter to our dear young sisters, the pupils at St. Mary's Hall, who I thought would be interested at hearing direct from a missionary quarter. I was interrupted in the middle, and have only just now been able to finish it. I value very greatly the interest they take in missions, and in our mission particularly, for I trust that there are many true daughters of Christ among them, and that they from time to time bring us, and the heathen to whom we preach, before the throne of grace. I am learning continually to desire more and more the prayers of God's people on our behalf ; we are so feeble, such faint-hearted Christians, with so little zeal for God, or love for souls, that I fear we greatly keep back the gifts of God to the poor heathen. But He will hear the united prayers of our

brethren, with ours,—all offered up as incense by our dear
Lord Christ, for our growth and renovation, and for an
outburst of life among the dead heathen ; I pray you to stir
up those whom you can influence to this exercise. I fear
Christians at home think too highly of missionaries, and
forget to pray for them. We greatly need grace. Satan
attacks us with most violence, as foremost in the van ; and
his attacks are not open or violent, but are the secret
temptations to deadness of heart, neglect of privileges,
worldly views, self-confidence, etc. He knows too well,
that if he can throw back the work of grace in us, he has
taken the most effectual means of checking the spread of
the Gospel by our means. I must, however, keep you
acquainted, though my letter must be short, with the notice
of our mission. We are now six workmen in all : first,
Mr. Noble, who has continued without a pause from the
beginning. His whole time and work are occupied with
his English school of sixty boys and young men, and with
the charge of the little Christian congregation of a dozen
souls. His missionary opportunities, though not wide-
spread, are great ; his influence with his scholars is powerful, and daily repeated, and, through them, a knowledge of,
and interest about, the subject of Christianity, is certainly
spreading through the town, among the upper ranks. He
has under him Mr. Taylor and Mr. Coombes. I managed
to get to the school the day before I sailed, to hear them
sing. It was painfully interesting to hear the poor heathen
lads, whose minds are awakening to divine truth, but who
have not yet accepted it, singing, "Oh, that will be joyful,
joyful," etc., and " *We* all shall meet at Jesu's feet, and meet
to part no more." And, again, that magnificent missionary
hymn, " Thou whose Almighty word," to the tune of " God
save the Queen." The school-room is in a very nice working
state : sometimes there are symptoms of life among some of
the scholars, but they melt away again. At present all is

P

still, and apparently dead; but it may be only the winter,
and so the immediate forerunner of a joyful burst of spring.
God grant such a glad season to us.   After Mr. Noble and
his assistant masters, come the Rev. J. Sharkey and myself.

He and I give all our time to conversing with, and preaching to the heathen, through the medium of their own language, both in the streets of the town and the villages all
around.   Our preaching in the town has already produced
so far a sensation, as to make people inquire, " What can
these people be taking all this trouble for ? "   And, in those
who see farthest, some uneasiness is produced in seeing us
persevering day after day, and carrying about and giving
publicly to high and low the knowledge of our religion.
They have already heard of the effects of this in other places
so as to anticipate an effect among their own neighbours,
which they do not like.   We also give some time daily to
the task of preparing tracts and a version of the Bible.
It is a glorious and joyful work : I would that our young
men in England knew it to be so.   However, in order to
know it, they need not inquire of us in India ; they need
only inquire of the four evangelists and the apostolic
writers, to see that missionary work is a joyful and blessed
work to him who engages in it.   Would that they believed,
not our report, but the report of the inspired writers on this
subject.   Next comes Mrs. Sharkey, who is busily engaged
with a girls' school of children of the lowest caste.   Two of
her pupils are Christians ; and in a few months more she
expects to have two more—daughters of one of the members
of our flock—who are now at a distance ; the rest, seven
in number, are heathens, except one Mohammedan.   The
school is only in its infancy, but it may be (and who shall
stay God's mercy ?) the beginning of great things.   By it
the Gospel is preached to the *poor* heathen girls.   Our
missionary circle closes with Mr. Darling, who only joined
us about four months ago as catechist.   He lives with me,

and is attached to my department of the mission, but is still
engaged in learning Telugu ; in which he makes the quicker
progress, from his familiarity with the kindred language of
Tamul. Here then you see the instrumentality which God is
pleased to employ against the kingdom of Satan in this
district : He is fully able to triumph over the strong one,
through means of it, feeble as it is; yet, as the sin of our
Church is great in doing so little toward the work (only
sending two men, and funds for the payment of four), He
may in judgment withhold the fulness of the outpouring of
His Spirit, till His people are roused to do more of their
duty. Nevertheless, the Telugu nation shall glorify God.
The redeemed who walk in white robes, and the elders who
sit on twenty-four thrones, are from amongst *all* nations and
tribes ; and there are Telugu chosen ones to be of their
number. There will be no more, but there will not be one
less than that number, whom God has elected, prepared, and
is calling, from among the inhabitants of these plains. With
thoughts like these we encourage ourselves.

Mr. Noble and all the rest of our party are blessed with
good health; so was I till the middle of September, when
God saw good to make His blessings run in another channel ;
for already I can say again, " It is good for me that I have
been afflicted." Remember me most affectionately to all
your family, of whom I frequently think, and please to
convey the enclosed letter to the pupils of St. Mary's
Hall, with very Christian regards to them.

Most affectionately yours,

HENRY W. FOX.

Madras: Jan. 13, 1848.

MY DEAREST SISTER,

I am writing to you from the same house in which I
wrote my first letter in India. I have been here nearly a

fortnight, after a three weeks' voyage from Vizagapatam, which, though unusually protracted, did me some good. As soon as I got here, I sought the advice of Dr. Sanderson. He always has inspired me with confidence in him, from the very careful and minute examination of a case which he makes at first, and his clear insight into the real ailment. After examining me, and watching me for a week, he spoke decidedly to me a few days ago, referring to his former experience of my constitution. He considers my liver organically affected, though slightly, and gives no hope of my recovering from this state on shore : thinks I may more or less completely recover from it by a voyage to sea for a few months, but believes I shall never be able to continue in India, and that my return to Masulipatam will be attended with great probability of a return of disease, and consequent risk of life. He says my constitution is unfit for the tropics, wanting *nervous energy,* so that when a complaint lays hold on me, I sink under it at once. This I know to be true by experience ; and indeed much of what he has said to me is confirmed by what I have heard from doctors about my health in times past, though unconnectedly and not so decidedly. I tell you all the worst, because I know you would wish me to reserve nothing from you, and at present there is no risk, so far as man can see, of life. I have pretty well decided to take a sea-voyage, perhaps to the Straits of Malacca, perhaps to the Cape of Good Hope, for a few months : not that Dr. S. thinks I shall return set up again for work, though he anticipates much good from such a step ; but I do it for my own satisfaction and that of others, that I may not forsake my missionary work too lightly : my own thoughts at present are that I ought to make every endeavour to stay by my work as long as I possibly can, even at some risk. I have asked the advice of —— and ——, whose judgment I value highly ; the former thinks I ought not to remain in India, to run the risk predicted by the doctor ; the latter advises a good sea-voyage, and after that, another experiment at Masulipatam, taking every and even peculiar precaution to avoid exposure. I shall be better able to decide when the time for decision comes, for God does not always make our distant plans clear to us ; only if we have sought His guidance, He will make the next step to be taken clear to us. I wish you therefore, dear sister, to help me in this matter both with your advice and your prayers. In case I return from a sea-voyage, recovered from my present state of health, and Dr. S. continues to affirm the same risk to attach to my attempting to renew my work at Bunder, ought I to run the risk or not? I wish to have an impartial judgment, as little influenced as you can by your own feelings of affection, and with such reasons as appear to you on the subject. Secondly, pray for me, that I may with a single purpose seek God's glory in my decision, that I may have no wishes or will of my own in the matter, and that He will guide me aright. Your letter directed to Madras, in reply to this, will probably arrive before I have to decide.

Your very affectionate Brother,

HENRY W. FOX.

TO THE REV. R. T. NOBLE, MASULIPATAM.

Madras : Jan. 18, 1848.

MY DEAR ROBERT,

This day last year I was on the point of setting out from Guntoor to rejoin you at Bunder, and to re-enter on my work in full health and spirits : to-day, what a change ! Broken down and enfeebled, and with prospects far from raising my spirits, I am beginning to write to you in preparation for retiring from my work : I can only say, God's will be done. He has shown me endless mercies in India : His goodness in bringing me and employing me here for

a little while has been great, and now if it is His will to
send me away to a less honourable position in His vineyard,
who am I that I should gainsay it? Only I would desire to
be humbled at His rejection of me: and I do pray, and
will continue to pray and to labour that He may send
out to you others more and more fitted for His work than
I am.

Your affectionate Brother in Christ,

HENRY W. FOX.

Madras: Jan. 22, 1848.

MY DEAREST ISABELLA,

I write to you by Marseilles with the view of preventing
you from writing by return of mail in reply to my last
letter; for I have come to the decision, earlier than I anticipated, of at once leaving India and proceeding to England.
On consideration, I saw, as I might have seen from the first,
that considering Dr. S. said his view of my case would
remain unaltered, however much I might be benefited by
a voyage to the Cape, England, or elsewhere, it was my
business, previous to starting on such a voyage, to make up
my mind regarding my future course; or rather that the
making such an experimental voyage and returning to India
was in itself a decision in opposition to the doctor's opinion.
I waited, however, for a few days till Dr. Sanderson called
in another and senior doctor, and they unitedly condemned
my residence in the country. Upon this I came to the conclusion above-mentioned, considering it to be my duty not to
run the risk predicted by competent medical judges, while an
important, though inferior, sphere of work lay open before
me in England. I trust I have judged according to God's
will. I have sought His guidance, and prayed that I might
be unbiassed, and I have used the means of asking a few
friends most competent to give advice. The giving up my
Indian work is very painful, as you will well know: but my

weak state of body, and callous enfeebled feelings, do not let me feel at present so much pain as I might. Indeed, I seem able to feel nothing, neither love nor hatred, joy nor sorrow, and I believe this is chiefly physical. I am not, however, worse, though feeling poorly. In all probability I shall embark in the steamer on the 13th of February, and proceeding from Alexandria by the Trieste and German line, which is now open, reach London about the end of March. I suppose I shall be just in time for the Clifton Church Missionary Society meetings : I hope to be stronger by that time, if it pleases God to bless the cool climate to my recovery.

Your ever affectionate Brother,
HENRY W. FOX.

TO THE REV. R. T. NOBLE, MASULIPATAM.

Steamer "Ripon," near Gibraltar : March 23, 1848.

MY DEAR ROBERT,

I wrote to Sharkey by the returning " Precursor," and we have not since then had an opportunity of writing to India. * * * I am just now emerging from the dream or cloud in which I have been bodily and mentally these last six months : for, during the last four or five days, I have begun for the first time to regain a little energy and vigour, as my bodily health began decidedly to improve. Until then the voyage has been to me, like the time on shore, full of discomfort, as distracting as pain, though not so hard to bear, and altogether prostrating every energy. The prostration of mind and heart has been as great as that of the body, and much more distressing. I have been quite unable to write, or to read any but the most trifling books ; the Bible has been generally a closed book to me, and my mind has wandered as I tried to read it. But now, thanks to God, I seem to be somewhat restored. * * * I had expected a much more speedy improvement: indeed, during the last few weeks, at Madras, I was looking forward with an intense longing to the day of starting, hoping that I should feel immediate benefit as soon as I embarked; but it seems as if my constitution had got too low to be resuscitated at once; and till I reached Egypt, I continued better and worse, but still very poorly. The change on landing at Suez was surprising: it had not been hot in the Red Sea, but nothing of chilliness had been felt, until we got into the little boat which took us from the ship, just at sunrise; and then the air was as sharp as on an English spring morning. The whole time we were in Egypt the wind blew from the north, and was very cold and keen, and consequently, we most of us caught colds, had red noses, and chapped lips. The change at first was very beneficial to me, but just before we left Alexandria (having been detained there four days) I caught an internal cold, which brought on my dysentery symptoms again, and reduced me very low. I am thankful to say, that the means employed stayed the disease in two or three days after I embarked again; and I have been daily regaining strength. I am now again able to pray, and to rejoice in God :—during my weakness I have been in a cloud, far from Him, neither humbled nor prayerful, but altogether listless. What poor creatures we are, and how vile are our bodies! and yet it has been a comfort and encouragement to me many times, that vile as my body is, and as I have felt it to be, yet Christ Jesus has redeemed it, and counts it precious. Certainly the truth of the resurrection of the body is a very precious one during sickness. In crossing the desert I suffered very severely: it still remains to me like a horrible dream, and I scarcely think I could muster courage to go through the trial again, under similar circumstances. It was curious, how differently the same thing affected a healthy body and a weak one. When I crossed in 1846, I reached Suez after twenty-four hours of jolting, quite fresh, having greatly enjoyed the amusement of the transit, but now I scarcely knew how to sit or lie ;—pained, and exhausted, and faint, I at one time felt desirous of being rather left alone in the desert, than of going forward ; but here, God who allowed the suffering, would not let it go too far, and I was able to feel confident, that as I trusted in Him, He would carry me through ; and He did so, so that I was not materially the worse for it, and had only to lie up the next day, during which we remained quietly at Cairo. Indeed, all through He has been showing to me His wonderful providences and mercies ; and when I think of the tranquil passage we have enjoyed, and the numerous comforts I have had, I see a Father's hand in it all.

Your affectionate Brother in Christ,
HENRY W. FOX.

To the REV. R. T. NOBLE, MASULIPATAM.

Durham : April 17, 1848.

MY DEAR BROTHER,

This first letter to you from me in England, opens again the wounds of separation : I daily feel more and more, instead of decreasingly, the sorrow of having left you all, and having been separated from the work of a missionary. It is no satisfaction to be told by friends that there is much want of the labours of Christ's ministers in England ; for this last reminds me how much greater is the want of such in India, and in all the rest of the heathen world, which want is increased by my return. I have, however, found something to rest on, in what has been suggested by two or three. " He who has brought you back from your own work in India will have provided some sphere in England, in which you may glorify Him." It is not my part to dictate how or where I shall do God's work, and it is my esistance to His will on this point that makes the sacrifice a hard one. * * *

Your affectionate Brother in Christ,

HENRY W. FOX.

Wadham College, Oxon : May 30, 1848.

MY DEAREST SISTER,

My heart is so disturbed and so full, that I long to write to you to relieve it. My return here is as painful, and more so, than it is pleasant. It is not that my time here was more happy than present times, for I could not so belie the grace of God which has been given me these eight years past ; but every scene and sound is recalling thoughts and feelings which have slumbered for long, and is reminding me that much has passed away which I never can have again in this life,—much elasticity, much joyousness, much brightness. This does not make me melancholy, for I have received things which are much better ; but it greatly disturbs me, and I cannot enjoy myself in beautiful Oxford in May : this perturbation will, I know, subside after a while. All these scenes carry me back beyond the happiest days which I have yet known, and so they cause painful feelings to arise : for they make me think of all that has passed since—my five years with dear Elizabeth, and my missionary life in India ; and till I go down to the grave myself, and till I am called away from all work on earth, these two recollections cannot but contain much that is bitter. My cessation from missionary work is still a fresh grief, and at times it is very hard to bear ; I knew it would be a trial, but I did not know how great an one, and sometimes I begin to think of going back again, but am checked by the strong assurance that I have, that I should return to India—but not to active work. How little do men know the real state of the case, when they think that the trial

consists of *going* to be a missionary; for with all its
palliations of returning to England, to home, friends, and
family, and children, it is the *coming* from being a missionary which is the real sorrow; and beautiful as are our green
fields and hedge-rows, they make me sigh to be back at dear
Bunder, even in the midst of this burning May. You will
see, as I do, that in these feelings there is very much of the
natural heart, and that they do not altogether spring from a
desire to advance Christ's kingdom: for if I had His
glory more truly at heart, I should more cheerfully submit
to His manifest will that I should no longer remain in
India. * * *

Your affectionate Brother,

HENRY W. FOX.

It was a great satisfaction to his friends, to find that
though my brother's constitution could not stand the
climate of India, it seemed to rally rapidly in his native
air; the voyage had done him much good, and as the
summer drew on, he seemed so much restored to his
usual state of health, that he began to consider in what
sphere of useful labour he should engage at home. At
one time he thought he would like to undertake the
charge of some populous parish in our crowded manu-
facturing districts, as having a population that in some
respects resembled the heathen.

During the summer, however, the Church Missionary
Society proposed to him the office of assistant secretary; this was so congenial to his feelings, and seemed
to hold out so promising a prospect of future usefulness,
in that cause which was nearest his heart, that after
mature consideration he gladly accepted the offer, and
at once entered on its duties. In addition to which, he

also assisted Mr. Tucker in his ministerial duties at Hampstead on Sundays.

To the Rev. Henry Venn.

Wadham College, Oxford : June 5, 1848.

My dear Mr. Venn,

I had intended to write to you on Saturday, on the very subject of your letter, which reached me yesterday. I have continued to consider the question very carefully since it was first brought before me, and I have daily sought the guidance of God in regard to it ; so that in coming to a decision upon it, so far as regards my side of the question, I feel much at rest, and I can trust that I have been directed aright. The decision to which I have come is to accept the post of assistant secretary, in case the committee see fit to propose it to me. As it has pleased God to remove me from direct missionary work, I view it to be my duty to employ myself, as much as I am able, and have opportunity, in advancing the cause of missions in England. I do deeply feel my inefficiency for so important a post as that which you lay before me, but in this point I rest upon your judgment and that of Mr. Tucker, who think that I may be of service to the great cause in it. If the committee should decide in my favour, I would ask of you and of the individual members of the committee, to intercede with God for me, that I may be rendered efficient for the work laid upon me, and especially that He will grant me a larger measure of His Spirit, that all I do may be done in a holy and spiritual tone. The high standard of holiness, which has always been aimed at by the Society (and which appears to me to form one of the prominent subjects for thanksgiving, this jubilee year), lays on me the greater responsibility, lest by my own lukewarmness I may do injury to it. I am glad that the sub-committee have placed the proposed arrangement on an entirely temporary footing : for I should desire that ample opportunity should exist for the committee to reject me, if they find cause to do so, from my inefficiency ; and for myself to resign my post, if I should see my course to lie in another direction.   *   *   *

Affectionately yours,

HENRY W. FOX.

TO THE SAME.

Wadham College, Oxford : June 5, 1848.

MY DEAR MR. VENN,

I have written to you a letter, in reply to yours of Saturday, which you may lay before the committee, in case you have occasion to do so, and I now write you a private letter. I shall be willing to work for the Society in any and every way in which it appears I can glorify God by advancing missions ; such, at least, is my present strong desire.   I feel, however, my own weakness, and though I am sure of the abundant aid of God, in working for Him, so long as I submissively and humbly seek His grace, yet I know not how long I shall do so, and whether I may not fall into a lukewarm state, and so fail of His help ; it is this thought which makes me desire the prayers of others to go along with mine, that I may, in my own soul, be kept near to God.

Affectionately yours,

HENRY W. FOX.

To H. STOKES, ESQ., GUNTOOR.

Church Missionary House, Salisbury Square :

July 7, 1848.

MY VERY DEAR FRIEND,

My thoughts have very often been at Guntoor, since my return to England ; and I was greatly rejoiced to see a good

account of yourself and your family in a late letter from you
to Mr. Tucker. With all the heat of India, and your hard,
anxious work as collector, I would envy your position if I
might ; for to be permitted to live in India appears to be a
great privilege, and to be removed from it and from missionary work, while it is a most righteous act of a loving
Father, is to me, I am sure, one of chastisement and warning.
With my returning health, my desires for, and love of India,
have returned : as long as I was suffering from disease, the
lowness of my spirits and an intense physical shrinking from
the very idea of an Indian sun, made my separation from
India a light matter ; but I have had many sorrowful seasons
since then. It was to me a very great comfort, to see in
your letter a good account of our dear brother Noble ; that
he is still permitted to go on without failing or fainting. I
have been very mercifully dealt with ; for my bodily health
is all but entirely restored, and my strength very much so ;
and though I may not preach to the Telugu villagers, I am
permitted in an indirect way to have a share in the great
work of missions, for I am associated as assistant secretary
with Mr. Venn and Mr. Tucker in the Church Missionary
House ; and, unworthy as I am of so great an honour, I feel
it a great happiness to be thus employed. I have but just
commenced my work, but I see great privileges in it : first,
I am led to become intimately acquainted with the details of
all the Society's missions in the four quarters of the world ;
then I am an agent in the Society commenced by Simeon,
John Venn, and other holy men of the last generation ; and
our committee-meetings are indeed those of Christian men.
Then I am brought into contact with many of the eminently
good men of London and its neighbourhood : and not least, I
am allowed the affectionate friendship and intercourse with
two such men as Mr. Venn and Mr. Tucker. When I
magnify my office, then I lower myself; for who am I, to be
thus blessed and set in so privileged a position ? Dear friend,

pray for us here at head-quarters, as well as for the missionaries in the field; it is not only wisdom and prudence that
we need, but holiness and a deep knowledge of God. The
Society which for fifty years has been kept in the truth, and
in a pure and earnest faith, is as holy (I had almost said) as
the ark of the Lord; and it seems well nigh a profanity to
touch it with such hands as mine. I know of no immediate
prospect of a missionary for Bunder; our universities are still
asleep. I visited Oxford for a fortnight, and though a little
advanced in missionary interest since I was there two years
ago, it is still barely above freezing point. We have numerous offers of men for the Church Missionary Institution, some
of whom are very promising : but the finance committee
are shy of allowing any fresh expenditure, while the general
funds are in so low a state. However, the accumulated subscriptions to the Telugu mission justify the appointment
of a missionary to Bunder, if we can find one, and I trust the
Lord will guide us in the search, and bring the right man to
us. * * *

Your affectionate, but unworthy, Brother in Christ,

HENRY W. FOX.

To THE REV. R. T. NOBLE, MASULIPATAM.

Hampstead : July 16, 1848.

MY BELOVED BROTHER,

I may well occupy a few minutes of the evening of this
day of rest, and of preaching the Gospel, in writing to you.
Never a day passes, without you and all our dear brothers
and sisters at Masulipatam being in my thoughts, and seldom
do I forget to pray for you; but on Sunday I remember you
most,—though by the time I am going to church, your afternoon is well advanced, yet I think of you, with that little
feeble flock around you; and never do I read the commencement of the Liturgy, but my heart is brim full with the

recollections of the Monday evenings, which just a year ago
we used to spend, in trying to prepare a version. Happy are
you to be allowed to go on with this work : not in wrath,
but in loving chastisement, and wise discipline for my sinning
soul, has God removed me from the glad work. The Lord's
Prayer raises up many recollections of the Sunday afternoon,
when I used to break it up for my poor servants ; and the
Ten Commandments carry me away into the streets and lanes
of Battayah, and Sarikilly, and Páta Ramanah pettahs. May
the Lord give you to see the fruits of your work : one soul
may be an inestimable treasure, and as Abraham to Isaac,
may make you the father of a great nation. I long and
yearn over the dear youths in the school, and I greatly desire
to hear that some of them have been strengthened by the
Spirit of God, to leave all for Christ. Venkatachillapati, and
the Venkatachellums, and Poorshotum, and Rangashai, how
do they go on? The sound of their songs on the morning
of November 9th still rings in my ears. And Mrs. Sharkey's
little girls, we must perhaps wait longer to see fruits in them ;
but, sooner or later, and exactly at the right moment, the
desert of Bunder shall blossom as the rose, and our dear Lord
shall be glorified in His new children. But I like to look
even further still, to that joyous day when He shall come to
take us home, free from sin, with nothing to make us weary
of loving Him—nothing to lead us to grieve Him. What a
prospect ! I long to be out of the power of sin : though it
does not any longer *rule* in me, it has yet a wonderful power
of warping me, and leading me to dishonour my Saviour. I
could say that, if I was always victorious, I should not care
for the length of the battle, but I grow weary of struggling,
and being buffeted, and often taken prisoner. What asto-
nishing long-suffering does God show towards us ; and what
infinite love that of Christ to us must be, which led Him to
die for us, though all the while He foreknew what poor
wretched Christians we should be. But we shall have an

eternity to praise and admire Him, and to recount to each, the tales of His goodness.   *   *   *

Your affectionate unworthy Brother,
HENRY W. FOX.

TO THE REV. T. G. RAGLAND, MADRAS.

August, 1848.

MY VERY DEAR FRIEND,

This is ——'s wedding-day, and the fact has reminded me that I must write a few lines to you, as he perhaps has not found time to write to you by this mail.   It is doubtless a joyful day for him, but yet it is more joyful to be married unto the Lamb, and our glad bridal-day will be when He comes to take us home.   I have come up to town from Clifton for a fortnight, preparatory to spending a fortnight at Oxford to see young men.   Since I wrote to you last, I have lost my dear father.   I was just able to see and speak with him the last day of sensibility; but he has only gone before, and my widowed mother and my brothers and sister and I shall soon follow him, to join the other dear ones laid up in Christ's treasury.   Yesterday there was a large committee at Salisbury Square, to make arrangements about the jubilee. A fund is proposed to be raised for the disabled missionaries' fund, for school and church-building, for education of missionaries' children, and for endowment of native congregations. It is to be a year of humiliation for *our* neglect, and of praise for God's wonderful works.   November 1, All Saints' Day, is the day chosen for all missionary friends of our Church, both in Great Britain and abroad, to unite in worshipping and glorifying God.   Come what will, that is a sure day for us : if we are here, we will join with the living saints ; if we have crossed the flood, it will be only one day out of our ceaseless worship.   *   *   *

Your very affectionate brother in Christ,
HENRY W. FOX.

Q

It was but a few months, in the providence of God, that he was permitted to prosecute his new duties ; but he was so fully absorbed in them, and threw so much of his heart into the work, as at least to give all that he had to bestow, in carrying on at home the plans of the Church Missionary Society.

The testimony of Mr. Venn on this point is as follows : " He entered upon the duties of his office in July ; and with so much efficiency, and in such a spirit, that his seniors in the office rejoiced in the hope that he was destined to carry forward the work with youthful energy, and to continue his beneficial aid after they should cease from their labours."

The period at which he entered upon his duties, as secretary to the Church Missionary Society, was a crisis of peculiar interest in the history of modern missions—it was the jubilee year, and preparations were making to celebrate that interesting event, the fiftieth anniversary of the Church Missionary Society, on the 1st of November.

It was with feelings of deep and lively interest that my brother entered into all the plans of the Society, in reference to this great event, and he looked forward with hope and joy to its commemoration, little supposing that when the 1st of November arrived he should be celebrating a more glorious jubilee in the courts above.

The following lines were written by him as a Jubilee Hymn, and they have since been set to music by the Rev. Peter Maurice, D.D., of New College, Oxford.

I.

I hear ten thousand voices singing
    Their praises to the Lord on high :
Far distant hills and shores are ringing
    With anthems of their nation's joy.
"Praise ye the Lord ! for He has given,
    To lands in darkness hid, His light ;
As morning rays light up the heaven,
    His Word has chased away our night!"

II.

On China's shores I hear His praises
    From lips which once kissed idol-stones :
Soon as His banner He upraises,
    The Spirit moves the breathless bones—
"Speed, speed His Word o'er land and ocean,
    The Lord in triumph has gone forth :
The nations heave with strange emotion,
    From east to west, from south to north."

III.

The song has sounded o'er the waters,
    And India's plains re-echo joy :
Beneath the moon sit India's daughters,
    Soft singing, as the wheel they ply—
"Thanks to Thee, Lord ! for hopes of glory,
    For peace on earth to us revealed :
Our cherished idols fell before Thee,
    Thy Spirit has our pardon sealed."

IV.

On Afric's sunny shore glad voices
  Wake up the morn of jubilee :
The Negro, once a slave, rejoices :
  Who's freed by Christ is doubly free—
" Sing, brothers, sing ! yet many a nation
  Shall hear the voice of God, and live :
E'en we are heralds of salvation :
  The Word He gave we'll freely give."

v.

The sun on Essequibo's river
  Shines bright midst pendant woods and flowers ;
And He who came man to deliver
  Is worshipped in those leafy bowers—
" O Lord ! once we, by Satan captured,
  Were slaves of sin and misery ;
But now, by Thy sweet love enraptured,
  We sing our song of jubilee."

VI.

Fair are New Zealand's wooded mountains,
  Deep glens, blue lakes, and dizzy steeps ;
But sweeter than the murmuring fountains
  Rises the song from holy lips—
" By blood did Jesus come to save us,
  So deeply stained with brother's blood :
Our hearts we'll give to Him who gave us
  Deliv'rance from the fiery flood."

VII.

O'er prairies wild the song is spreading,
  Where once the war-cry sounded loud ;
But now the evening sun is shedding
  His rays upon a praying crowd—
" Lord of all worlds, Eternal Spirit !
  Thy light upon our darkness shed
For Thy dear love, for Jesu's merit,
  From joyful hearts be worship paid."

VIII.

Hark ! hark ! a louder sound is booming
  O'er heaven and earth, o'er land and sea :
The angel's trump proclaims *His* coming,
  Our day of endless jubilee—
" Hail to Thee, Lord ! Thy people praise Thee :
  In every land Thy name we sing :
On heaven's eternal throne upraise Thee,
  Take Thou Thy power, Thou glorious King ! "

CHAPTER X.

ALTHOUGH my brother was not permitted to be present at the celebration of the jubilee of the Church Missionary Society—having been already removed to take part in choral strains of a more exalted character in the courts above—yet his antici-pations were more than fully realised when the day came round.

The 1st of November, 1848, was a day much to be remembered for the time to come, as one on which the blessing of God was freely bestowed ; as one which did much towards enlarging the hearts of men at home, and laying deeper the foundations of the missionary cause amongst us. Many groundless prejudices were removed; many ears listened for the first time to the claims of the heathen upon our Church and nation ; many a church and parish were opened for the first time to the Church Missionary Society ; whilst not a few of our cathedrals had their time-honoured walls consecrated, as it were, afresh by this sacred cause—for well may it be asked, How could those splendid piles, with their massive pillars, vaulted roofs, and fretted windows, be more highly honoured or converted to better use, than when

within their walls were celebrated the high notes of
jubilee praise; and the glory of God, the advancement
of our Redeemer's kingdom, the conversion of the
world, formed the noble theme of the preacher's
discourse?

But the energy of his mind was too great for his
bodily strength, and he was tempted by the ardour which
he felt for the work in which he was engaged, to exert
himself beyond the bounds of prudence. This brought
on a relapse of his Indian complaint, which con-
siderably reduced his strength. In the month of
September he visited Durham, intending to take a
few weeks of recreation and rest; he reached home
on the 14th, in a very feeble condition. The record
of his few remaining days is fully detailed by one who
watched with unwearied assiduity over him during his
last illness, and having been committed to paper whilst
these events were fresh in her memory, will impart a
more lively and interesting impression of those closing
scenes, than could be otherwise given.

MY DEAR GEORGE,

According to your wish I send you a few particulars
respecting the last days of our beloved brother Henry;
having had, from being almost constantly with him during
the last three weeks of his life, more opportunity of witnessing his faith and patience to the end, than any one else.
After attending one of the committee meetings of the
Church Missionary Society, on Monday, the 11th of
September, in London, he imprudently started for the
north by a night train, being anxious to make the most
of a short absence from his usual routine of labour, during
which, besides visiting his own family in Durham, he

intended in the pulpit and on the platform in various
places, to advocate the missionary cause.

After spending a day with the family of his much-loved
and revered master, the late Dr. Arnold, at Fox How, he
reached Durham on the middle of Thursday, the 14th of
September. We met him at the station, and I was painfully
struck by his worn and debilitated appearance. He confessed
himself extremely unwell, and willingly allowed us, upon
reaching home, to send for medical advice. He was pro-
nounced to be exceedingly unwell, suffering from diarrhœa,
which had been upon him several weeks, and very unfit for
the work before him. Still it was not imagined, that by
going through it, he would endanger his life. His name
was advertised for two sermons to be preached at South
Shields, and four consecutive meetings at different places
on the four following days. We hoped that the two
days' rest before him would restore him in some measure,
especially as in part he was suffering from cold caught on
the journey.

On Saturday, the 16th, he was sent in my mother's
carriage to Shields in preparation for the Sunday duty.
In a letter he wrote to quiet our anxiety about him, he
told us he had felt so ill, during the previous service, he
feared he should have been quite unable to acquit himself in
the pulpit, either morning or evening; but that God had
wonderfully helped him.

Next day he addressed a very large and crowded meeting
at Bishop Wearmouth, and the following morning, the
Sunday-school teachers assembled at the house of the
rector, after which he returned to Durham, in preparation
for the meeting to be held that evening. I was grieved to the
heart to see him arrive, at four o'clock, exhausted to a degree.
He went to bed, and got up only to attend the meeting,
where it was arranged that he should speak first, and then
retire immediately, which he did. Most touching was his

appearance, " thrown aside as a useless wreck," as he himself
feelingly said ; pale and languid, he yet spoke with his usual
simple earnestness and energy, his countenance beaming with
that peculiar expression of love to God and man, for which it
was so remarkable.

He returned home, and every attention was paid to his
health, which, anxious as we felt, we had no idea but rest
and proper measures would speedily restore.   The next two
days he kept his room, after which he never left his bed, the
disease gaining ground rapidly, and laying such firm hold of
his constitution as baffled all efforts to overcome it.

For several days, however, our fears were not roused, so
that we indulged in speaking of plans for his taking a long
and needful season of rest, in order to his perfect restoration
to health, a prospect which to his family looked very pleasant,
as securing to them for a considerable season the society of
one so dear and profitable to them.

During these days, I had scarcely any intercourse with him,
besides seeing that his comfort was attended to, he being
ordered to be left perfectly quiet, and unexcited by conversation or reading.   His weakness was very great, so much
so, that upon asking him if he would like a little prayer one
night, he said it must be very short ; he was so weak.   The
following evening on my commencing, he put his hand on
mine, saying, " I am too ill, I cannot bear it."   Still our fears
only arose slowly and gradually.

After some days he asked me if the doctors thought him
in danger.   I truly replied, not so,—but that his state was
certainly critical.   He then made me promise I would tell
him in case they thought worse of him.   At this period of
his illness, he expressed a desire to recover, that he would
rather recover and labour in God's service.   I asked him if
he were willing to depart.   " Oh yes, willing, I hope, if it be
God's will, which is best ; only, if He sees well, I should
prefer remaining."

Another time he said, "For *me*, it is far better to depart, but I am only a young man yet, and I might work in God's service, if He raised me up. Yet when I think of my own deceitful heart, and the power of the world, I tremble, lest I should not stand firm." I said, we must trust God for life, as well as death. He who had begun the good work could finish it. "Yes," he replied, "and then we have the promise of the Holy Ghost to uphold us, and sanctify us—yes, to sanctify us."

Upon my remarking, whilst giving him some food, "What an aggravation to sickness poverty must be, where there can be none of those alleviations you have," he replied, "Oh, God is merciful, very merciful, and full of love, more than we can count up." I added, "How dreadful it must be to endure sufferings, caused by sin, such as intemperance." He added, "All suffering is from sin ; mine is from sin, perhaps some particular sin—I don't quite see what." He wondered how those who had not the consolations of the Gospel could endure suffering.

About the same time I believe he expressed to you very ' humbling views of himself—how, with great privileges, he had been only a very ordinary Christian, and lived far beneath the standard he ought.

He also said to me, " I have not worked enough by faith. I have overworked myself, and made myself ill. God has punished me by this sickness." He meant he had not sufficiently trusted God to do His own work, in His own way, independent of his personal exertions, thinking, if he did it not, it would be left undone. He firmly resolved to amend in this point, if God raised him up, and not again to labour beyond the strength given him.

Except once, he scarcely after this first week of his ill-ness alluded to himself, except in connection with Christ's wonderful love to him. It made me think of the promise, " He that humbleth himself shall be exalted." Humility,

genuine humility of that rare and Christ-like kind, which
lays self so low, as to put it out of sight, so as not to be perpetually brought before fellow-sinners' eyes and ears, in self-
abasing complaints, was one of his peculiar characteristics.
Self was sacrificed, I had almost said annihilated in him, and
Christ exalted. He had risen above self, almost above the
remembrance of the sinner, in the love for the Saviour of
sinners. He realised his completeness in Him; his life being
hid with Christ, he was conscious of his union with Him, and
in this he gloried, viz., Christ in him, the hope of glory. It
was a very high and holy state of mind, feeling his own
nothingness so completely, as to seek and find fulness in
Christ. And that fulness was his comfort and strength, his
joy and crown of rejoicing. Therefore, I believe it was, that
as he drew nearer to heaven, we heard so few of those self-
abhorring complaints, so often poured out by God's children.
He had risen above these, so as to be swallowed up with the
sight of Christ's work, and in that he rejoiced with joy
unspeakable, and full of glory.

During the days on which he made the remarks already
noted, he mingled much of praise and thanksgiving, together
with such expressions of love to God his Saviour, as made
me again and again feel as if I had never loved Christ at all.
In fact, the one great striking feature of his illness, as of his
life, I may truly say, was his abounding love to his Saviour.
It literally filled his heart, and nothing came in competition
with it : "Him first, Him last ;" He was indeed the Alpha
and Omega with him. In his weakest and most tried
moments, the name of Jesus would bring a smile of happiness across his worn and suffering features. I wish that
thousands could have partaken of the privilege I enjoyed
of being an eye-witness of his faith and love. Words cannot
describe it. A few disjointed expressions of his own cannot
picture it. It was the whole tone and bearing of his mind,
his conduct, and his looks, which bore such striking witness

to the Spirit of Christ which was in him. It was beautiful beyond description.

But his habitual tone of mind was shown very affectingly in the wanderings of mind caused by fever; proving that he had indeed put on Christ, and that the mind which was in Christ, was in him. And here I may remark, that as in his sober moments, so in these wanderings caused by disease, there was a remarkable absence of excitement; the mind was occupied with unrealities, but still there was a striking calmness and quietness of tone. In fact, he was remarkable for a deep, steady earnestness of character, which is opposed to the flickerings of excitement. It always struck me that he "spoke because he believed;"—that he acted on conviction and the exercise of a sound judgment. All that knew him must remember the peculiar calmness, gentleness, and I may say repose of his manner. This continued throughout his illness.

To give an instance of how his soul was filled with love to God and man, even when wandering, I will mention the following. He asked the servant, who was at the time in the room, if she saw "that sheet of white paper on the bed"? There was nothing. "That," said he, "is the plan of salvation, laid out all plain and clear for the heathen; there is no crease or rumple upon it to prevent their taking it, and it is offered to them." Then, in a sad tone, after a pause, "But alas! alas! I see none coming to lay hold on it."

But to return to my narrative. He was too weak, during the whole of his illness, to bear continuous reading or praying. One or two verses of Scripture at a time, however, and an ejaculatory prayer to meet his wants, were great comforts to him. In this way I repeated to him a great portion of the promises of the Bible; some of them many times over: and most affectingly now are they associated in my memory with him, as having raised the eye of faith, and brought many a smile of angelic happiness across his countenance.

Early in his illness, upon repeating from John iii. 36, "He that believeth in Him hath everlasting life," he said, with a solemnity of tone and look I shall never forget, "I *have* believed, I *do* believe." This was the secret of his strength and comfort throughout his illness, and it was striking that he should have said this to show it at the very commencement.

The second Sunday before he died, upon my remarking, "It is the close of the Sabbath, and there remaineth a Sabbath (rest) for the people of God," he said, "And what a Sabbath! perfect rest! when shall I get there? It is that little stream which divides us and makes us shrink. Earth has such hold of us."

This was on his thirty-first birthday, the 1st of October. He had felt too ill for several days to see his children, but now begged they might come. They came, bringing him nosegays of flowers, gathered from their own little gardens, wishing him, in child-like glee, "Many happy returns of the day." "Perhaps," said he, "it will be the last." I did not think it then; hope still predominated with us. After the children left him (and he could only bear their presence a few minutes), he said, "Dear little things, how they wind themselves round one's heart." His affection for his children was very deep and tender, which made his readiness to leave them and commit them with faith to the God of the fatherless, more striking.

Reading to him a portion out of the Book of Revelation, he said, "The second and third chapters are so full of rebuke and exhortation, full of beautiful passages. I read them with R. just before I left Madras. I never met with any one of my own age so full of Christian experience as he is. He did not talk *about* religion, he talked *Christ*. We do not speak enough about Christ. It is because our hearts are not full enough of Him."

Reading to him Jer. xxxi. 3 he repeated, "An everlasting love. 'I have drawn thee.' Yes, *drawn*, against our wills."

One morning, upon the medical man's reminding him of the many mercies he enjoyed in his present illness compared with what he had had in India, he said, " Yes, God is indeed good to me, He sends me innumerable mercies. His love is indeed wonderful ! wonderful ! wonderful ! To send His Son to die for such creatures as we are ! Surpassing love !" Then, in a low tone, his eyes shut, and a pause between each word, he repeated, " Love ! Love ! Love !"

This is a specimen, I may say, of his general tone of mind. Innumerable times did he express himself in a similar manner, respecting the love of God, and His great goodness to himself and to all men. His heart seemed literally *filled* with the love of God shed *abroad* in it by the Holy Ghost. I now regret I was unable to note down more of his sweet expressions of love and faith ; those I give you, I put down at the time, they are his own words. On my saying, " We shall see Him as He is," he said, " See Him ! see Him ! Oh, it will be glorious !" He then went on to speak of the blessedness of heaven : " No crying, no death, no curse, no sin." We then spoke of the happiness of being there. Surely, even then, he had a foretaste of its glory. His heart seemed filled with joyful anticipations, and the poor suffering body could not keep it from mounting into the third heaven, into which he almost seemed to carry me along with him.

A doubt of his interest in Christ never arose, nor did a cloud for a moment ever come between him and his clear view of his Saviour. I had, in my own mind, fears, whether in the hour of nature's greatest weakness, Satan might not be allowed to try him, as he often does God's children ; but no, blessed be God ! all was bright to the end. Once when he seemed much depressed and oppressed by suffering and weakness, I said, " In going through the dark valley, Satan often distresses God's people." He quickly replied, "Thank God, he has never been allowed to distress me."

This was the day before he died, and I feel assured, the same peace continued to the end.   Do not imagine, however, there was not conflict; this, I believe, will only cease when we put off this corruptible, and put on the incorruptible. His faith was never shaken, but it was tried.   Deeply did he feel those seasons, when, from extreme weakness, he could hold no sensible communion with God.   He seemed to reckon his nights bad, or good, in proportion to the degree in which he enjoyed the light of God's countenance.   He generally answered my inquiries by "I have not been able hardly to pray. I could not break through; I was too ill."   Once he said, "Sometimes I can lift up my heart to God, at other times it is so dead. To look to Christ on the cross, *that* is the way to get comfort and help from the Saviour of sinners."

The taking to pieces the earthly tabernacle was, as I imagine it always is when taken down gradually, very painful.   Once, on my repeating, "O Lord, I am oppressed, undertake for me," he repeated in a tone of deep feeling, "Lord, *I am* oppressed, *I am* oppressed, undertake for me, undertake for me!"

At such seasons the texts—"The eternal God is thy refuge, and underneath are the everlasting arms"—"Yea, though I walk through the valley of the shadow of death, I will fear no evil, for Thou art with me, Thy rod and Thy staff, they comfort me;" were full of comfort to him.   Sometimes he said to me, "Read me some strong passages."   Another time, "Read me something about going through."   I repeated from Isa. xliii. 2: "When thou passest through the waters, I will be with thee; and through the rivers they shall not overflow thee; when thou walkest through the fire, thou shalt not be burned; neither shall the flame kindle upon thee. For I am the Lord thy God, the Holy One of Israel, thy Saviour."   This text, and many others from Isaiah, were of great comfort to him, and I often repeated them to him.

Once or twice he said, " Oh, it is *very* painful, *very* painful,"
—but he never expressed any sense of suffering or unrest,
without adding, either " God's will be done," or " God's will
is best." Frequently did we hear him in low and earnest
tones calling upon Jesus. At the commencement of his
illness he seemed to be peculiarly sensitive to the fear of
sinning by impatience. Many times he said to us, " Pray
that my patience fail not ; " and most fully was the prayer
answered.

Never was there a word, or sign, or look, which betrayed
a failing of perfect patience. We felt, from his words and
conduct, that God's will was indeed sweeter to him than his
own ease and comfort. Neither was he passing through these
trying days without profit. He said to me, " I do feel
thankful, the last fortnight I have gained so much more
knowledge of Christ, I could not have believed illness
could have done so much for me. You know I used to say,
I felt illness unprofitable." He at other times told me
how he had gained deeper views of the love of Christ since
laid on his sick bed. He seemed to have a constant sense
of his smaller as well as greater mercies. Whilst bathing his
hands, I remarked, " You see, God sends many alleviations
to your sufferings."—" Oh yes, tender mercies, wonderful
mercies ! He makes all my bed in my sickness. He just
gives me all the comforts I need." Another time : " I
never wake but I think of fresh mercies—God's mercies
are innumerable." If you had seen the happy, grateful,
heavenly countenance with which he uttered all his praiseful,
grateful sentences, it would have engraven them on your very
soul.

God was glorified greatly in His servant, for it was manifest
to all that it was His power which shone forth so brightly in
him. The second coming of Christ was a subject which was
much in his thoughts, and one his heart longed for. Speaking
of it I said, " If He comes not soon, we may first go to

Him." " Yes, but His coming is more blessed." On speaking
of his entering into glory, he said, " Not full glory yet, I
shall rest with Christ." He dwelt with much more joy on
the time when Christ would come, and the consummation of
all things be completed. " Oh, if He might come in our day !
How glorious ! how one longs for it." His heart seemed filled
with the joyous anticipation.

Although we had not yet given up hope, his illness was
assuming a more and more serious aspect, while he who was
the subject of it seemed daily nearing heaven. His mind
increasingly dwelt with holy joy on the probable prospect of
soon being with his Saviour.

He literally was without carefulness. After reading to
him the concluding portion of 1 Cor. xv., ending, " Thanks
be to God, who giveth us the victory," he exclaimed,
" Victory ! yes, victory ! Oh, that it might be to-night ! " It
was the first time he had expressed a decided wish to go, and
I said, " Do you wish to go ? " He turned his face toward
me, and replied, with an angelic smile, " Oh yes, it would
be so much better to be with Christ ; " adding, however,
that he thought God would raise him up, so many friends
were praying for him, and instancing God's answering prayer
in the release of Peter from prison. It was a great gratifica-
tion to him to know he was prayed for by many friends and
congregations on his last Sunday, at Durham, Shields, Clifton,
Brighton, Hampstead, and Edinburgh. He generally left
the choice of portions of Scripture to me, though he sometimes named the subject he desired, according to his need ;
but he once asked me to read him the first two verses of the
third chapter of the first epistle of John, after which he
repeated, " Sons of God,—let me dwell on that, *I* am a son
of God, yes, a son of God ! " He looked up as he said it,
and seemed lost in happy contemplation.

At another time, speaking of the conclusion of the eighth

R

of Romans, and that love of Christ from which nothing can
separate us, he said, " I seem to have gone deeper into this—
this wonderful love of Christ."

" This is the one thing God has shown me more of in this
illness. This wonderful love of Christ to sinners—such
love ! " I spoke of the shortness of time, the length of
eternity. " Ah ! and *such* an eternity *too*," he exclaimed,
" and *such* brightness, and such glory—we cannot reach it—
we cannot comprehend it now—it will be far, far above
our present powers of conception." Such remarks were the
more striking from his state being throughout one of much
lethargy and physical depression—with a total absence of
excitement. A large portion of his illness was passed in
unrefreshing sleep.

All I have recorded was before hope was given up. On
Tuesday, October 10, worse symptoms appeared, but it was
not till the following morning the medical man expressed his
decided opinion that he would not recover. It so happened
that this was the only time I missed seeing him during
Henry's illness. After he was gone, Henry sent for me and
said, " George has been with me, and is much cast down
about this ; he tells me that Mr. J—— thinks me worse, and
that I shall not live long : did he say so to you ? " I replied,
" I missed seeing him." I confess my heart rather trembled ;
I feared that now the near and certain approach of death was
brought before him, its terrors might at first dismay him,
and I was quite unprepared for what followed, when he
went on to say, " When he comes again, I wish you
particularly to ask him, and if he says the same thing,
are you all prepared to join me in praise ? " I was overcome,
and hid my face. He continued, " I fear I ask a hard
thing of you." I replied, " God has made us *willing* to
part with you. He can enable us to praise Him." He went
on to say, " Oh, it will be glorious ; so glorious ! "

After this his whole heart seemed fixed upon the joys to which he was going; the prospect looked to him inexpressibly bright. This seemed to him a day of peculiar joy; for as yet the body, though very weak, was not so painfully oppressed as it afterwards became.

When I went into his room the next morning, he said to me, " I am very weak, can scarcely speak ; but oh, happy ! happy ! happy ! " He now thought his time might be short, and desired to see his children. They got on the bed and kissed him ; he said, " That is your last kiss. God bless you ; if you wish to see papa again, you must come to heaven, where you will find him and dear mamma and little Johnny ; now, good-bye."

He was calm and not overcome. I remembered his deep emotion when he parted from them to return to India, two years before. The struggle—and it was a bitter one—was gone through at that time : the sacrifice had been made, and God spared him the pain of a second.

One of the servants told me that, whilst sitting up with him one night, he began to repeat from the Revelation, " What are these which are arrayed in white robes, and whence came they ? " then pausing, as if memory failed him, she concluded the passage, " These are they which came out of great tribulation, and have washed their robes and made them white in the blood of the Lamb." Then he said, " Ah ! there will be many from India, many from the Telugu nation." He then spoke of the approaching Jubilee, how he had written for it, preached for it, prayed for it, adding, in a joyful tone, " It will be a glorious Jubilee for me."

I may here mention his dying testimony to the cause to which he had sacrificed his life. After reading to him the first three verses of Isaiah xl., I remarked it was a privilege to have been called, even in a small measure, to " prepare the way of the Lord." He replied, "Yes, there seems a special blessing resting on it; I often thank God that He called me to be a missionary to go abroad." On his mother's asking him whether he repented having given his life to missionary work, he said, "No, never! if I had to live over again, I would do the same." This he said only a day or two before he died, when he knew he was, humanly speaking, losing his life in consequence of his labours abroad and at home in that cause,—a cause so glorious, even the rescuing of immortal souls from sin and Satan, that it was dearer to him than life itself, through love to his Redeemer.

And now his work on earth seemed done, and truly "his soul was in haste to be gone." Every symptom that spoke of the nearness of death was precious to him, and raised a smile of joy. Once he complained that the extra clothing on his feet produced no warmth : then turning his eyes on me with a smile, he asked, "This is a *good* sign, is it not?" Any little thing I could name to him as a sign of approaching dissolution was a pleasure to him. Strange did it seem to be affording him comfort, by telling him of various little signs of the nearness of death ; but so it was. Still there was no impatience, but perfect submission to God's will. Once he said, "It matters little, a day or night, more or less ; God's time is best." He liked me to repeat to him his favourite Baxter's saying, respecting his own death, "When Thou wilt ; where Thou wilt ; as Thou wilt."

He was detained nearly two days and a night longer than he had been led to suppose. On Saturday morning he said to me, "For half an hour in the night I thought I was just going to be at rest, but I rallied again. God's will be done, God's will be done, God's will is best." I said, "You have peace in Jesus?" "Yes, *in Jesus*, He is the dying Saviour!"

On the medical man's saying, the same morning, when he

visited him, " I had hoped to have found you released," he
replied, " Mr. J., *perfect* submission of our wills to God's,
that is the thing."

He had told Mr. J., the night previous, that the only
thing that distressed him was " seeing your and our dear
mother's grief." He said to her once, " Why have you been
crying, dear mother? Have they told you I am going? it
is right you should know. Oh, mother, it will be so joyous !
To meet father and Lizzy, and all who have gone before."
In general, however, this happy anticipation of seeing
departed relations was swallowed up in the higher joy of
seeing that Saviour whom, not having seen, he had so truly
loved.

On my reminding him, as a cordial to his bodily suffering
and weariness at the moment, " that he would soon see his
dear wife," he replied, " To see Him that was pierced for us,
that is the thing ! " Another time, speaking himself of the
happiness of finding so many dear ones whcm he had loved
on earth, in heaven ; after a pause, he said, " But we shall
there be so taken up with Christ, we shall have little
thought for other things." Another time he remarked to
me, after speaking of some dear relations now in heaven,
" We think much of those few, but there are so many more :
such a glorious company of saints to see and be with,—
St. Paul, St. Peter, Hezekiah, Henry Martyn. It will be
so blessed to meet them."

As he grew weaker and weaker, he, at times, seemed much
oppressed, and I said, " You must not faint ; " he answered,
" I sometimes feel as if I should." I replied, " I do not
mean your body, but your spirit must not fail." " There is
no fear of that, it is all joy." Another time, when my heart
ached for him, more to reassure myself than for his sake, I
asked, " Have you peace ? " " Yes, peace ; the only anxiety
is to be gone : but God's will is best, that is the best thing,

perfect submission to His will." As the outer man decayed, the inner man grew stronger ; it was a love and faith made perfect which had cast out fear. To his dear mother he said, " In due time we shall meet in Jesus ; we shall see Him as He is, very beautiful ! very beautiful ! "

Once he said, " It is a hard thing to die, to pass through ; nothing but the Lord's promises could enable us to do it ; " then, in a firm tone, " but they are sure and *stedfast.*" He seemed to lose all sense of time, which seemed often immeasurably lengthened. I said, " Time seems long when suffering. You have scarcely been three weeks confined to bed yet ; " he went on, " and by the time these three weeks are completed, I shall in all probability be in heaven."

Speaking of Christ, he said, " It would be ten thousand times better to be with Him ; perhaps I may see Him to-morrow." The happy calmness of tone and look with which he expressed himself throughout was striking ; it was the result of a firm conviction of the certainty and reality of the truths he believed, and the glory he anticipated. It was as if he was speaking of soon joining a loved parent or brother upon earth, only his feelings were holier, higher, more blessed. I may again repeat, I never witnessed any thing like excitement in him ; it was the sober certainty of waking bliss, which filled his heart ; and there was a reality about it that made me almost feel as if faith were turned into sight.

He was now getting very near putting off this mortal body ; his hands were like ice, he begged me to come closer to him, he could not see me. " My sight is going—it is coming back." " It will come back in eternity," I said. For the last two days he could hardly bear me to absent myself from him ; and if I left the room, would send for me, and have me sit close to him ministering to his bodily and spiritual wants. " How different your hand is to every

GRAVE OF THE REV. H. W. FOX, ST. MARY'S,
IN THE SOUTH BAILY, DURHAM.

one else's," he said, as I bathed his forehead with Eau de
Cologne. "Do you like it best?" "Oh yes." I had left
him a few minutes, he sent after me. When I came, "Oh,
Isabella, I want some of your comfort." I said, "You mean
God's." "Yes, read me some passages." Once, previously,
I had taken up Clark's "Promises," and he said, "Not that
little book, the real Bible." Once he remarked, with a
happy smile, "There (in heaven), there will be no Bible."
During this last day he frequently exclaimed, "Lord, why
tarriest Thou? Come, Lord!"—but always adding, "God's
will be done," or "God's time is best."

Whilst sitting quietly by him, he exclaimed, "How
happy! If it please God I may just sink away thus, it will
be a great mercy." At three o'clock of this last day he
said, "O Lord! gracious Lord! loving Jesus! how gracious
He is. Oh, let me go to-day! O Lord, Thou knowest
best! Are there two or three hours yet before God comes?
pray that He will come."

And now the last enemy was nearly conquered, for
"death," as he himself had remarked, "is called an enemy."
He had for the last two days and nights frequently seemed
near going, so that even now I scarcely knew whether he
might not still linger for a while, though my prayers were
joined with his, that if it were God's will, his happy soul
might speedily be released. I heard him faintly saying to
himself, "Jesus, Jesus must be first in the heart." I said,
"He is the first in yours." "Yes, He is." These were his
last words. I felt his firm grasp of my hand relaxing, his
pulse was gone; his breathing became slow and more faint.
I sent for you and my mother, and soon after your arrival he
gently ceased to breathe, and was with his Saviour.

"Blessed are the dead that die in the Lord, from henceforth, for they rest from their labours, and their works do
follow them."

I did not think I could have praised God under the blow ;
but He did enable me, and does, and ever will, I trust,
enable us all to join in thanksgiving, for that He permitted
His servant so to glorify Him in life and death, and us to
be witnesses of his faith and patience.   May we be the
followers of him, as he followed Christ !

OB : 14 OCTOBER, 1848.

AGED 31.

APPENDIX.

———◆◇◆———

AFTER my brother's death, an organisation was formed in connection with Rugby School, entitled "THE FOX MEMORIAL," which has been continued to the present day.

Considering the length of time which has elapsed since the decease of my brother Henry, and the large number of his personal friends who have been removed by the hand of death, it is very gratifying, and has somewhat surprised me, that the fund, instead of diminishing, has materially increased during the last decade of years.

A sermon has been preached in the school chapel at Rugby every year since his death, and this annual sermon has now become one of the established institutions of the school, and takes its place among the associations of their boyhood, which old Rugbeians carry with them to all parts of the world.

It may be interesting to place on record a copy of the original appeal, and of the members of the committee, many of whom are now deceased.

FOX MEMORIAL.

THE friends of the late Rev. H. W. Fox, being desirous of testifying their high estimation of his singleness of mind and unwearied labours as a missionary, and sympathising with him in his earnest wish "that Rugby School might become interested in the cause of missions," commenced an effort shortly after his death, to establish and maintain a

mastership at one of the native schools in South India
for promoting Christian education, to be called

THE RUGBY FOX MASTERSHIP,

proposing further to connect it with Rugby,

1st. By having an annual report of the school sent
thither;

2ndly. By an annual sermon to be preached in the
chapel on behalf of the object;

3rdly. By making a collection towards its support
amongst the boys.

Dr. Tait has given the plan his cordial support from
the beginning, and has already preached a sermon on its
behalf in Rugby School Chapel. As he is shortly about to
quit his present sphere, it may be a satisfaction to many to
know that his successor, the Rev. E. M. Goulburn, also
looks favourably upon the design, and purposes, if spared
to enter upon the duties to which he has been appointed,
to give it his hearty support.

It was hoped that the benefits resulting from the intro-
duction of this missionary element into one of our public
schools, would, under the blessing of Him whose Holy
Spirit alone can give real success to the design, be incal-
culable; and therefore the plan was commended not only to
the friends of India and of the Church Missionary Society,
but to all who long to see the kingdom of Christ advancing
in our schools, and through them in our universities, and
throughout the land.

To effect this object, a committee was formed, and it
was proposed to raise by donations a sum of £1,500, and
a further income of £70 or £80 by annual subscriptions.
An appeal was made, which has been so far liberally
responded to, that, up to the present time, donations have
been received amounting to £750, besides £45 16s.
from Rugby School, and £57 16s. 6d. in annual subscriptions.

It will thus be seen that above £700, besides an addition
to the annual subscriptions, are still required to secure a
permanent income.

The money raised is reckoned as part of the Church

Missionary Society's Jubilee Fund, and the appointment of the master rests with the committee of that Society, They have for many years desired to send a schoolmaster to Masulipatam, to assist the Rev. R. T. Noble in his native school, but have been unable to meet with a suitable person; at length, however, by the blessing of God, they have found one, whom they believe to be fully qualified for his duties, and him they purpose appointing to the office of Rugby Fox Master at Masulipatam.

His name is Nicholson. He was born in India, educated in England, and was for some time master of a school; he is at present preparing for holy orders in the Missionary College at Islington, and will sail for India, it is expected, next month.

The way being thus opened, by the good providence of God, for fulfilling the purposes of the Fox MEMORIAL, the committee would commend it to the liberality and the prayers of all who are interested in Christian missions.

FREDERICK GELL, *Secretary.*

CHRIST'S COLLEGE, CAMBRIDGE:
Dec. 1849.

The following are Members of the Committee:—

BUCKOLL, Rev. H. J., Rugby.
CARUS, Rev. W., Romsey.
ELLIOTT, Rev. H. V., Brighton.
EMERIS, Rev. J., Gloucester.
FRENCH, REV. T. V., University College, Oxford.
GELL, Rev. F., Christ's College, Cambridge, *Secretary.*
HALES, Rev. R. C., Secretary to the Oxford Association of the Church Missionary Society.
HATHAWAY, E. P., Esq., Lincoln's Inn, London.
HAYNE, H., Esq., Clifton.
M'BRIDE, J. D., D.C.L., Principal of Magdalen Hall, Oxford.
PRICE, B., Esq., Rugby.
SIMPKINSON, Rev. J. N., Harrow.
SYMONS, Rev. Dr., Warden of Wadham College.
TAIT, Rev. Dr.
TUCKER, Rev. J., Fellow of Corpus Christi College.
VENN, Rev. H., London.

Subscriptions to the Fox MEMORIAL can be paid at Messrs. WILLIAMS, DEACON, & Co.'s Bank, Birchin Lane, London.

The following are lists of the preachers and of the collections from the commencement :—

PREACHERS.

1848.—Rev. Dr. Tait, Head Master, now Archbishop of Canterbury.
1850.—Rev. Dr. Goulburn, Head Master, now Dean of Norwich.
1852.—Rev. H. Highton.
1853.—Rev. J. Tucker.
1854.—Rev. E. W. Benson, now Bishop of Truro.
1855.—Rev. Dr. Goulburn.
1856.—Rev. J. N. Simpkinson.
1857.—Rev. C. E. Oakley.
1858.—Rev. Dr. Temple, Head Master, now Bishop of Exeter.
1859.—Rev. R. Lawson.
1860.—Rev. T. V. French, now Bishop of Lahore.
1861.—Hon. and Rev. Canon Lyttleton.
1862.—Rev. P. S. Royston, now Bishop of Mauritius.
1863.—Rev. W. Tait.
1864.—Rev. T. L. Claughton, now Bishop of St. Albans.
1865.—Rev. R. E. Bartlett.
1866.—Rev. C. Evans, now Canon Evans.
1867.—Rev. E. W. Benson.
1868.—Very Rev. Dr. Goulburn, Dean of Norwich.
1869.—Rev. J. H. Gray.
1870.—Right Rev. Dr. Gell, Bishop of Madras.
1871.—Rev. J. Sharp, Head Master of Noble High School.
1872.—Rev. H. E. Fox, son of Henry Watson Fox.
1873.—Rev. G. F. W. Munby.
1874.—Rev. E. H. Bradby.
1875.—Rev. T. V. French, now Bishop of Lahore.
1876.—Rev. J. Frank Bright.
1877.—Right Rev. E. Parry, Bishop of Dover.
1878.—Ven. Archdeacon Sir Lovelace Stamer, Bart.
1879.—Rev. Canon Evans.

COLLECTIONS.

		Collected in Chapel.			Donations.			Ann. Subs.			Interest.			Total.		
		£	s.	d.	£	s.	d.	£	s.	d.	£	s.	d.	£	s.	d.
First Year..	1850	46	3	0	767	5	6	58	8	0				871	16	6
Second ..	1851	21	3	8	67	10	0	58	16	0	20	1	2	167	10	10
Third ..	1852	34	6	11	119	1	6	78	8	0	31	0	0	262	16	5
Fourth ..	1853	25	2	0	19	6	6	72	1	0	30	0	0	146	9	6
Fifth ..	1854	38	4	0	10	15	6	85	7	0	30	0	0	164	6	6
Sixth ..	1855	39	11	10	6	1	0	78	6	0	30	0	0	153	18	10
Seventh ..	1856	31	8	0	26	3	0	89	16	0	30	0	0	177	7	0
Eighth ..	1857	23	17	11	24	16	0	96	19	6	30	0	0	175	13	5
Ninth..	1858	19	2	6	18	19	6	97	15	0	30	0	0	165	17	0
Tenth ..	1859	19	15	0	19	17	6	97	7	6	30	0	0	167	0	0
Eleventh ..	1860	30	9	2	111	12	0	85	10	6	30	0	0	257	11	8
Twelfth ..	1861	36	19	1	30	0	6	74	9	6	33	0	0	174	9	1
Thirteenth .	1862	30	13	5	8	14	0	99	15	0	33	0	0	172	2	5
Fourteenth .	1863	29	10	6	4	19	6	85	1	3	33	0	0	152	1	3
Fifteenth ..	1864	29	16	5	15	17	0	94	4	6	33	0	0	172	17	11
Sixteenth ..	1865	23	18	2	7	3	0	123	0	6	33	0	0	189	1	8
Seventeenth	1866	22	19	0	6	8	6	108	3	0	33	0	0	170	10	6
Eighteenth .	1867	29	15	7	17	1	0	109	12	6	33	0	0	189	9	1
Nineteenth .	1868	25	2	11	113	11	0	106	16	0	33	0	0	278	9	11
Twentieth..	1869	38	9	2	4	16	8	118	13	0	42	0	0	203	18	10
Twenty-first	1870	32	11	2	13	13	8	101	17	0	42	0	0	190	1	10
,, second.	1871	27	0	5	7	13	6	89	16	0	39	0	0	163	9	11
,, third..	1872	32	12	11	21	7	10	133	17	8	39	0	0	226	18	5
,, fourth.	1873	21	4	0	14	0	8	119	1	6	39	0	0	193	6	2
,, fifth ..	1874	25	3	6	2	6	0	142	12	10	39	0	0	203	10	4
,, sixth ..	1875	30	0	0	16	5	1	179	6	0	39	0	0	264	11	1
,, seventh	1876	31	3	9	8	5	0	185	2	0	39	0	0	263	10	9
,, eighth .	1877	27	14	6	2	16	0	206	2	9	39	0	0	275	13	3
,, ninth..	1878	32	11	2	2	16	0	222	17	10	39	0	0	297	5	0
Thirtieth ..	1879	27	1	6	3	6	0	202	8	6	39	0	0	271	16	0
Thirty-first.	1880	30	5	2	2	10	0	207	12	3	39	0	0	279	7	5
														£6,471	1	5

It will thus be seen that the sum of £6,471 has been contributed since the commencement of the Fund to the present time.

It may be stated that the office of Rugby Fox Master at Masulipatam has been occupied by a succession of six masters, who have usefully filled the post. One of them, the Rev. John Sharp, like my brother, was educated at Rugby and Oxford. He assisted Mr. Noble for four years in the school, and when the terrible cyclone of Nov. 1, 1864, with all that followed it, had brought that devoted missionary to his grave, Mr. Sharp succeeded him as head master, and continued so till April, 1878. The present occupant of the post is the Rev. A. W. Poole, of Worcester College, Oxford.

In addition to the valuable aid which the Rugby Fox Mastership has rendered to the cause of Christian missions in South India, I cannot but believe that the maintenance of the association and the annual sermon for so long a period has exercised a useful influence at home, and tended to develop in some degree that growth of interest in the missionary cause by which the present generation has been distinguished. May this long continue to be the case, and may the work, both at home and abroad, continue to enjoy the blessing of God for many years to come.

G. T. FOX.

DURHAM: *September*, 1880.

For EU product safety concerns, contact us at Calle de José Abascal, 56–1°,
28003 Madrid, Spain or eugpsr@cambridge.org.

www.ingramcontent.com/pod-product-compliance
Ingram Content Group UK Ltd.
Pitfield, Milton Keynes, MK11 3LW, UK
UKHW010346140625
459647UK00010B/852